Ethics Management
for Public Administrators

Ethics Management for Public Administrators

Leading and Building Organizations of Integrity

Second Edition

Donald C. Menzel

M.E.Sharpe
Armonk, New York
London, England

Library of Congress Cataloging-in-Publication Data

Menzel, Donald C.
  Ethics management for public administrators : leading and building organizations of
integrity / by Donald C. Menzel. — 2nd ed.
      p. cm.
  Includes bibliographical references and index.
  ISBN 978-0-7656-3260-9 (hardcover : alk. paper) — ISBN 978-0-7656-3261-6 (pbk. : alk. paper)
  1. Public administration—Moral and ethical aspects. 2. Civil service ethics. I. Title.

  JF1525.E8M46 2012
  172′.2—dc23   2011037556

Printed in the United States of America

The paper used in this publication meets the minimum requirements of
American National Standard for Information Sciences
Permanence of Paper for Printed Library Materials,
ANSI Z 39.48-1984.

IBT (p)   10   9   8   7   6   5   4   3   2
IBT (c)   10   9   8   7   6   5   4   3   2   1

For Kristi Lynn,

David Scott, and Kay

—travelers together!

Contents

Preface and Acknowledgments

In a sense, I began writing this book more than 20 years ago, when I initiated a series of empirical studies to find out what makes individuals in complex public organizations behave in an ethical manner. We have plenty of theories about why people do the wrong thing, sometimes ending up criminals; however, we know much less about why people in organizations do the right thing. I am not certain that my search has been fully successful, but I believe it has been sufficiently revealing to fill the pages of a second edition of this text.

Ethics Management for Public Administrators is about leading and cultivating organizations of integrity. It is written for college and university students contemplating careers in public service, as well as for elected and appointed public officials, administrators, and the thousands of career public servants in the United States and abroad. Educators who are responsible for guiding men and women through the labyrinth of professional public administration as a field of study and practice will also find this book useful.

In addition, this book deals with issues and controversies facing students and practitioners of public administration who must prepare themselves for brave new ethical futures. After all, the study and practice of public administration in the United States was forged in an age of corruption, patronage government, and—in the words of the famed New York City Tammany Hall politician Senator George Washington Plunkitt—"honest graft." Although that age is more than a century past, many issues and controversies remain that will surely form the ethical futures of twenty-first-century public administration. What those futures will look like is difficult to say with confidence. Still, lawmakers, political executives, and career public managers dedicated to building public trust and confidence in U.S. governments must make every effort to sort through the important ethics issues that all too frequently become front-page headlines and grist for the 24-hour cable news cycle.

So you might ask: "What does the second edition bring to the table?" The answer is straightforward—new valuable information and insights into leading and building organizations of integrity. Among other things, two new chapters have been developed. Chapter 3, "Leading with Integrity" recognizes that tools for building organizations of integrity are useless in the hands of those who do not understand what it means to lead with integrity. Thus, this chapter, and insights offered by practitioners that are threaded throughout the volume add significance to the book. The second new chapter, Chapter 6, "Local Government Ethics Management in Action" provides the reader with an in-depth picture of what it takes at ground zero to meet the challenges of ethical governance.

What else is new in this edition? Ethical happenings and issues at the local, state, and national levels, especially the U.S. Congress, are recounted. This includes a discussion of new laws, procedures, and findings. The utilization of hotlines, blogs, and social media as ethics management tools have been added as well. At the international level, an entire new discussion of ethics management experiences in Africa is included in Chapter 9. Finally, new skill building case exercises have been added to several chapters. This second edition brings together ideas, information, and insights in a comprehensive manner that is unrivaled by any other book.

Acknowledgments

I am indebted to a number of persons who kindly read and critiqued all or part of earlier versions of this manuscript. Professors James Bowman at Florida State University and Jonathan West at the University of Miami provided valuable insight and encouragement very early in this effort. So, too, did Professor Curtis Wood at Northern Illinois University. Others academics who offered sound advice, information, and support include Terry Cooper at the University of Southern California, Carol Lewis at the University of Connecticut, J. Edwin Benton at the University of South Florida, Rick Green at the University of Utah, H. George Frederickson at the University of Kansas, Pamela A. Gibson at Troy University, Frank Anechiarico at Hamilton College, Jamil Jreisat at the University of South Florida, Robert Smith at Kennesaw State University, Susan Paddock at the University of Wisconsin, and Carl Southwell, University of Southern California. Dr. Stuart Gilman at the United Nations Office on Drugs and Crime was also very helpful.

Thanks and appreciation are extended as well to the many state and local ethics officials who kindly responded to my queries about their programs, among them Gavin Anderson, Deputy District Attorney, Salt Lake County, Utah; Walter C. Ayers, Director of Communication, New York State Commission on Public Integrity; Martin Black, former City Manager, Venice, Florida; Amy Calderwood, Ombudsman-Director, King County Office of Citizen Complaints–Ombudsman, Seattle, Washington; Mark Davies, Executive Director, New York City Conflicts of Interest Board; Kevin C. Duggan, former city manager, Mountain View, California; Christina Prkic, Staff Attorney, Miami-Dade County Commission on Ethics and Public Trust, Florida; Matthew Conquergood, Assistant to the Ombudsman, King County Office of Citizen Complaints–Ombudsman, Seattle, Washington; Frank Edmunds, City Manager, Seminole, Florida; Alan S. Johnson, Executive Director, Palm Beach County Ethics Commission, Florida; Eric Johnson, Director of the Office of Budgeting and Finance, Hillsborough County, Florida; Kim Leinbach, City Manager, Temple Terrace, Florida; Susan Moore, General Counsel, Georgia Municipal Association; James Spinello, Clark County, Nevada; Joseph M. Stahura, Mayor, Whiting, Indiana; John St. Croix, Executive Director, San Francisco Ethics Commission; Carla Miller, Ethics Officer, City of Jacksonville, Florida; Nicole A. Gordon, Executive Director, New York City Campaign Finance Board; Pat Bean, former County Administrator, Hillsborough County, Florida; Patrick R. Brannigan, former Deputy Director of the Office of Citizen Complaints in the Department of the Public Advocate, State of New Jersey; Sarah Lang, Director, Department of Human Resources, Tampa, Florida; Steve Berlin, Deputy Director, Board of Ethics, Chicago, Illinois; Dorothy Eng, Director, Board of Ethics, Chicago, Illinois; Catherine Clemens, Executive Director, King County Board of Ethics, Seattle, Washington; and Steve Brown, Mayor, Peachtree City, Georgia; Kevin Woodhouse, Deputy City Manager, Mountain View, California.

Finally, I wish to thank my wife and best friend, Kay, for her patience, support, and good cheer as the hours and months passed while writing and revising this book. Our moments struggling over the use of the home computer brought forth a new laptop for her and a realization of the extent to which we have become techies. Much appreciation as well to Emmy and Sammy, who provided canine relief (woof, woof) from the sometimes tedious nature of a second edition revision.

Ethics Management
for Public Administrators

1
Ethics Management

If men were angels, no government would be necessary.

—James Madison, *The Federalist #51*

Men and women are not angels, nor are they devils. Nevertheless, it is human nature to be ambitious and self-serving—and, as Alexis de Tocqueville added in his classic nineteenth-century account *Democracy in America* (1840/2000), Americans "enjoy explaining almost every act of their lives on the principle of self-interest properly understood" (Mayer 1969, 526). The doctrine of enlightened self-interest means "every American has the sense to sacrifice some of his private interests to save the rest" (Mayer 1969, 527).

Men and women of ambition continue to seek power and act out their lives, driven by "self-interest properly understood." Of course, not all do so, and when self-interest consumes the public interest, much trouble is in store. Those who govern—elected, appointed, and career public officials—are constrained by a myriad of laws and regulations intended to ensure that the public interest is not sacrificed on the altar of self-interest. Still, it is impossible to construct enough laws and rules to check the behavior of human beings both in and out of government. Thus, self-constraint is thought by many to be the answer to ethical governance. But what are the self-constraints? Where do they come from? How do you know they work? Answers to these questions about human behavior have occupied the attention of philosophers for centuries.

This chapter introduces the important but largely neglected subject of ethics management. It also provides an overview of organizational perspectives that can lead to the development of effective ethics leadership and management strategies. There is no magic potion that can be applied to transform public organizations into organizations of integrity. Building an organization of integrity—*workplaces where individuals treat each other with respect, take pride in their work, care about one another, promote accountability, and place the public interest over individual and organizational self-interest*—requires substantial time, resources, and commitment. No small challenge, is it? Yet it must be met. Perhaps most significant is the role public administrators take on the front line of this challenge.

Ethics in Government

Government is not in the business of producing ethics, as Dennis F. Thompson reminds us (1985). Rather, it is in the business of producing public goods and services such as justice, transportation, air and water quality, consumer and occupational safety, national security, and protection from the misfortunes of age, poverty, or race, to name a few. Thus, managers and elected officeholders are charged with providing those collective goods and services deemed desirable but often not provided by private-sector firms.

Why, then, do so many people—managers included—believe that ethical governance is so important? The answer is disarmingly straightforward: Without ethical governance, the effective production of public goods and services is not likely to occur; or, as is so commonly illustrated in the experiences of undemocratic and developing countries, the costs and consequences are so great that a vast majority of the population cannot afford whatever goods and services are produced. Moreover, ethical governance is vital to effective and democratic government. *"Ethics may be only instrumental, it may be only a means to an end, but it is a necessary means to an end"* (Thompson 1992, 255; italics added). In other words, well-meaning public managers and policy makers must realize that public policies and organizations cannot be achieved in an ethical vacuum. Indeed, such a vacuum is likely to swallow up even the most well-conceived policies, plans, and day-to-day operations of government.

This apparently undeniable law linking ethics, public management, and governance has not always taken precedence in the United States. Indeed, as Americans fast-forward into the second decade of the twenty-first century, there is reason to wonder whether such an iron law really exists. Do public managers and elected officeholders understand the vital link between ethics and good governance? Does anyone care if they do, or have we entered an era of "anything goes" governance so long as somebody else will pay for it?

Former U.S. comptroller general David M. Walker (2005) paints an ethically troublesome picture of the U.S. government's "don't pay as you go" mind-set—a way of thinking that prevailed in Washington for much of the first decade of the new millennium, bringing with it enormous implications for future generations. The government's liabilities and net obligations as of September 30, 2004, according to Walker, totaled $43 trillion and were rising rapidly. That number translates into a $150,000 burden for every American and twice that amount for every full-time worker. By 2040, "the federal government could be reduced to doing little more than paying interest on the national debt" if the nation's fiscal policy remains on autopilot (Walker 2005, 347). This is not an ethical future that anyone wants. "We have a stewardship responsibility to future generations," writes Walker. "At the end of the day, we should be able to look our children and grandchildren in the eye and say we did everything we could to pass on an America that is better off and better positioned for the future than when we found it" (351).

President Barack Obama has also taken note of the nation's lapse in responsibility. In his inaugural address (Obama 2009), he exclaimed: "What is required of us now is a new era of responsibility—a recognition on the part of every American that we have duties to ourselves, our nation and the world; duties that we do not grudgingly accept but rather seize gladly, firm in the knowledge that there is nothing so satisfying to the spirit, so defining of our character than giving our all to a difficult task."

Challenges to Ethical Governance

The vast majority of public servants are conscientious, dedicated, competent, ethical individuals pursuing public service careers with integrity and pride. Yet, as we move into the new millennium, the ethical challenges facing those who preside and administer over government organizations have become increasingly complex. Among other things, the boundary between those things public and those things private has largely disappeared, leaving in its wake much uncertainty about how to do the right thing in the right way. The age of privatization is upon us and, with it, the increasing inability of citizens, elected officials, and organizational managers to distinguish between public and private organizations, public and private managers, and public and private ethics.

Governance and Government

Governance is a dynamic, inclusive concept that encompasses a wide spectrum of organizations and individuals engaged in making, implementing, and evaluating public policies. This includes government bodies, elected and appointed public officials, administrators and middle managers, rank-and-file members of public organizations, nonprofit organizations, interest groups, political lobbyists, and profit-making corporations and their chief executives. *Government* refers to institutions such as three branches of the U.S. government and the rules and laws that determine how the work of government gets done.

The ethical challenges of privatization are no less daunting than those ushered in first by the Internet and later by mobile and web-based social media technologies. The future is here; it is now. It is both a virtual "now" and a very real "now." Not only must elected officials and public managers, like their private-sector counterparts, understand and harness information technology (IT) within their organizations, they must be able to understand and manage the human-technical-organizational dynamics that IT brings to the workplace. For example, organizational leaders cannot ignore the depersonalization of relationships in the workplace due to the arrival of e-mail. Nor can they ignore the desire of employees to carry out their duties in high-performing organizations with strong ethical cultures.

The knowledge explosion wrought by the electronic age of computers and high-speed interactive communication has truly transformed the world, giving meaning to the global village and citizen in ways unimaginable a mere decade ago. The globalization of economies, communication, education, commerce, and even warfare and peace are redefining the nation-state and presenting numerous challenges to public officials in the United States and abroad. Public organizations, like private profit-making firms, must add value to their products and services in order to withstand the ever-increasing pressures of worldwide competition. Responsive, high-performing organizations are a necessity, not a luxury. Government agencies are not immune to these pressures, and political executives and career public managers know this. They also know that the forces of globalization can tempt governments to devalue the ethical overhead that is part and parcel of getting things done. Getting things done and staying competitive can be—but are not necessarily—compatible with high ethical standards.

Leading and building an organization of integrity has become ever more difficult since the 2008–2009 economic calamity that threatened to bring down governments and economies across the world. The fiscal austerity that followed has motivated governments—local, state, and national—to downsize, and the resources needed to build and sustain strong ethical cultures are ever more scarce. All too often under financial conditions like these, ethical initiatives are put in reverse; those who serve as "watchdogs" of the public interest are viewed as "fifth wheels," with some thrown under the bus. Consider, for example, the New Jersey Office of the Public Advocate, which was abolished on June 29, 2010, when Republican governor Chris Christie signed into law legislation eliminating the agency.

A person with sound moral character is said to possess *integrity*. When applied to an organization, integrity refers to an environment in which decency, fairness, and honesty abound and respect for others transcends self-serving interests. Building an organization of integrity involves cultivating and balancing a range of competencies and virtues that improve judgment in decision making.

Ethics Management Is Important

Why is ethics management important? Rarely has this question been asked or satisfactorily answered.[1] Why? Because in the past, government reformers and scholars focused heavily, if not exclusively, on the core values of efficiency, economy, and effectiveness.[2] Moreover, it was generally assumed that administrators would be men and women of strong moral character and integrity. Look, for instance, to the words of nineteenth-century civil service reformers such as Woodrow Wilson. In his famous essay of 1887 titled "The Study of Administration," he said that we must clear "the moral atmosphere of official life by establishing the sanctity of public office as a public trust . . . [thereby] opening the way for making it businesslike" (1887/1941, 494). "The ideal for us," he argued, "is a civil service cultured and self-sufficient enough to act with sense and vigor . . ." (501). Thus, there was little reason to be concerned about the need to add a fourth "e"—ethics—to the holy trilogy of efficiency, economy, and effectiveness. But times change. Ethics has become both academic talk and office shoptalk. Indeed, it is increasingly common to find public administration graduate programs offering ethics courses and public organizations providing in-house ethics training.

The effort to curb wrongdoing in government is driven by several factors. First, incidents of wrongdoing in the United States and abroad have drawn increasing public and media attention. Corrupt acts at the highest levels of government in local, state, national, and international arenas have not vanished from the earth. Indeed, a persuasive argument can be made that corruption has held steady in developed countries and is rampant in many developing countries. No community or nation is immune to its ruinous effects. Thus, the "why" of ethics management can be tied to stamping out wrongdoing.

At the same time, there is a second compelling argument for organizations to embrace high ethical standards—an argument tied to the realization among private- and public-sector managers that productive, high-performing organizations are value driven. And, most important, these organizations place ethics high on their list of values. Insofar as such a link exists between ethics and organizational performance, prudent managers and scholars have focused on understanding the dynamics of the ethical workplace. Additionally, they have examined how professional associations armed with ethics codes can help them cultivate an ethical culture.

Is Ethics Management Possible?

The possibility of ethics management has become a reality only in recent decades, although interest in ethics in Western culture can be traced to the age of antiquity (8 B.C.) and in the Orient to the Chinese sage Confucius (551–479 B.C.E.). The Greek philosopher Aristotle (384–322 B.C.E.) wrote about moral virtues such as courage, honesty, temperance, and responsibility. Virtue ethics, as this approach came to be known, has inspired and motivated human beings in vastly different cultures for centuries. Confucian ethics is considered similar to virtue ethics, although his teachings emphasized self-cultivation and reasoned judgment.

Other philosophers such as the German Immanuel Kant (1724–1804) offer an alternative to virtue ethics. Kantian ethics focuses on duty as exemplified in the famous categorical imperative: "Act only according to that maxim by which you can at the same time will that it should become a universal law" (Kant 1785/1989). An act is accorded moral worth if the motive is principled. Ethical humans are duty bound to do the right thing.

The Englishman John Stuart Mill (1806–1873) offers yet another view, asserting that one can know if an act is right or wrong only by its consequences. Thus, utilitarian ethics as espoused by Mill calls for acts that result in desirable ends. The well-known maxim, "Do the greatest good for the greatest number," continues to undergird the ethics philosophy of many. The view that moral ends justify immoral means is no more acceptable from a public ethos utilitarian perspective than is the view that moral means can be used to justify immoral ends.[3]

These philosophies—virtue ethics, duty-based ethics, or utilitarianism—rarely serve as pure operating philosophies in day-to-day living. As the public administration ethicist Terry L. Cooper (2006b) explains, "We identify, or assume, certain principles of duty that are important to us and relate those to the consequences we anticipate by following that duty. The result is that we almost never act purely on the basis of duty to principle, nor purely by calculating the consequences."

Given these philosophies, reasonable questions include: How would we characterize the prevailing ethos of American public administrators? Do administrators subscribe to one of these views? More than one? None? While it is risky to generalize, the answer is that most public administrators draw on all of these ideas but are closer to what might be called *pragmatic utilitarianism*—that is, they are constantly exploring decision alternatives that generate satisfactory outcomes for their (a) elected bosses, (b) employees, and (c) citizens. A public service ethos presupposes that administrators promote the public interest over those of their employees and elected bosses, but doing so is not always so straightforward or clear.

These great philosophers beget an intellectual legacy and presence that remain significant in the twenty-first century. Though different, they share a common bond in identifying and holding the individual responsible for right and wrong behavior. Consequently, moral agency—the capacity to make a choice between right and wrong—is key to understanding ethical choice and behavior. Telling a lie when under physical duress, for example, illustrates a lack of moral agency.

Definitions of *ethics* and *morals* are provided in the following box. While both ethics and morals are concerned with right and wrong, it is important to note that there is a difference. On the one hand, the term *ethics* presupposes that an action has taken place or a certain behavior exists. It is this behavior that matters and, in the end, defines right or wrong. On the other hand, *morals* can exist independent of behavior. Former U.S. president Jimmy Carter's statement in a *Playboy* magazine interview during the 1976 presidential campaign illustrates this point rather well. Candidate Carter said: "I've looked on a lot of women with lust. I've committed adultery in my heart many times." Jimmy Carter confessed to an immoral act in his mind (Scheer 1976).

Definitions of Ethics and Morals

Ethics are values and principles that guide right and wrong behavior. The Golden Rule—do unto others as you would have them do unto you—is an example of an ethical principle that guides behavior. *Morals* are core beliefs about life, humanity, and nature. Beliefs about going to war, executing criminals (capital punishment), abortion, adultery, and gay lifestyles are moral issues.

An Ethical Oversight

The intellectual legacy of the great philosophers has spawned a blind spot in our understanding of contemporary ethical behavior. What has been largely overlooked is the *context* in which ethical decisions are made. The scope of questionable decision making grew ever more evident in the mid-twentieth century, as the work and play of humans in all walks of life became wholly enmeshed in complex organizations. Social scientists began to study and write about life and morality "in the shadow of organization," as Robert B. Denhardt (1981) puts it. Individual morality became dominated by the prevailing ethos of the organization, leading to the belief that what is right for the organization is right for the individual. The organizational imperative—do whatever is in the best interests of the organization—requires employees to be obedient to the decisions of superiors, to be technically rational, to be good stewards of other people's property, and to be pragmatic, contend W.G. Scott and D.K. Hart (1979, 1989). Above all, "managers must be amoral in order to obtain the most benefits for their organizations" (1989, 34).

Empirical studies also began to focus on the organizational context of (un)ethical decision making.[4] For example, studies of whistleblowers have flourished.[5] One study by Lovell (2003, 201) paints a picture of organizational life in which "the fear of impairing one's future career prospects was a significant factor shaping the muteness of many of the managers about their respective ethical dilemmas." Lovell's research points to the suppressing influence that organizational imperatives can have on moral agency. Suppressed whistleblowing, Lovell contends, is an enduring and troubling phenomenon in modern organizations.

Rosemary O'Leary (2006) adds to this literature with a set of provocative cases about career administrators in state and federal agencies who engaged in what she calls the "ethics of dissent." These seasoned public officials found themselves at odds with their political superiors over significant public policy issues. Rather than resign, all worked behind the scenes to correct what they perceived to be flawed public programs—programs that did not advance the public interest. Most were successful at this form of guerrilla warfare, as she describes it.

Case studies of ethics stress and decision distress also began to appear over the past two decades.[6] Frederickson and Newman (2001), for example, explored the decision by Gloria Flora, a high-ranking manager in the U.S. Forest Service, to resign her position. She "exited with voice" and, according to the investigators, is a moral exemplar. The incident had to do with Flora's judgment that, as the supervisor of a national forest in Nevada, she could no longer carry out her stewardship duties in the face of powerful economic and political pressures to exploit protected federal lands—pressures from interests in mining, timber production, and livestock grazing. Flora's more than 20 years of service with the U.S. Forest Service was terminated with less than three years from vestment in the civil service retirement system. She paid a high price, emotionally and financially, for her moral courage. Frederickson and Newman ask, why would she do this? The answer—because she could not compromise her strong belief to do the "right" thing. "She was motivated to act as she did out of a sense of responsibility" (2001, 360).

Ethics is often regarded as something that cannot be taught or "managed" in the age of high-tech, performance-driven organizations. However, the results of many recent studies are casting considerable light on what we know and do not know about ethical behavior in complex organizations. There is, of course, still much more to learn. Nonetheless, a sufficient body of knowledge can be drawn on to learn how to lead and build organizations of integrity.[7]

"In fact, ethics has everything to do with management.... Managers who fail to provide proper leadership and to institute systems that facilitate ethical conduct share responsibility with those who conceive, execute, and knowingly benefit from corporate misdeeds" (Paine 1994, 106).

The Ethics-Performance Linkage

Efforts to probe the ethics-performance linkage in public administration began in the early 1990s. Burke and Black (1990), for example, conducted an exploratory study of organizational ethics and productivity by surveying 69 executives and managers, approximately one-third of whom were from the public and nonprofit sectors. Their findings did not demonstrate a conclusive empirical link between ethics and performance but did motivate the authors to recommend that agencies create "a leadership group focused on identifying ethical concerns and productivity measures" (Burke and Black 1990, 132). Bruce (1994) also used survey research to study the ethics of municipal clerks. Municipal clerks, she found, are generally a highly ethical group who feel that city employees are principled and productive. She contended that managers and supervisors have a "substantial influence on employee ethics and, by extension, on organizational performance" (251).

Menzel (1992, 1993, 1995) has also probed the ethics-performance link. He surveyed different populations—city and county managers in Florida and Texas and city and county employees in two Florida local governments. One study (1993) included the question: "Do ethical climates of public organizations reinforce or detract from organizational values such as efficiency, effectiveness, excellence, quality, and teamwork?" Menzel hypothesized that as the ethical climate of an organization becomes stronger, the five aforementioned organizational performance values will be strongly supported. His findings led him to accept the hypothesis that an organization's ethical climate has a positive influence on its performance.

Similar results are reported by Berman and West (1997) in their study of the adoption of ethics management strategies. City managers reported that "commitment to workforce effectiveness and the adoption of pay-for-performance policies are associated strongly with ethics management practices." In addition, the researchers found that "efforts to decrease absenteeism and to adopt a customer-orientation also are significantly associated with ethics management" (26).

The business community is very much aware of the ethics-performance linkage. Running a business solely on the basis of profit making is no longer the be-all and end-all it once was. Calls for a value-based approach to managing high-performance business enterprises leave little doubt about the importance of ethical values for good business. "Ethical dimensions must be in-built in management thinking, management strategy and performance analysis" (Stainer, Stainer, and Gully 1999, 776).

Ethics-Induced Stress

Other research (Menzel 1996a) has focused on the organizational consequences of ethics-induced stress in the public workplace. Menzel defined ethics-induced stress as a form of cognitive dissonance between an employee's personal ethics and the ethical climate found in the employee's workplace. He asked: Does ethics-induced stress lower employee productivity? Does it result in less job satisfaction? Greater conflict? More employee turnover? Drawing on surveys of city and county managers in Florida and Texas, he found strong statistical associations between managers' high levels of ethics-induced stress and impaired organizational performance. Specifically, as the level of ethics-induced stress increases, job satisfaction decreases, organizational conflict increases, and employee turnover is greater.

Managers as Ethical Leaders

Must managers of public organizations be ethical leaders to have good government? Perhaps, although it might be argued that if good government can be achieved with morally mute managers—managers who do not feel a responsibility to promote ethics or morality in government—then it may be possible to have government that gets the job done efficiently, effectively, and economically. A chilling possibility? Yes. But now consider the question rephrased: If public managers were unethical, would we have good government? Probably not—perhaps definitely not. Conventional wisdom suggests that good government—government that gets the right things done right—cannot be achieved by men and women who lack ethical or moral values or fail to govern or manage on the basis of those values.

Ethics Management in Practice

Public administration practitioners live with ethical and unethical realities day in and day out. This places them in the unique position of being able to practice ethics management and, on occasion, to experience the consequences of ethics management. But do they really practice ethics management? And, if they do, how? Gary B. Brumback (1998) offers some advice. There are four key components of ethics management: hiring, performance, training, and auditing. He stresses the need to hire the "right" people. But who knows how to hire the right people? Should some kind of ethics screening be conducted? Yes. According to Brumback, hiring authorities should

1. review background investigation policies and procedures to determine if they are ethical, can be improved, and are used for the right (seductive) jobs;
2. build the agency's reputation for integrity . . . and then stress that reputation to recruits;
3. not use surreptitious screening and explain the policy to recruits; and
4. ask new hires to pledge a commitment to ethics in government in the oath of office. (66)

Once hiring decisions are made, Brumback contends that "factoring ethics into the process of managing performance is the best way to ensure that work objectives are achieved in an ethical manner, and that other on-the-job behaviors are ethical" (1998, 66). Performance evaluations can and should include an ethics dimension. Assertions that "ethics is not performance" or "ethics is too subjective to be measured" are bogus arguments, he believes.

Ethics management should also emphasize training programs. Employees throughout a public organization are vulnerable to ethics lapses. Thus, a continuous, ongoing program in ethics training amplifies the message that ethics matters. "Above all," Brumback (68) asserts, "tell people what the preconditions of unethical behavior are, what the bottom line of ethics is, and what the agency and each individual can do to make ethics a work habit."

Another component in managing ethics in public organizations is an audit. An audit, whether based on a survey of employees or an assessment of occupational vulnerability, should be conducted periodically. Stephen Bonczek (1998), a city manager with hands-on experience in Michigan, Texas, and Florida, strongly supports the use of an audit to let employees know the positive as well as the negative effects of their efforts. He also believes that managers should "review with their employees all decisions on ethical issues, asking, what did we do right? What did we not do that we should have done? What should we do in future, similar situations?" (78). He encourages managers to use weekly staff meetings "to review all discussions and decisions for ethical implications" (78). Bonczek fully believes that a strong ethical climate has a positive influence on organizational performance and productivity.

Leading with Integrity

"Organizations in difficult times may suffer from the lack of a clear vision for the future and the lack of credible leadership. In roles as a mentor and as the chief executive and adviser to elected and appointed boards and councils, I have found that the commitment to lead with integrity requires the willingness to define and live by clear principles and values in order to build trust and the willingness for others to follow.

"Relying upon the expertise and advice of others requires the ability to also admit one's own mistakes and limitations and to seek and accept the thoughts and ideas of others. Having the flexibility to reach identified goals through a variety of paths can help build that trust and the credibility needed for sustained success."

—Martin P. Black,
AICP, ICMA-CM, former city manager, Venice, Florida

Proactive Ethical Risk Taking

The advice offered by these managers is directed at the "how" of ethics management. Others suggest more. Donald G. Zauderer (1994) adds that integrity includes taking risks to oppose unjust acts (don't just go along); communicate truthfully (do not intentionally deceive others); deal fairly (do not provide others with special advantages or disadvantages because of their affiliations or positions); honor agreements (keep your commitments); accept personal responsibility when things go right or wrong; forgive individuals for mistakes or wrongdoing (don't hold grudges or strive to get even); exhibit humility (avoid unbridled ambition and emphasis of rank and status differences); respect the dignity of individuals by giving earned recognition (don't treat employees simply as vehicles for getting the work done); and celebrate the ability and good fortune of others (suppress envy).

The Council for Excellence in Government (1992–1993) urges every individual in government to recognize that public service is a public trust and that he or she must accept two paramount obligations: (1) to serve the public interest, and (2) to perform with integrity. Furthermore, top leaders in public organizations must advocate and exemplify these core values and obligations. Employees' performances, the council asserts, should be evaluated in light of these standards. Leaders should also make every effort to ensure that their organization recruits workers with strong ethical values.

Chris Wye (1994) shares the council's view of the role that top leaders should assume in promoting ethical organizations. "At every level in the organization, but especially at the top," Wye (45) contends, "effective leadership is an essential ingredient for maintaining the highest standards of ethical conduct in an organization." Nonetheless, Wye worries that the present course of action in the United States has been to focus on the "moral minimum," not the "moral maximum." Through the use of and reliance on laws and regulations to restrict certain types of behavior, the line between that which is acceptable and that which is unacceptable has become the default for defining a bare moral minimum. "Shouldn't we," he asks, "spend at least some time encouraging good behavior?"

Managers Speak Out

James S. Bowman's (1977, 1990, 1997 [with Williams]) surveys of public administration practitioners also shed light on the general understanding of what ethics management is and how prevalent it is. When asked by Bowman in 1989 if their agencies had a consistent approach toward dealing with ethical concerns, nearly two-thirds of the surveyed managers said they did not. When he asked the same question in 1996, a smaller (58 percent) yet still-high percentage of respondents replied in the same fashion: "My agency does not have a consistent approach toward dealing with ethical concerns." Do these responses suggest that there is little ethics management in the public sector? Possibly—but not necessarily. Consider the findings reported by Berman, West, and Cava (1994) and Berman and West (1997).

In 1992, Berman and colleagues surveyed more than 1,000 directors of human resource agencies in municipalities with a population over 25,000 in order to find out (1) what ethics management strategies are employed, (2) how they are implemented, and (3) how effective they are. Their results confirmed Bowman's findings about the lack of a consistent approach—if consistent means "formal." A minority of cities surveyed reported using formal ethics management strategies while a majority claimed that their cities relied primarily on leadership-based strategies, which are informal. They found four categories of ethics management—two they labeled as formal, one informal, and one a combination of formal-informal.

Formal ethics management strategies involve mandatory employee training, the use of ethics as a criterion in the reward structure, and the adoption of organizational rules that promote the ethical climate, such as requiring financial disclosure and approval of outside activities.

Informal ethics management strategies involve reliance on role models and positive reinforcement and are behaviorally based (Berman, West, and Cava 1994, 189).

Code-based and regulatory-based strategies are the two formal strategies used by a large number of cities. Adopting a code of ethics or establishing guidelines for standards of conduct is part of a code-based strategy. Advocates of codes typically presume that codes contribute to a healthy, and therefore higher-performing, organization. Bowman's surveys (1990, 1997 [with Williams]) of practitioner members of the American Society for Public Administration show that the members strongly embrace codes and believe that they have a positive influence on organizational life. Bruce's research (1994) also adds to the believed real-world impact of codes. Her study of members of the International Institute of Municipal Clerks found that clerks "rank a code of conduct as the most powerful way a city can prevent corruption" (29). Using ethics as a criterion in hiring and promotion or requiring approval of outside employment constitutes part of a regulatory-based strategy. Leadership-based strategies, such as demonstrating exemplary moral leadership by senior management, constitute an informal ethics management strategy. Employee-based strategies that incorporate ethics training, protect whistleblowers for valid disclosures, or solicit employees' opinions about ethics constitute a mixed strategy.

Does reliance on an informal strategy, which most cities claim they have, result in ineffective ethics management? Not necessarily. Berman, West, and Cava's research indicates that moral leadership strategies are more effective than regulatory- or code-based strategies in enabling cities to achieve ethics management objectives such as avoiding conflicts of interest, reducing the need for whistleblowers, and fostering fairness in job assignments.

Responses to Ethics Failures[8]

Ethics lapses and failures occur; they are part and parcel of contemporary life. When they happen, what else might be done? At the macro level, codification of acceptable behavior in the form of state law or local ordinance is common practice. Many states and cities have opted for ethics laws and regulatory bodies or boards. Megacities like Los Angeles and Chicago, for example, have established ethics commissions to investigate real and alleged cases of wrongdoing. The U.S. government has also taken action, having established the Office of Government Ethics (OGE) with the Ethics in Government Act of 1978. Now, more than 30 years later, several thousand full- and part-time ethics officials can be found in the federal executive branch (Gilman and Lewis 1996, 521).

These efforts have not gone unnoticed. Several investigators have attempted to assess what difference ethics laws and commissions make in states and communities. R.L. Williams (1996), for example, studied the Florida Commission on Ethics to assess the agency's effectiveness in training officials, conducting ethics audits, investigating complaints, and encouraging an ethical climate. Based on unstructured interviews with commissioners and archival records of the agency, he concluded that the Florida Commission on Ethics was largely ineffective in all four areas. "Unfortunately," Williams (71) says, "the commission apparently serves more effectively as a punitive agent than as an agent of constructive change."

Menzel (1996b) also studied the Florida Commission on Ethics, but from a different vantage point—the view from the street. He surveyed persons who had filed ethics complaints (legally referred to as complainants) and public officials who were the objects of complaints (legally referred to as respondents), asking three questions:

1. What is the relationship between how an ethics complaint is handled and citizen trust or distrust in government?
2. Do persons who file ethics complaints have a positive or negative experience? Are those experiences satisfactory and therefore build trust and confidence in government? Or are those experiences unsatisfactory and therefore contribute to the erosion of public trust and confidence in government?
3. What are the outcomes of the ethics complaint making?

The study involved mail surveys of 303 complainants (144 responded) and 555 respondents (161 responded) completed between 1989 and 1992. Menzel found that complainants were much more likely to say they were dissatisfied with the outcome of the complaint they filed than were respondents who were the object of the complaint.

Furthermore, neither complainants nor respondents differentiated process outcomes from substantive outcomes, and both groups seemed to equate how they were treated with how the complaint-making process turned out. Menzel (1996a, 80) ultimately concluded that "the ethics complaint-making process in Florida may be widening rather than closing the trust deficit."

Trust Building[9]

Closing the trust deficit between the public and government agencies is a legitimate and needed activity, and one that ethics managers should embrace. Figuring out how to reduce the trust deficit is no small challenge. However, research by Berman (1996) is suggestive. He sought to find out how much trust there is among local government officials and community leaders, what municipal strategies are employed to increase trust levels, and how socioeconomic conditions may influence perceptions of trust in local government. Berman surveyed city managers and CAOs (chief administrative officers) in all 502 U.S. cities with a population of more than 50,000 to obtain their perceptions of trust levels. He found that "community leaders have only moderate levels of trust in local government" but that cities with a council-manager form of government experience a significantly higher level of trust than do cities with the mayor-council form of government (33).

Leading with Integrity

"It's most important today for local government administrators to be guided by ethical principles, honesty and moral standards. I do not recall a time when political rhetoric was so deceiving that news agencies found it necessary to produce 'Fact Checks' on political pronouncements. In order for citizens to have faith in government, there must be a sense of trust. Local government professionals may foster such trust by actions that are based upon ethical values."

—Frank Edmunds (2011),
City Manager, Seminole, Florida

Berman identified three principal trust-building strategies—communication, consultation and collaboration, and minimization of wrongdoing. Communication strategies emphasize providing information about the cities' programs and performance. Consultation and collaboration strategies involve engaging community leaders via partnerships, meetings, panels, and so forth. The minimization of wrongdoing strategies emphasizes the adoption of ethics codes, the provision of ethics training, and the like. Strategies vary from community to community, and no single one appears to be more effective than the others. However, there is some evidence that "using a range of strategies by local officials increases trust, even though the impact of individual strategies is modest" (34). Socioeconomic conditions, Berman concludes, influence trust levels. Positive conditions in a community such as high economic growth and cooperation among local groups inspire trust in government. "Negative community conditions, such as economic stagnation, low income levels, racial strife and high levels of crime reduce economic and political resources . . . for dealing with community problems," contributing to a distrust of government (34).

A well-functioning democracy cannot survive without citizen trust and confidence in those who govern. Thus, behaviors or acts by officials that diminish citizen trust and confidence are a direct threat to democratic governance. While trust is a renewable resource, "it is much easier to destroy than to renew" (Bellah et al. 1991, 4). Many factors can destroy trust in governmental institutions, but none destroys it easier or faster than unethical behavior or blatant corruption by public officials.

> "Democracy requires a degree of trust that we often take for granted. . . . It is much harder to build trust than to lose it. But that is our problem in the United States: we have begun to lose trust in our institutions. . . . The heritage of trust that has been the basis of our stable democracy is eroding" (Bellah et al. 1991, 3).

Several trust-building strategies are pursued by the Miami-Dade Commission on Ethics & Public Trust. For example, the commission sponsors a Model Student Ethics Commission Program that "is designed to teach and to engage students in the policies and issues concerning ethics, good governance and accountability in the administration of government. Students will review case studies regarding ethical dilemmas, identify solutions to various ethical issues within the local to international arenas and participate in mock public hearings to discuss/debate public policy issues" (Miami-Dade County Ethics Commission 2005a). A second strategy is an ethics education and training program for companies doing business with local government. Free monthly ethics workshops are conducted in the business workplace. The objective is to increase the "company's understanding about best business practices and the ethics rules as they relate to contracting with local government" (Miami-Dade County Ethics Commission 2005b). A third strategy is directed at candidates for municipal office and covers topics such as reporting and filing requirements, the role of the campaign treasurer, and the Ethical Campaign Practices Ordinance.

Organizational Perspectives on Ethics Management

Theories of organization and governance provide different perspectives on the development of effective ethics management strategies. Traditional *bureaucratic theory,* which stresses hierarchy, rules and regulations, standard operating procedures, and work classification, fits comfortably with a compliance-oriented ethics management strategy.[10] Know the rules of acceptable/unacceptable behavior and stay out of trouble, this perspective demands. The bad news is that much of what passes for ethics management in government is exactly this—compliance oriented. But, as it is argued throughout the book, this approach is inadequate because it minimizes moral agency.

Transaction-cost theory, which emphasizes decision making under conditions of asymmetrical information exchanges, offers another perspective. Gerald Garvey (1993, 25) describes transaction-cost theory as an effort to reduce "especially the costs of gathering and processing information, as the driving factor in rational human beings' never-ending quest for efficiency." Organizational life is viewed as a series of exchanges within and outside the organization. The principal goal is to minimize transaction costs; that is, strive for greater efficiencies and therefore lower the cost of getting work accomplished. Thus, anything that raises the cost of work in the organization is undesirable, including (1) information that is inadequate or uneven (some organizations have more information than others) and/or (2) corruption or unethical behavior. This view would treat unethical behavior as a cost factor that should be reduced, minimized, or eliminated altogether. Consequently, management must embrace measures that accomplish this goal. Such measures might include "one-shot" ethics inoculations, which require members of the organization to attend an ethics seminar from time to time, or more long-term investments in training.

One limitation of transaction-cost theory is that it can be very reactive, not proactive. Another limitation is that it may put too much emphasis on an instrumental view of ethics. Thus, organizational attention to ethics practices and behaviors become a means to an organizational end—productivity.

Transaction-cost theory draws attention to moral hazards in the workplace. Every occupation contains opportunities that can be corruptible. Police, for example, are always vulnerable to favors and bribes. Planners in public organizations are vulnerable to the influence of developers, including the prospects of post-public employment. Pentagon procurement officers are vulnerable to defense contractors' offers of travel, vacations, and employment.

Organizations can also be viewed as *learning systems* that have the capability to adapt to changes in the environment. Peter Senge advances one popular theory in his best-selling book, *The Fifth Discipline: The Art and Practice of the Learning Organization* (1990). A learning organization, Senge advises, is one "where people continually expand their capacity to create the results they truly desire, where new and expansive patterns of thinking are nurtured, where collective aspiration is set free, and where people are continually learning to see the whole together" (3). The learning organization engages members who work as teams to accomplish organizational objectives and, most important, to learn from one another. This system's view and thinking puts the accent on the whole of the organization, not just the parts. Thus, it offers a long-term view of the organization's well-being that is contrary to the more common emphasis on short-term performance.

A learning theory approach is attractive from an ethics management perspective for several reasons. First, specific steps taken to promote ethical behavior are not treated as one-shot efforts. For example, ethics training, although directed at specific members of the organization, is viewed as beneficial because those who have received the training will influence others. Stated differently, the learning process extends beyond the individuals who are trained. Second, the long-term emphasis of a learning organization would buffer attempts to cut back on, say, ethics training when organizational resources are threatened. Training activities are commonly reduced when organizational budgets are challenged. Despite these positive features of the learning organization, fashioning an effective ethics management strategy is quite challenging. As Mark K. Smith (2001) points out, "while he [Senge] introduces all sorts of broader appreciations and attends to values—his theory is not fully set in a political or moral framework. . . . His approach largely operates at the level of organizational interests."

Recent trends in *governance by networks* provide yet another perspective on building organizations of integrity. Stephen Goldsmith and William D. Eggers (2004, 7) point out that "in the twentieth century, hierarchical government bureaucracy was the predominant organizational model used to deliver public services and fulfill public policy goals . . . but its influence is steadily waning." Rather, governments are relying ever more frequently on networks to deliver public goods and services. The growth of third-party government "is transforming the public sector from a service provider to a service facilitator" (Goldsmith and Eggers 2004, 10). Outsourcing, contracting, privatization, and the commercialization of public-private partnerships are, as the authors put it, "the new shape of government." Networked government promises greater speed, flexibility, and responsiveness in meeting the needs and demands of the public. The implications for ethical governance and the development of effective ethics management strategies are difficult to predict with confidence. However, the blurring of public-private-nongovernmental boundaries, as the networked model posits, calls for the development of creative ethics management strategies.

Another significant organizational perspective derives from research on *organizational cultures.* This perspective has a long and respectable heritage dating to the organizational theorist Chester Barnard's (1938) famous observations about informal organizations—that is, what happens in organizations is impersonal and not reflected by the organizational chart. In the same era, Mary

Parker Follet (1924), a social worker and management consultant, wrote at length about the importance of group relationships in organizations, noting that authority in organizations derives from relationships among its members.

Interest in culture as a conceptual lens for viewing organizational behavior languished for decades after Barnard and Follet drew attention to it. In the 1980s, however, with the publication of popular books such as *In Search of Excellence* (1982) by Thomas J. Peters and Robert H. Waterman, and *Theory Z: How American Business Can Meet the Japanese Challenge* (1981) by William G. Ouchi, there came a renewal of interest in culture as a determining influence in organizations. Values, these scholars argue, must be understood, cultivated, and drawn upon to build high-performing organizations.[11]

Viewing organizational life though the values embedded in its culture has much to offer in leading and building organizations of integrity. The ethical culture of the organization then becomes an important subset of values that constitute the overall organizational culture. Managers who have a firm grasp of this culture understand the importance of ethical values and practices in contributing to the effectiveness of the organization and are likely to devote time and energy to building and sustaining an organization of integrity. A culture perspective, therefore, is among the more promising organizational perspectives to consider when devising a successful ethics management strategy.

Building an Ethical Culture[12]

But how can managers build ethics and integrity into the organizational culture of their agencies? The quick answer is, not easily! Creating and sustaining an ethical workplace takes many hands and much time. It is not that public organizations are staffed with unethical workers; over the years, though, many fall prey to a series of false assumptions about the role and place of ethics in agencies. So, the administrator who wants to build ethics into the organizational culture must first dismiss the following false assumptions.

Ethical Values Are Personal and Are Not Expressed Within the Organization

Part of the mythology of working in the public sector is that employees should not act on their values and beliefs because to do so would undermine their ability to be fair and impartial. In other words, it is okay to have personal values and ethics, but do not bring them to the workplace! This approach will breed ethical complacency and eventually contribute to ethical lapses within an organization.

*Ethical People Always Act Ethically Regardless of What Goes On
in the Organization*

To suppose that ethical people will not experience ethical lapses is a false assumption. Recruiting ethical people is certainly an important first step, but it is not sufficient to ensure that ethical government will result. Employees with sound ethical intentions still need support and reinforcement in the workplace.

*Ethics Discussions in Public Organizations Contribute Little, if
Anything, to Productivity, Morale, or Problem Solving*

Many managers may believe that it is nice to talk about ethics in the workplace but that such talk matters little when it comes to getting the job done. This is another false assumption. Indeed, time devoted to ethics discussions or formal training might be viewed as a major distraction from time that could be devoted to providing services in a more cost-effective fashion. Growing empirical evidence shows a significant correlation between the presence of a strong ethical climate and the emphasis the organization places on values such as efficiency, effectiveness, quality, excellence, and teamwork.

It is important for managers to develop strategies that encourage dialogue on issues with ethical implications and to provide an approach toward establishing an ethical workplace. The creation of a shared value system based on principles requires meaningful and serous dialogue through an inclusive, not an exclusive, process. The involvement of employees in training and development seminars that allow for questions and confrontations will give individuals the confidence needed to take action, resolve problems, and raise productivity.

*Ethics Cannot Be Learned, Taught, or Even Discussed in Any
Meaningful Way*

There is a widespread belief that ethics are acquired in one's youth, and therefore, any effort to teach or learn about ethics as an adult is fruitless. A corollary is that one can learn ethics only through the crucible of personal experiences. These views reduce ethics to whatever values and life experiences workers bring to the workplace and are hardly reassuring to managers who wish to build ethics into their organizational culture.

Neither ethical persons nor workplaces are entirely products of past experiences, whether personal or organizational in nature. This "naturalist" view of how an ethical sense is acquired or transmitted must be rejected. Rather, ethical behavior must be viewed as learned behavior that can be relearned and modified, if needed.

> Ethical behavior is learned behavior, and managers can build organizational processes and strategies that contribute to this learning effort. Initiatives such as including ethics stories in newsletters and holding seminars on ethics training, for example, might not transform unethical employees into good organizational citizens, but they can facilitate decisions that reflect organizational values and purpose. When training is successful, employees become aware of options and have the knowledge and resources to select and carry out the right choices.

Creating and Distributing a Written Ethics Policy Eliminates Any Further Responsibility of the Organization or Its Leaders

False! While it is important to have guidelines and to provide them to employees, this action alone will fall short of guiding behavior and can do little to change it (when such change is needed). Building ethics into the organizational culture does not occur in a single shot. It is a continuous process that finds expression in many ways. A written statement of principles is an important beginning point, and no organization should be without one. Equally valuable, however, are the moral cues sent out by members of top management. Managers who do not "walk the ethical talk" will soon experience a credibility gap that employees will see as hypocrisy—"do as I say, not as I do."

Appearing to Do Wrong and Actually Doing Wrong Are Different Matters

While true from a factual perspective, this claim is inconsequential when it comes to building ethics into the organizational culture. The belief that a person's ethics should be judged not by appearance but by facts does not reflect the power of perception. Appearing to do wrong when we have done nothing wrong may have the same negative impact as actually doing wrong. The appearance of impropriety erodes employee and public trust in public agencies and weakens the principles of accountability. It may, for example, be legal for a manager to invest in a business that does business with her agency, but she will have difficulty convincing a skeptical public and workforce that she is not using her position for personal gain. The appearance of impropriety is inescapable, regardless of the reality. Appearances matter!

Practical Wisdom

Beyond dismissing these false assumptions, administrators should rely on both formal and informal ethics management strategies to strengthen their agencies' ethical environment. Managers do not need to run through a daily checklist to achieve an ethical workplace. No algorithm or methodology will cultivate an ethical organizational culture. Still, the literature reviewed here suggests that managers should take a systemic and comprehensive approach to fostering ethics in the workplace. Evidence collected to date, although limited, points to the need to incorporate a wide range of ethical practices into the total fabric of an agency. Doing so is likely to have a lasting imprint on ethical life in the organization. Moreover, managers are likely to enjoy the benefits of a sustained ethical workplace by encouraging employees to participate in professional associations, finding creative ways for ethical behavior to be rewarded, establishing an ethics conscience within their organizations, adopting a code of ethics or statement of principles, providing for ethics training or dialogue, and "walking the talk."

Organizations of integrity are places where human beings carry out their daily duties with pride and respect for others. Practitioners whose viewpoints were examined in this chapter especially embrace this view. Character, integrity, accountability, moral competency, and exemplary behavior are words that one finds threaded throughout the practitioner literature. The U.S. General Accountability Office exemplifies these core values in practice. If you visit Washington, DC, as former Comptroller General David M. Walker points out, you can see three core values etched over the entrance to the GAO's headquarters—accountability, integrity, and reliability.

Ethical governance is not an oxymoron. Ethical workplaces can be found in many federal agencies, states, cities, counties, and special districts. Yet, one size does not fit all. So, how do government leaders and professional managers know which size to pick? Perhaps the advice that President John F. Kennedy offered is a helpful starting point: the ultimate answer to ethical problems in government is honest people in a good ethical environment. Honest people can certainly contribute to an ethical workplace, but more is needed—a strong ethical environment. The components of such an environment include exemplary ethical leadership, a community that cares about its least advantaged citizens, and a management profession that values integrity and demands high standards of performance.

But how does one create a strong ethical environment? Certainly not from the manager's bookshelf, as helpful as that might be. Rather, an ethical setting is built and maintained the same way a new home is built—stick by stick, nail by nail, day by day. Ethical organizations require the same kind of care, competence, and attentiveness to maintain what has been established. Ethical governance cannot be conjured up with the wave of a wand or a magic elixir. Without a strong infusion of ethical leadership and management in organizations, good government is not likely to exist. Federal, state, and local government officials and appointed public managers can—indeed must—do everything within their power and imagination to build ethical organizations.

Key Themes

Six key themes are threaded throughout the chapters that follow. First, scandal is the most common trigger for bringing about ethics reform. Nearly every instance recounted in this book about a city, county, state, or national government adopting an ethics ordinance or law or code to foster integrity in governance was preceded by a scandal. And more often than not, the scandal involved elected officials, not appointed administrators. Public managers, nonetheless, often are viewed as "guilty by association" and become the target of bureaucratic reform while actual political reform is left untouched. Ethical governance must encompass both political and bureaucratic spheres of action.

Second, ethics issues and efforts to remediate them are not limited to the American experience. As Chapter 9 on international ethics management illustrates, these matters are ubiquitous. Moreover, creative solutions are needed to address ethical shortcomings on a global basis; such solutions must allow for cultural differences while maintaining a universal standard of ethical behavior.

A third theme is that leading and building organizations of integrity is not a one-shot affair. Rather, it is an ongoing process: one might say that it's the journey, not the destination that matters. Still, the destination is very important, even if it is not reached. Earlier in this chapter, the destination was characterized as a workplace "where individuals treat each other with respect, take pride in their work, care about one another, promote accountability, and place the public interest over individual and organizational self-interest." This is the idea and ideal of an organization of integrity. Have you worked in such an organization? Probably not. Would you like to work in one? Does this question even need to be asked?

A fourth theme is that a compliance approach to building an organization of integrity is not sufficient. Indeed, in its most pernicious form, this path can lead to the lowest common denominator—if it's legal, it's ethical. This "low road" approach will never lead to an ethical workplace. Rather, the workplace becomes one in which rule evasion and dodging go hand in hand with a "gotcha" mentality. Members of the organization must always ask themselves, what is the right thing to do? and then follow the ethical "high road." Rules and regulations may help answer this question, but they will never be sufficient. Each person must strive to ensure that his or her ethical compass is working correctly. Having a floundering ethical compass is the surest way to get lost in the quagmire of today's complex organizations.

Key Themes

1. Scandals trigger ethics reform.
2. Ethics issues are universal.
3. Leading and building organizations of integrity is an ongoing process.
4. A compliance approach to leading and building an organization of integrity is not sufficient. The "high road" of aspirational ethics must be taken.
5. Ethics management tools must be used in a systematic, comprehensive manner.
6. Leading with integrity is essential.

The fifth theme is: there is no checklist for building organizations of integrity. The tools described in Chapter 4—training, codes, ethics audits, hotlines, and human resources management—are powerful devices when joined together in a systematic, comprehensive manner. Ethics managers must balance the use of each tool much the same way an orchestra conductor must distill harmonious music from diverse musicians and instruments. No single tool can transform the sour notes of unethical behavior into the reassuring culture of an organization of integrity.

The sixth and perhaps most significant theme is that organizations of integrity can only be built by leaders with integrity. Easy to do? No. Essential? Yes. Ethical managers aren't born; in fact, managers can *learn* to lead with integrity, by allowing no room for moral muteness in talk or behavior. Followers know when a leader embraces high ethical standards and promotes integrity in the day-to-day affairs of the organization.

Achieving an ethics-driven workplace is difficult but not impossible. There are ways and means to strengthen an organization's ethical culture, and it seems rather foolish not to employ those means to build organizations of integrity.

Plan of the Book

This book takes a public management perspective toward leading and cultivating organizations of integrity and encourages managers to take a proactive posture toward governing. Administrators and their elected bosses are not content to simply "let things happen" but seek out best management practices and knowledge to make the wheels of governance turn more smoothly.

Do we know enough about leading and cultivating ethical cultures in organizations to guide managers toward ethical management practices? Without question. Considerable research has been conducted on this subject since the early 1990s, yielding data that can be tapped for best practice ideas. Among other things, the accumulated scholarship provides ideas and recommendations for resolving ethics and values conflicts, managing ethics-induced stress, fostering strong ethical climates, preventing ethics failures, and even changing organizational cultures to make them more integrity friendly and responsive to the needs of employees and the community of which they are an integral part.

This chapter provided an introduction to ethics management. Chapter 2 follows with a discussion of the U.S. constitutional and administrative environments in which public officials grapple with the challenge of leading and building organizations of integrity. Chapter 3 explores the "ins and outs" of leading with integrity, including some instances of failing to lead with integrity. Chapter 4 describes and assesses the tools available to elected and appointed officials who are committed to building ethical organizations; among others, these include ethics training, audits, codes, hotlines, and oaths. Chapter 5 presents a "big picture" view of this largely unmapped terrain. Chapter 6 takes the reader inside three cities (Tampa, Chicago, New York City), four counties (King County, Washington; Palm Beach, Florida; Salt Lake County, Utah; and Cook County, Illinois), and two consolidated city-counties (the Unified Government of Wyandotte County and Kansas City, Kansas, and Jacksonville-Duval County, Florida) to examine "ethics management in action."

Chapter 7 canvasses legislative and administrative measures taken by the American states to encourage ethical behavior and discourage unethical behavior. It also assesses state ethics laws, commissions, and boards in three states—Florida, Illinois, and New York. This chapter is followed by a similar effort in Chapter 8 to examine U.S. Congress, American presidents, and the federal judiciary from an ethics-based perspective.

Chapter 9 examines the international world of ethics management, with particular attention focused on Europe, Asia, and Africa. The final chapter, Chapter 10, outlines the challenges confronting citizens and public officials committed to ethical governance, including (1) the limitations brought about by the privatization movement, (2) the enormous challenges of Information Age technology, (3) the impact of globalization on workplace ethics, and (4) the effectiveness of professional ethics education.

Accompanying each chapter are two skill-building exercises that allow the reader, working either alone or as a member of a small group, to engage in "hands-on" active learning. The exercises cover a wide range of issues and settings. Some are presented in a city or county setting; others are presented in a state, national, or international context. All are designed to stimulate the reader to think about the day-to-day world of ethics management and to explore the intricacies and complexities of the subject matter.

Summing Up

Can we talk about governing ethically or managing ethics in the same way we discuss managing budgets, policies, or people? The answer is a resounding "yes!" Indeed, the single act of developing and adopting a code of ethics, as Bowman (1981) documented more than 20 years ago, is managing ethics in the workplace. Thus, ethics management is not a new enterprise; it is an old one. What is new is how we think about it. If we view it as a systematic and consistent effort to promote ethical organizations, as Article IV of the American Society for Public Administration (ASPA) Code of Ethics declares, then there is such a thing as ethics management. Ethics management, however, is not synonymous with "control." *It is not the act of controlling coworkers' behaviors.* Rather, it is the cumulative effect of ethics-building actions taken by managers—actions designed to engender an ethical sensitivity and consciousness that permeates all aspects of getting things done in a public service agency. It is, in short, the promotion and maintenance of a strong ethics culture in the workplace. And, "success in creating a climate for responsible and ethically sound behavior requires continuing effort and a considerable investment of time and resources" (Paine 1994, 112).

Ethics Management Skill Building

Practicum 1.1. A Late Night Surprise!

Dennis, the city manager of a financially strapped municipality, is working uncharacteristically late at night. The offices are empty and quiet. As he is leaving, he notices a sliver of light coming from the door of the new budget director, Susan. He decides to stop in and praise her for her excellent report in which she discovered errors that will save the city millions of dollars, projecting a budget surplus for the first time in years. As he approaches her office, he can see through the gap in the partially opened door that she is in a passionate embrace with Gary, the assistant city manager. The city's employment policy forbids dating between employees, threatening dismissal to those who do.

The city's code of ethics requires Dennis to enforce this policy, yet at the same time he does not want to lose either or both of his valuable employees. It would be difficult if not impossible to bring in someone else with their experience and credentials for the amount of money the city can afford to pay in salary.

Questions

1. What should Dennis do? Should he report Susan and Gary, in accordance with policy? Is it his ethical duty to do so?
2. Should he overlook the situation, believing the city will be best served in the long run? Is this a pragmatic utilitarian approach?
3. Should he speak to each of them and threaten to tell his elected bosses if they don't end the relationship? Would this cause other employees to pay more attention to the city's code of ethics?
4. Does Dennis have any right to interfere in a personal affair between two consenting adults?
5. Is this a management problem? An ethics problem? Both?
6. Can ethics problems be separated from management problems? Why or why not?

Practicum 1.2. Moral Management?

Assume that you are the top elected official of a county constitutional office, such as the clerk or property appraiser. As part of your campaign to become elected, you promise that you will hold employees of the organization to a code of conduct that will not jeopardize the credibility and integrity of the office. A week after you take office, you learn that several married employees are engaging in intimate behavior that offends your sense of morality and is causing disruption in the agency.

The agency's written policy is quite clear. It states:

> Agency personnel, whether married or single, shall not develop an association with another member whom they know or should have known is married to another person. Married members also shall not develop an association with agency members who are single. Excluded from this are members who are separated and residing apart from their spouse, or those who have legally filed for divorce. For the purpose of this policy, "association" means residing with, dating, or entering into any intimate relationship with.

Questions

1. What do you do? Do you turn your head and hope the situation disappears? Is this solution in the best interest of the organization?
2. Are you obligated to enforce the agency's written policy?
3. Do you call the employees to your office and have a conversation about adultery?
4. Do you consider revising the agency's written standard of conduct?
5. What changes would you make in the existing policy?

Notes

1. This discussion relies on Menzel (2005a).

2. See Richard J. Stillman, *Preface to Public Administration: A Search for Themes and Direction,* 2d ed. (Burke, VA: Chatelaine Press, 1999), for an excellent overview of the evolution of public administration practice in the United States.

3. An insightful discussion of philosophical perspectives in administrative ethics is contained in Part II of Terry L. Cooper, ed., *Handbook of Administrative Ethics,* 2d ed. (New York: Marcel Dekker, 2001). This discussion covers virtue ethics as well as deontological and teleological approaches to administrative ethics.

4. The first serious attempt to bring empirical research to bear on administrative ethics took place in 1991 at Park City, Utah, when H. George Frederickson organized a conference for this purpose. The conference papers were published in *Ethics and Public Administration,* ed. H. George Frederickson (Armonk, NY: M.E. Sharpe, 1993).

5. See Brewer and Coleman Selden (1998); Folks (2000); Perry (1993); Glazer and Glazer (1989); Jos (1989); Miceli and Near (1985).

6. This discussion relies on Menzel (2005a).

7. For an in-depth review of the public service ethics literature, see Menzel (2011).

8. This discussion relies in part on Menzel (2001b).

9. A thorough discussion of trust building is presented by David G. Carnevale's *Trustworthy Government: Leadership and Management Strategies for Building Trust and High Performance* (San Francisco, CA: Jossey-Bass, 1995).

10. Max Weber is widely recognized as the intellectual father of modern bureaucracy. Weber identified six key characteristics of bureaucracy: (1) official duties are fixed by rules, laws, or administrative regulations; (2) offices are arranged hierarchically, with a clearly ordered system of super- and subordinate relationships; (3) management is based on written documents; (4) management is selected and promoted via the merit principle; (5) the official is a full-time employee; and (6) management follows general rules that are stable and can be learned (Gerth and Mills 1946).

11. For an excellent overview of issues and research on organizational cultures from a sociobehavioral perspective, see Benjamin Schneider, ed., *Organizational Climate and Culture* (San Francisco, CA: Jossey-Bass, 1990).

12. This discussion draws in part on Menzel (2001b).

2

Constitutional and Administrative Environments

Where a man assumes a public trust, he should
consider himself a public property.

—Thomas Jefferson, quoted in *A Winter in Washington*

The Founding Fathers believed that democratic governance required leaders with impeccable moral and ethical credentials. Those who occupied office, whether appointed or elected, were expected to demonstrate the highest degree of integrity and conduct themselves in honorable ways. A democratic government—one that is open and accessible to popular will and thought—could be achieved only through the good works of morally committed men and women. According to Louis C. Gawthrop (1998) in *Public Service and Democracy: Ethical Imperatives for the 21st Century,* the 55 men who gathered in Philadelphia in 1787 to draft the Constitution for a new republic wove a garment threaded with ethical values and moral virtues. Those values "constituted an indivisible presence in all of the practical and pragmatic decisions made concerning the structure and functions of the new government" (38).

A cursory examination of the historical record—the Constitution and the *Federalist Papers*—to identify the framers' expectations of the qualifications one must possess to hold office suggests that, beyond age and residency requirements, members of Congress (especially the Senate) should have "stability of character" and be "truly respectable." A morally imbued constitution required nothing less than morally imbued officials to ensure that a true democracy would prosper. Still, the framers recognized a darker side of the human spirit—ambition, greed, and revenge. In *The Federalist #6*, Alexander Hamilton asserts that in creating a government of the people we must not forget that "men are ambitious, vindictive, and rapacious" (1787). James Madison shared Hamilton's view, arguing in *The Federalist #51* that "ambition must be made to counteract ambition" (1788). Checks and balances, the separation of powers among the three branches of government, and the division of power between the national government and the states (federalism) were put forward as the structural means to "counteract ambition." And, as Madison so eloquently proclaimed, "In framing a government which is to be administered by men over men, the great difficulty lies in this: you must first enable the government to control the governed; and in the next place oblige it to control itself" (*The Federalist #51*).

This chapter examines the foundations of the U.S. Constitution and its implication for ethical governance. Particular interest is focused on the evolution of government ethics in the United States.

Government of, by, and for the People

The framers' clashing views of human nature and the need for government conducted by upright persons were borne out in the early decades of the new republic. George Washington's secretary of war, Henry Knox, found himself deeply in debt as a result of an extravagant lifestyle and gambling obligations incurred by his wife (Gilman 1995b). In 1791, in an effort to cope with his debts, Knox engaged in land speculation in Maine that resulted in lawsuits challenging the transactions. Friends came to his legal rescue, and he later rewarded them with recommendations for public office (1995b, 63). Embezzlement was also a problem in the early republic. "A pointed example," Gilman (1995b, 64) notes, "is the embezzlement case of Dr. Tobias Watkins, a close friend of President John Quincy Adams (1824–1828) and a high-ranking officer in his administration." Dr. Watkins was later tried and imprisoned by the Jackson administration.

These transgressions, however, paled alongside the rampant patronage bestowed on political followers when Andrew Jackson (1828–1836) occupied the White House. Jacksonian Democracy, as historians dubbed it, meant that the common man could lay claim to any job in the federal government. And, perhaps most important, the credentials for this claim were neither the possession of moral character nor workplace competency; rather, they were rooted in political and personal connections. Thus, the *spoils system*—whereby those who won political office rewarded their friends and supporters—came to the fore.

Patronage politics was to dominate much of American government—city, state, and national—for the next five decades. Even during the Civil War (1861–1865), President Abraham Lincoln spent much of his time receiving and responding to federal job seekers. The war itself bred numerous accounts of corruption ranging from exorbitant fees for the purchase of rifles to public expenditures for the purchase of meat in food rations for soldiers. "Corruption in the procurement of war supplies led to the dismissal of Secretary of War Cameron and the passage of the first set of conflict-of-interest statutes" (Gilman 1995b, 66). Widespread corruption, as Gilman (1995b, 65) notes resulted in "America's development of a legal foundation for ethical behavior." Conflict-of-interest statutes were drafted in the postwar years under the Grant administration in an attempt to stop federal officials from "participating in negotiations that might bring financial benefits to the employee either directly or indirectly" (Roberts 1988, 12).

Still, government by incompetent, immoral, and unethical officials approached epidemic proportions by the end of the nineteenth century. Courthouses and state capitols became breeding grounds for the corrupt and ambitious. In New York City, for example, the Boss Tweed gang and a string of Tammany Hall political successors handed out jobs and dollars with impunity. Among the more famous personalities was New York state senator and ward boss George Washington Plunkitt, a son of Irish-American immigrants who entered politics to amass and lose a fortune in his lifetime (1842–1924). Plunkitt's ethics—or more appropriately, lack of ethics—eventually became the anathema of good government reformers.

"This civil service law is the biggest fraud of the age. It is the curse of the nation. There can't be no patriotism while it lasts. How are you goin' to interest our young men in their country if you have no offices to give them when they work for their party?"

—Senator George Washington Plunkitt (1903)

Despite the lively condition of big city political machines and patronage government in the second half of the nineteenth century, reform was launched with the passage of the Pendleton Act of 1883 (also known as the Civil Service Act). This new law aimed to inject "merit" and "political neutrality" into the operations of the national government, presumably leading to a modern civil service imbued with an ethical impulse. Joining the reformers, then Princeton professor Woodrow Wilson (1887/1941, 217) called for "a civil service cultured and self-sufficient enough to act with sense and vigor"—a system in which "administration lies outside the proper sphere of politics" (210). The result of civil service reform, Wilson argued, is "but a moral preparation for what is to follow. It is clearing the moral atmosphere of official life by establishing the sanctity of public office as a public trust" (210).

Administration, Science, and Ethics

Wilson sought to ensure that the American system of government remain effective and moral. His plea to remove the running of government from the "hurry and strife" of politics required two additional considerations: (1) that the field of administration be viewed as a "field of business," and (2) that efforts be undertaken to build a "science of administration" (209). These pronouncements, when taken together, provide an embryonic definition of public management and, as the industrial age roared into the twentieth century, found an intellectual home with the emergence of the *scientific management* movement founded by Frederick Taylor.

Taylor, an engineer who believed that America suffered enormous inefficiencies in the workings of its factories and its government, advocated "one best way" to accomplish work. He introduced tools such as time-and-motion studies to find that one best way. The application of scientific management principles in industry and government, Taylor argued, would lift America out of its wasteful and unproductive habits to the benefit of all. His call resonated with government reformers and with members of the movement to create an impartial, merit-based civil service. Inefficiency, after all, was closely identified with corruption and other misdeeds that prevailed in America's cities and states. Moreover, in creating a "neutral" cadre of public servants to carry out the work of government, the proper emphasis would be placed on work processes, not on personal or political friendships.

Scientific management is an approach to management that emphasizes the application of "scientific" knowledge to work processes. Frederick W. Taylor (1856–1915), an engineer and the father of scientific management, published *The Principles of Scientific Management* in 1911.

A science of administration and Taylorism, as the scientific management school became known, became the model for the evolution of public management and administration. The ethic associated with this paradigm was utilitarianism (or instrumentalism—getting the job done right benefits the greatest number), and it found overt expression in the evolution of the city management profession. Staunton, Virginia, appointed the first person ever with the title of city manager in 1908. The manager was expected to be competent, politically neutral, and well versed in getting the city's streets repaired and its sewer and water lines working properly. This separation of management from politics was exactly what Wilson had in mind, and the fact that the prevailing ethic was utilitarian was not especially concerning to anyone. Indeed, utilitarianism fit very well with a work ethos. It also fit well with the evolution of the City Managers' Association, which was established in 1914, although it should be noted that the association recognized early on that it was important for its members to live by a strict code of ethics.

Morally Mute Public Management

Efforts to turn administration into a scientific practice began to waiver with the onset of World War II, but they continued to stir the imaginations of managers and organizational theorists well into the 1960s. Science, progress, and modern management, inextricably interwoven, had become dogma by the late 1930s (Stillman 1999). The scale, planning, and execution of the war effort brought a new reality and thinking. The politics-administration dichotomy drew unfavorable attention as policy makers administered wartime programs and administrators became heavily involved in policy making. The planning, coordination, and execution of programs and policies were not driven by scientific principles but by the necessity to get the job done quickly, efficiently, and effectively. And, with the advent of nuclear weapons, and resulting concerns about their destructive potential, many observers began to question whether progress needed to be redefined.

The war years contributed to a proactive management style and led to the so-called "golden years" of federal government employment in the 1940s and 1950s. Gone was some of the theoretical baggage, especially the identity of managers as "neutrally competent" problem solvers. Neutrality, as epitomized through local, state, and federal civil service, had grown larger than the Wilsonian legacy of removing partisanship from government work. In conjunction with the ethic of utilitarianism and Weberian norms of impartiality and hierarchy, neutrality meant (1) either public servants had no claim to values (personal, social, political), especially insofar as they might enter into the carrying out of one's official duties; or (2) at best, as a professional, one could make an argument for a preferred course of action but was expected to fall into line once a policy decision was made by organizational or political superiors. The end result of these influences was the emergence of amoral management—organizations led by men and women who may have been moral but refused to voice their beliefs.

Indeed, as managers and organizations became more morally and ethically sterile, a movement was launched to do something about it. In the late 1960s, at the height of civil unrest and diminishing confidence in the ability of the United States to become a Great Society, a group of young academics gathered in Upstate New York at a retreat called Minnowbrook and put forth a call for a *new public administration*. This "new" public administration would be one in which administrators and managers accepted responsibility for promoting social justice and equity. This value-infused movement was seen by many as an antidote to the perilous plight of the morally mute manager.

What was new about the *new public administration?* Namely, that administrators could and should become proactive in promoting the welfare of the less-advantaged members of society. The old public administration required administrators to be obedient and passive purveyors of the wishes and demands of their elected superiors.

For a variety of reasons, the new public administration did not have as great an impact as some had hoped. Terry L. Cooper (2001, 12) asserts, however, that "when one surveys the history of administrative ethics during the last hundred years it seems clear that this movement made an important contribution to the emergence of a field of study focused on ethics in public administration . . . [especially] around a commonly shared ethical concept—social equity." Nonetheless, the proactive posture of the new public administration made many managers and public officials question whether it was a proper role for nonelected officials to be so presumptuous in defining the public interest. After all, is that not the responsibility of legitimately elected officeholders?

Low Road, High Road, or No Road?

There's a saying with relevance to the role and place of ethics in public management during the past several decades: "If you don't know where you're going, then any road will get you there!" The tumultuous 1960s came to a close with a quest to make managers more relevant morally and ethically, but then there was Watergate—and its aftermath. The secret White House tapes not only revealed that President Richard M. Nixon had conspired with others to cover up a politically motivated break-in of the Democratic Headquarters at the Watergate Hotel, but they also showed that the president's moral compass was broken. President Nixon's resignation in 1974 spawned a wave of legislative initiatives in Washington, DC, and the states to prevent wrongdoing in government and punish those who choose to break the law. State after state enacted ethics laws and established ethics boards or commissions, with some given substantial powers to investigate alleged cases of wrongdoing by officials. At the federal level, Congress enacted the Ethics in Government Act of 1978—a law that, among other things, created the U.S. Office of Government Ethics and the controversial independent counsel, whose broad investigatory powers were put on display in Kenneth W. Starr's 1998 investigation of President Bill Clinton's financial and personal affairs.

Efforts to legislate the ethical behavior of local, state, and federal officials, including high-ranking appointed managers and often frontline members of the government workforce, have produced dubious results. There is precious little empirical evidence that ethics laws, ordinances, or boards have given us good government. Indeed, some say that this legislation allows officials to employ the lowest common denominator in deciding right and wrong behavior. That is, by stating in law what constitutes various punishable offenses, lawmakers have given elected and appointed officeholders the opportunity to define ethics as "behaviors and practices that do not break the law," but may come close to it. Stated in the vernacular, if it's not illegal, it's okay. This approach has been appropriately labeled by John Rohr, a noted ethics scholar, as the "low road" to ethics. The low road features compliance and adherence to formal rules. "Ethical behavior," Rohr asserts in *Ethics for Bureaucrats: An Essay on Law and Values* (1989, 63), "is reduced to staying out of trouble" and results in "meticulous attention to trivial questions."

> "While compliance systems can work, their failure is surprisingly high, often at great expense to employers. But the primary danger of compliance systems lies in their contortion of the decision-making process. Suddenly, instead of thinking about doing the right thing, employees focus on calculating the costs and benefits of compliance versus noncompliance—and about trying to outsmart the system" (Bazerman and Tenbrunsel 2011, 113).

But is the low road the only road? It is hard to argue that it's the "best" road. In fact, many scholars believe it is even a poor substitute for "no road." What, then, might be a more agreeable or desirable alternative? The "high" road to ethics behavior for public managers, C.W. Lewis and S.C. Gilman argue in *The Ethics Challenge in Public Service: A Problem-Solving Guide* (2005), is the path of integrity: "Relying on moral character, this route counts on ethical managers individually to reflect, decide, and act" (16). Such an approach blends the acceptance of personal responsibility for one's behavior with honorable intentions and personal integrity—that is, adherence to moral and principles. But to whose morals and principles should one adhere? Herein lies the challenge of the high road.

The legislative flurry to enact ethics-based laws in the 1970s is regarded by some as an important step forward. However, insofar as this step fosters the "low road" of compliance to ethical behavior, it may actually be a tiny step at best. To be sure, scholars are not advocating a blanket repeal of ethics laws and ordinances. Rather, they are calling for an awakening, perhaps a reawakening, of what might be referred to as the "moral sense" that exists in every single human being. A tall order? To be sure. Indeed, it is one that is fraught with real-world challenges that were amply illustrated in the decade of the 1980s.

The thrashing around to find an ethical road for public managers and elected officeholders to follow fluctuated throughout the "me" generation of the 1980s. Scandals on Wall Street, in the U.S. Department of Housing and Urban Development (HUD), and in the White House with the Iran-Contra affair (a clandestine arms deal with Iran that occurred during Ronald Reagan's presidency) sent ethical compasses spinning wildly. Why would an inside trader like the notorious Ivan Boesky risk his reputation and a prison sentence to skim off millions of dollars in illegal stock trades? Why would Samuel Pierce, the head of HUD under Reagan, sell out to the highest bidders? And, why would Reagan, a popular American president, deny involvement in an illegal and covert scheme to fund anticommunist activity in Nicaragua by selling arms to an unfriendly Iranian regime?

The answer to the first two questions is greed, with some overtones of Plunkitt ethics—"I saw my opportunity. . . ." The Wall Street and HUD scandals clearly involved men and women of ambition and avarice. Some believe that these incidents were merely symptoms of the 1980s "me" mentality. Neither government officials nor private-sector managers and CEOs seemed immune to the question, what's in it for me?

The Iran-Contra affair of the mid-1980s involved the secret and illegal sale of high-priced missiles to Iran by the Reagan administration to support the Contra rebels in Nicaragua—a move that had been banned by the passage of the Boland Amendment. The Contras were fighting to overthrow the Socialist-led Sandinista government in Nicaragua. Top administrators in the Reagan White House tried to funnel proceeds from the Iranian arms sales to the guerrillas bent on toppling the Sandinista regime. At the same time, U.S. officials believed that the arms deal would move Iranian leaders to use their influence to win the release of the American hostages in Lebanon.

Lying, as in the Iran-Contra affair, was equally troublesome and symptomatic of the moral malaise that seemed to gain ground in 1980s America. This particular scandal was especially disturbing because the chain of command from the president through his top security advisers, and eventually Lieutenant Colonel Oliver L. North, seemed to be an unbroken lie bound together by patriotism, duty, and blind loyalty. As North explained to Congress, "Lying does not come easily to me. But we all had to weigh in the balance the difference between lies and lives" (U.S. Senate 1987). That President Reagan actually lied is arguable, however, given the congressional testimony of Admiral John M. Poindexter, the President's national security adviser. Testifying before a joint Senate and House hearing in July 1987, Poindexter stated: "I made a very deliberate decision not to ask the president [about whether arms should be sold to Iran to raise money for the Nicaraguan Contras to fight the Socialist-controlled Nicaraguan government] so that I could insulate him from the decision and provide some future deniability." In other words, Poindexter purposely withheld information from Reagan about the money-for-arms transactions against which Congress had specifically legislated. Lying? No. Evasiveness? Yes. Poindexter provided the president with *plausible deniability* that, in effect, undermined the constitutional responsibility of the highest elected official in the nation.

Plausible deniability is the act of withholding information from a superior so that he or she will be able to speak in a truthful manner about an issue. Admiral Poindexter provided President Reagan with plausible deniability by withholding information about the sale of illegal arms to Iran to raise funds in support of the Contra guerrillas.

The ethical angst of the 1980s spilled into the world of public management, as well—so much so that a number of countermeasures were initiated. One was the promulgation in 1984 of a code of ethics by the American Society for Public Administration (ASPA). ASPA was established in 1939 by men and women of the New Deal generation to promote professional values and ethical behavior in public service. Yet it took more than 40 years to build the consensus needed to adopt a code. Another countermeasure was the recognition by many schools of public affairs and administration that it was time to place ethics courses in their curricula. By the end of the 1980s, 40 schools had added an ethics course to their graduate program of study (Menzel 1997). The National Schools of Public Affairs and Administration (NASPAA) took a related initiative in 1989, when a new curriculum standard on ethics was introduced. Schools seeking accreditation, NASPAA asserted, must demonstrate that their programs have the capacity and means to "enhance the student's values, knowledge, and skills to act ethically."[2]

Scholarship on administrative ethics also expanded significantly in the 1980s with an unprecedented number of ethics books and journal articles appearing in print.[3] Additionally, the International City/County Management Association released an influential volume titled *Ethical Insight, Ethical Action: Perspectives for the Local Government Manager* (Keller 1988), and the long-running periodical *Public Administration Review* published insightful articles.[4]

These collective efforts by individuals and professional associations constituted a major push to ensure that men and women who entered public service could contribute to ethics and competency in government. Whether these results have been achieved remains an important but mostly unanswered question. In fact, the pluralistic nature of these initiatives, in combination with the rethinking of administration and management in the 1990s, may have diffused the presumed desirable outcomes.

Administration as Management

The discussion thus far has assumed that public administration and public management are essentially the same—getting the job done in an efficient, effective, and economical manner. Therefore, it might be presumed that any discussion of ethics is relevant to either. During the past several decades, however, the meaning of *managing* and *administering* public programs and organizations has changed sufficiently to warrant a reexamination of what it means to be a public manager or administrator and to reassess the ethical implications associated with each role.

What kind of changes occurred, and where did they come from? The most important change was the swelling of management and the shrinking of administration as operating concepts and practices in public affairs. One might go so far as to say that public administration, in its most traditional fiduciary sense, has been pushed aside in favor of a public management defined as business management. Entrepreneurialism, get me results, just do it, pay for performance, contracting out, competition, satisfy the customer, outsource the work—these are all examples of the language of managerialism. Echoes of Woodrow Wilson's assertion that administration is a field of business administration? Perhaps.

Another important change is the erosion of the significance of "public" in public service. When institutions of higher education began to recognize the importance of educating men and women for public service careers, the line between governmental and nongovernmental employment was fairly clear. Thus, the rise of MPA (master's of public administration) degree-granting programs responded to the need to supply city, state, and national governments with talented and capable administrators. The degree, however, was supposed to convey more than the competency of its holder. It was presumed that an MPA degree recipient understood why competent administration was essential in a democracy and why he or she, in bringing competence to administration, was also serving the public interest. Normative commitments to promoting democratic governance and the public interest explain precisely why graduate degrees in public administration are rarely named MGAs—master's in government administration.

Nonetheless, times change, and over the past 30 years it has been increasingly difficult to separate public-sector from private-sector employment—not to mention the enormous growth of third-party-sector employment (nonprofits, special districts, and quasi-public agencies). The result, some believe, has been an unwitting redefinition of the MPA degree to emphasize competency only. H. George Frederickson argues in *The Spirit of Public Administration* (1997) that this approach is wrongheaded and potentially dangerous. A democracy, he contends, requires a democratic administration—that is, one in which managers and workers are competent and morally committed to serving the public. Redefining "administration" as "management" poses some risks to that model and raises questions about "managerial" ethics, especially those of a utilitarian nature.

As noted, the 1980s saw a renewal of interest in public-sector ethics issues and problems. This decade also witnessed the steady blurring of private-sector and public-sector lines; unending bashing of bureaucrats and bureaucracy by the media and Republican presidents (remember, it was Ronald Reagan who quipped "Washington is not the solution to our problems: It is the problem!" (January 20, 1981, Inaugural Address); and a steadily growing belief in the application of private-sector management tools to public-sector management problems (Quality Circles, Total Quality Management, Team Building, and so on). Thus, when management consultant David Osborne and former city manager Ted Gaebler published *Reinventing Government: How the Entrepreneurial Spirit Is Transforming the Public Sector* (1992), the stage was set for even more dramatic changes in our thinking about administration and management. The "reinvention" movement, as it is often called, was galvanized when President Bill Clinton assumed office in January 1993. Ten months later, the Clinton administration released *Creating a Government That Works Better and Costs Less: The Report of the National Performance Review* (Gore 1993), a document that embodied the spirit and soul of reinventing government per Osborne and Gaebler, by promising to turn the federal government into a hard-working, cost-effective machine.

Quality Circles and Total Quality Management (TQM) are management techniques that were first applied in private profit-making firms to improve product quality and sales. Quality Circles were popular in Japan in the early 1960s and later used in the United States. They involved small work groups who met regularly in the factory or business to discuss production problems and their solutions. Total Quality Management emerged in the 1980s as an organization-wide approach to improving the quality of products and services. TQM is widely employed by private firms, government agencies, and nonprofit organizations.

The *new public management* school calls for managers to steer organizations, not row them; to empower citizens and coach workers through teamwork and participation; to thrive on and promote competition; to reject rule-driven organizations in favor of mission-driven organizations; to seek results not outcomes; to put customers first; to foster enterprising and market-oriented government; and to embrace community-owned government.[5] New public managers (NPMs) are also likely to find the privatization of public goods and services an attractive alternative and adopt new management tools such as benchmarking, strategic planning, reengineering, and Total Quality Management (TQM) as the situation warrants. This new way of thinking about management requires public managers to take the lead in pursuing economical, cost-effective solutions to administrative problems. Gone is the era of the administrator who merely responds to citizen complaints and demands rather than meeting the customers' needs, who fixes problems after they arise rather than preventing their development, and who promotes the public interest per the new public administration or some other passé value set.

So, what are the implications of the new public management for ethical behavior and practices? Actually, the NPM school is somewhat silent about the place of ethics or morality in public management, and this silence has prompted some observers to worry a great deal about what might be ahead. Larry Terry (1993, 393–394), an outspoken opponent of new public management, believes that NPMs go too far in embracing entrepreneurial values such as "autonomy, a personal vision of the future, secrecy, risk-taking, domination, coercion, and a disrespect for tradition." Frederickson (1997, 22) also worries that NPMs' acceptance of utilitarianism—much as in years past when the tenets of science were believed well suited to public administration—will reduce the public interest to the "sum of atomistic individuals." A public interest so defined is, essentially, no public interest at all, only competing interests. Furthermore, Frederickson cautions against turning citizens into customers, a process that might very well result in a collective escape from responsibility, a reduction in civil discourse, and an alarming increase in individuals and groups vying against each another to extract promises and favors from government. Frederickson is equally concerned about the effect of the reinvention movement and privatization on public affairs.

> Government . . . is being reinvented to put together public-private partnerships, "empower" citizens with choices, and so on. In sum, it is now fashionable to degovernmentalize on the promise of saving money and improving services. If previously governmental functions are shifted to the private sector or are shared, it is a safe bet that corruption will increase. It is no small irony that government is moving in the direction of privatiza-

tion at the same time that there is a rising concern for governmental ethics. (Frederickson 1997, 171)

Gawthrop (1999) has spoken about the risks of debureaucratizing government and treating public service as merely work. In *Public Service and Democracy* (1998) Gawthrop is unrelenting:

> We are faced with a new reality in which the citizen has been reinvented into the customer; interest groups—broadly defined to include private-sector contractors, suppliers, and so on—have been re-designated stakeholders, and, most significantly, public servants have been recast in the mold of entrepreneurs. In the process of reconfiguring public bureaucracies, however, little attention is being given to how this new reality conforms to the ethical-moral values and virtues that are deeply embedded in our democratic system. (17)

This new reality represents a break from the old but no less reassuring reality of the administrator as a detached, dispassionate rational provider of objective information and advice to elected bosses. Good men and women with good intentions who allowed themselves to be seduced by a sense of duty as competent purveyors of neutral information became neither moral nor immoral actors. Rather, they became amoral and therefore incapable of contributing to ethical or democratic governance. Notions of faith, hope, and love, Gawthrop (1998, 87) contends, are not "generally recognized as significant components of public administration in America today. Instead, it is the logic of utility that still provides the basic rationale for the classical management tenets of efficiency and control."

Despite the enormous influence of the old and new management realities, Gawthrop is an optimist, not a pessimist, about public service, ethics, and democracy. A moral impulse, he contends, must suffuse bureaucracy and democracy if the common good, as promised by a democratic society, is to be achieved. But from where does this moral impulse radiate? From the public? Elected officeholders? Administrators? Gawthrop places his confidence in administrators if, and only if, they can break out of "the habits of the self-serving good which allow public servants to pursue a procedural, quasi-ethical life" (139). In other words, an ethical life rooted in procedural correctness—avoiding conflicts of interest, disclosing financial information relevant to one's office holding, and conducting public affairs in the sunshine— is, in Gawthrop's view, a hollow ethical life at best. At worst, a procedural, quasi-ethical life produces a "government of persons without fault, operating in a society without judgment, through the ministrations of a Constitution without a purpose" (139).

Ethics is morality in action, according to Gawthrop (1998, 122). Therefore, it is a mistake to separate morality and ethics, even though it is done quite often. Ethics defined only as compliance—"tell me what is right; what is wrong; what is legal; what is not permissible"—is also unacceptable. It is imperative that public administrators and managers understand that ethics is morality in action and that there is a moral dimension to democracy.

One other issue that might be amplified considerably by NPMs is the challenge of managerial discretion. John Rohr considers this an enduring issue in public affairs that remains unresolved. Take the following question as an example: "How can a democratic regime justify substantial political power in the hands of people who are exempt by law from the discipline of the ballot box?" (Rohr 1998, 6). He has dared to "solve" this unsolved problem in his book *To Run a Constitution: The Legitimacy of the Administrative State* (1986). The oath of office, Rohr asserts, legitimates a degree of professional autonomy for the public manager and "can keep this autonomy within acceptable bounds" (1986, 69). Rohr reminds the reader that the oath of office is more than a mere promise; it is a morally binding commitment to uphold the Constitution. As such, it is a "statement of professional independence rather than subservience" (72). The oath guides autonomy and deters public managers from becoming maximizing bureaucrats.

A *maximizing bureaucrat* is an appointed public official whose single-minded goal is to expand his or her agency's authority, resources, and power.

As appealing as Rohr's solution might appear, it is not without problems. For example, not all managers take an oath of office. Members of the federal government do, but this is not the case with all state or local managers. Then there are those who manage nonprofit or quasi-government corporations, positions that do not necessarily require an oath. Finally, there is the bleak reality that those who do take an oath of office still might not grasp Rohr's contention that an oath places self-imposed limits on the exercise of discretion.

An Unfinished Portrait

Ethics in American public administration has a long, evolutionary history. The portrait sketched here remains unfinished in light of the changes and challenges in managing twenty-first-century public organizations. These changes are in no small measure exacerbated by the forces of privatization, globalization, computerization, and the rapidly moving world of information technology.

The threat of the resurrection of the morally mute manager is real and must be taken seriously. The new public management movement has yet to define itself ethically or morally. Rather, it has aligned itself with a pernicious brand of moral muteness that reduces citizens to customers and public service professionals to businesspeople whose major task is to make citizen-customers satisfied with what they want and receive from government. This pathway, as Gawthrop reminds us, is certainly not a pathway to the common good. It even raises the question of whether such an approach can avoid the worse pitfalls of unethical behavior and practices in government.

Moral courage is the willpower to do the right thing with the knowledge that it will cause pain for another person or for members of one's organization.

Public managers who do *not* understand why the word *public* cannot be removed from their job descriptions or cannot grasp why managerial/ethical competency are essential to effective governance should ply their trade in less demanding occupations.[6] "No web of statute or regulation," as President John F. Kennedy (1961) put it, "can hope to deal with the myriad possible challenges to a man's integrity or his devotion to the public interest" (Lewis 1991, 14). And, according to the then U.S. comptroller David M. Walker: "We need more leaders with three key attributes: courage, integrity, and innovation. . . . We need leaders who have the integrity to lead by example and to practice what they preach" (2005).

Even more is needed to build and sustain organizations of integrity. We turn next to an examination and assessment of the tools that public administrators can use to transform their organizations into high-performance agencies that embrace ethical governance.

The Evolution of Government Ethics in the United States

1792–1828: Character and Integrity in Governance

George Washington set the moral tone of the new government by insisting that public officeholders be men of integrity and high moral character. He served as an exemplar of the values he exalted and appointed men to the federal bureaucracy who were reputed to be persons of character as well as competence (Henry 1995, 240). Some appointees, however, possessed questionable character at best.

1828–1870: Age of Patronage Governance

The election of the Tennessee populist Andrew Jackson to the office of the president of the United States in 1828 ushered in patronage politics and the spoils system. Government jobs were handed out freely to friends and political supporters. Corruption reached alarming levels as time passed and political machines in New York, Philadelphia, and Chicago put down deep roots among immigrants needing help.

Postmaster General Amos Kendall developed the first code of public ethics for the U.S. government in 1829.

1870–1900: Antipatronage Movement

In 1883, U.S. Congress passed the Civil Service Act (also known as the Pendleton Act), which called for a federal civil service system based on competence and merit in appointments and advancement. Federal administrators were to conduct themselves in a politically neutral manner. The law followed the assassination of President James A. Garfield in 1881 by a disappointed office seeker.

In 1887, then Princeton professor Woodrow Wilson penned the famous essay "The Study of Administration" (1887/1941), which calls for the separation of politics and administration. Civil servants were expected to carry out their duties in an efficient and ethical fashion.

1900–1930: Zeal for Government Integrity

Demands to end corruption and advance good government resulted in a zealous approach to reform the entire political system, not just the bureaucracy. Progressive reformers advocated removing partisanship from officeholding, especially at the municipal level; staggering election cycles so that local elections were not held in the same year as state or federal elections; eliminating ward-based districts and replacing them with at-large districts; establishing independent commissions and authorities; ending patronage appointments.

Theodore Roosevelt waged a vigorous campaign to end patronage appointments as a U.S. civil service commissioner (1889–1895). He led efforts to investigate fraud and political abuse in government and expose corrupt government officials. As president, he championed the expansion of competitive civil service, which was increased from 110,000 to 235,000, approximately 63.9 percent of the whole executive civil service. And for the first time, the merit system surpassed the spoils system in numbers of jobs in the executive service (U.S. Office of Personnel Management n.d.).

The early twentieth century also witnessed the adoption of new local government models such as the council-manager plan, which recognized the growing need for professional public management. New professional associations sprang up with the founding of the International City Managers Association (ICMA) in 1914. Thirty-two local governments in the United States and Canada became charter members as the ICMA became the front line in the battle for good government. A decade later (1924), the ICMA adopted the first public service code of ethics for local government administrators.

In 1914, the Society for the Promotion of Training for the Public Service was created. It was "a forerunner of the American Society for Public Administration, which was established in 1939" (Henry 1995, 23).

University of Chicago professor Leonard D. White published the first edition of his textbook *Introduction to the Study of Public Administration* in 1926, creating a benchmark for public administration as a professional field of study and practice.

Scientific management, as described by its inventor Frederick Winslow Taylor (1919), demanded greater planning, specialization, standardization, and "one best way" to accomplish the work of the organization. As a moral code, Taylor claimed that scientific management "aids the worker in general intellectual and moral development" (Fry 1989, 63). But the reality is quite different. The worker is trained to follow orders and be obedient. Attention to moral self and ethical behavior gives way to moral muteness and amoralism.

1930–1960: Administration as Science

Decades of strife, war, and recovery ushered in new views, attitudes, and realities of government and governance. Government was widely viewed as a positive instrument for social and economic advancement. Can-do administrators armed with the science of administration occupied senior posts in government and became social engineers. Many brought to their work a philosophical view of ethics that was both pragmatic and utilitarian.
States began to focus on ethics issues in this period. In 1954, New York became the first state to adopt an ethics law after a series of scandals involving the bribery of public officials by organized crime.

1960s: Rise and Demise of Can-Do Government

The 1960s witnessed the can-do government of the Great Society launched under President Lyndon B. Johnson. By decade's end, the steady erosion of public trust and confidence in government had taken its toll, and government was no longer seen as an instrument to advance social justice and improve the average American's quality of life. Social upheaval, spawned by disillusionment with the Vietnam War and the inability of the federal government to resolve difficult social problems, pushed administrators into a defensive and ethically challenging corner. By decade's end, growing concern with the irrelevance of public administrators motivated a call for a "new" public administration. Administrators were challenged to reconnect themselves ethically and morally and commit themselves to placing social equity at the forefront of the public interest. Most failed to respond.

The first government-wide executive order on standards of conduct affecting all executive branch employees was promulgated on May 8, 1965 (Executive Order 11222).

1970s: Ethical Meltdown

In 1972, Republican operatives attempted to break in to Democratic National Headquarters at the Watergate Hotel in Washington, DC. The unsuccessful burglary attempt spawned a cover-up that shocked the nation and forced President Richard M. Nixon to resign from office in 1974. A year earlier, Vice President Spiro T. Agnew had been charged with accepting bribes and falsifying income tax returns. He entered a plea of "no contest" to the income tax falsification charges and was forced to resign. Agnew was fined $10,000 and placed on probation for three years.

The U.S. Congress enacted the Ethics in Government Act in 1978 to prevent future Watergates. Many states followed the lead of Congress and enacted ethics statutes before the decade's end.

1980s: Into the Ethical Wilderness

Despite the flurry of legislation to discourage unethical behavior at all levels of government, problems continued in both the private and public sectors throughout the 1980s. Wall Street scandals involving insider trading brought attention to the ugly underbelly of the "me" generation and eroded public trust in America's financial institutions. Scandals rocked the federal government and reached the highest office of the land with the Iran-Contra affair—an illegal arms deal orchestrated in the name of anticommunism—during the Reagan administration.

The American Society for Public Administration unveiled its first public service code of ethics in 1984 with a decided emphasis on the public interest. Laws were enacted to regulate and investigate charges of unethical practices at the state and local levels and included provisions dealing with gifts, outside employment, and post-employment rules.

Congress passed the Ethics Reform Act of 1989, placing greater restrictions on federal employees in the solicitation and acceptance of gifts, outside earned income from professional services, and financial reporting.

President George H.W. Bush issued Executive Order 12674 in 1989, outlining "Principles of Ethical Conduct for Government Officers and Employees." For the first time, as many as 250,000 federal employees received annual training on the laws and regulations (Gilman 2005, 73).

The legal-punishment trend toward outlawing corruption and cracking down on unethical behavior intensified, but not everyone viewed this as a positive development. Frank Anechiarico and James B. Jacobs describe the decade as dominated by a "panoptic vision," one in which public employees were regarded as similar to "probationers in the criminal justice system" (1994, 468).

1990s: Benign Neglect and Reawakening

Governmental ethics and reform moved to the sidelines in the early 1990s as the first Gulf War occupied the attention of both the public and President George H.W. Bush. Democratic nominee Bill Clinton was elected president in 1992, and the "reinvention" of the federal government got under way in 1993 with much sound and fury. Vice President Al Gore, in charge of the reinvention process, issued a report in October outlining a government that would work better and cost less. The Gore report called for reforming the federal bureaucracy, not political institutions, and failed to mention the need for ethical governance. Benevolent neglect of government ethics prevailed during this time.

In 1998, the Bill Clinton–Monica Lewinsky scandal ensnarled all within its reach, especially President Clinton. The White House was lambasted by critics for moral indignities that eventually placed the president on the path to impeachment. The country recoiled at the tawdry details publicized during the Senate impeachment trial in 1999 as questions were raised about the president's behavior, including his lying under oath. Clinton was eventually cleared of the charges.

2000s: Restoring Ethical Governance?

George W. Bush was elected president of the United States in 2000 with his campaign promise to restore "integrity in the White House." He put the country on the road toward a moral America. The White House pushed for restrictions on stem cell research and abortion. After 9/11, a wartime president emerged with an agenda that challenged the moral fiber of the nation. By 2005, accusations of White House deception, misinformation, secrecy, domestic spying, torture, and leaking classified information abounded.

In October 2005, President Bush ordered ethics training for all executive office personnel.

2010 and Beyond

Ethical governance in America remains a work in progress. At the national level, President Barack Obama moved swiftly after taking office on January 20, 2009, launching a call in his inaugural address for a "new era of responsibility" by issuing Executive Order 13490, "Ethics Commitments by Executive Branch Personnel." Noncareer political appointees are expected to sign a pledge that they will not accept gifts from lobbyists or act on matters involving a former employee or former client. Furthermore, the pledge requires a signature that "I agree that any hiring or other employment decisions I make will be based on the candidate's qualifications, competence, and experience" (Executive Order 13490). State and local governments are on the move as well, although a patchwork of laws, regulations, and reform initiatives remains an apt description.

Summing Up

In this era of postmodernism, it is unclear what type of ethic might infuse American government. The economic collapse of 2008–2009 set in motion what is now known as the Great Recession, which—in combination with globalization—has resulted in much ethical soul searching within and outside government. The American public has become increasingly suspicious of those who govern and, in many instances, a degree of distrust and outright cynicism has surfaced that has not been experienced in decades. While these developments may produce more laws, rules, and regulations to restore integrity in governance, ethical governance requires much more than compliance.

Ethics Management Skill Building

Practicum 2.1. When the Chief Asks You to Lie

Chuck is the captain of one of the city's fire stations. The fire station is in serious need of repairs—a critical portion of the station has settled, causing it to become unusable. Meanwhile, a tropical storm has blown across the city, causing heavy damage and flooding. The area in and around the city has been declared a disaster area, and both state and federal disaster officials are assessing damage for emergency relief. The fire chief has advised federal and state officials that the damage to the station was caused by the storm. Prior to relief officials arriving to assess the damage at the station, the fire chief calls Chuck to advise him of their impending arrival and tells Chuck to inform the relief officials that the damage is a result of the storm.

While not stated, annual evaluations are due next month, and the chief is known to use the evaluations to reward loyalty and punish those who do not follow his wishes. Due to a previous illness in the family, Chuck is dependent on the salary increase associated with his annual evaluation to keep up with inflation.

Questions

1. Should Chuck lie for the chief? If Chuck turns his head and does what the chief wants, is he culpable of moral muteness? Or is he being unethical?
2. Should Chuck complain to the chief that he is being put in a position that he cannot agree with?
3. Should Chuck pass the lie onto another staff member by asking him or her to deceive the assessment team?
4. What ethics management strategy would you employ to prevent situations like this from occurring?

Practicum 2.2. Moral Courage

Imagine you are an inspector in the Village Engineering Department and have the responsibility to inspect the sidewalks of residents whose streets are being resurfaced. The village policy is clear—residents who live on streets that are partially resurfaced must pay up to $1,000 per home for their sidewalks to be replaced. But, residents on streets that are fully resurfaced are not required to pay. Your job is to determine how much a resident who lives on a partially resurfaced street must pay to replace the sidewalk. The technical criteria to determine the cost difference between a full resurface and a partial resurface are murky. Moreover, as the inspector, you have found it frustrating to try to explain the system to residents who are impacted by it. It is your strong belief that the required fee is too great of a burden, particularly for a large percentage of the residents who are retired. After years of expressing your frustrations to the director of the engineering department and having them ignored, you decide to take the matter directly to the mayor.

The engineering director does not find your conversation with the mayor amusing. Indeed, he becomes quite angry with you for going around him to the mayor and having his policy decision questioned. He instructs you to proceed with collecting money from residents and lobbies the mayor to support the current policy. You continue collecting checks and contracts from residents but decide not to cash them or process the contracts because you feel the mayor will rule in your favor. And you are right. The mayor concludes the system is unfair, and resident contributions are eliminated for all sidewalk replacement projects.

On hearing the mayor's decision, you return the unprocessed checks and destroy the contracts. The director, not having budgeted for the change, instructs you to continue with the old policy for the upcoming construction season and to initiate the new policy the following year. Concerned about losing your job, you lie and say that you had not collected any money. You feel it would be impossible to collect the money for the upcoming project year as the change in policy had already been announced in the local press.

In the meantime, the director investigates and finds that the money had indeed been collected and subsequently returned. In his opinion, this action was contrary to a direct order. You admit lying but claim that you had merely followed the wishes of the elected officials. The director gives you a pink slip, thus terminating your employment with the village. You decide to appeal the decision to the assistant administrator.

Questions

1. Imagine you are the assistant administrator. What should you do?
2. Was the director right to fire the employee for her behavior? Was the director acting out of his anger at having his decision overturned?
3. Did the inspector exhibit moral courage? Did she act in the best interest of the community?
4. Is it ethical to disobey an order when you feel it is the right decision? Should the inspector be disciplined?

Notes

1. The discussion in this chapter draws in part from Menzel (2001a).
2. NASPAA has adopted a new approach to accreditation that emphasizes "values," including ethical values. See Chapter 10 of this volume and Raffel, Maser, and Calarusse (2011).
3. See Burke (1986), Cooper (1982, 1984, 1987), Denhardt (1988, 1989), Gawthrop (1984), and Rohr (1989).
4. See Cooper (1987), Hart (1984), Frederickson and Hart (1985), and Thompson (1985).
5. New public management has spread internationally. See Lawton and Six (2011) for a thorough discussion of developments.
6. See Bowman and West (2011) for an overview of the field's roots and future.

3
Leading with Integrity

*It is wrong to use immoral means to attain moral ends [and] it is just as
wrong, or even more so, to use moral means to preserve immoral ends.*

—Reverend Martin Luther King, Jr., "Letter from Birmingham Jail"

So you want to lead with integrity—who doesn't? Building an organization
of integrity requires leading with integrity. But what does it mean to lead with
integrity? How is it done? LeRoy F. Harlow (1914–1995), who served as the
city manager of five communities in three different states, "walked the talk"
with this integrity philosophy—do not fear others or losing your job, just
do the right thing . . . and do not do favors. Armed with a B.S. in industrial
engineering from Iowa State University and an M.S. in public administration
from the University of Minnesota, Harlow moved west to become the first
city manager of Sweet Home, Oregon (pop. 3,300), a war-boom logging and
lumbering town that had the local FBI reputation as the "toughest town in
Oregon" (Harlow 1977, 2).

Sweet Home, Oregon

During the 1980s, Sweet Home experienced a major decline in population
and industry as environmental issues forced the closure of sawmills and
logging operations. Throughout the 1990s, using grant dollars provided
by the federal government, Sweet Home's downtown corridor was revitalized, small businesses were encouraged to relocate there, and assisted
living facilities were built to accommodate a retiring community. The city's
population in 2000 was 8,016 (City of Sweet Home, Oregon, 2011).

Harlow's early career in Sweet Home was followed by city manager jobs
in Albert Lea, Minnesota (a city that enjoyed a reputation as progressive and
up-and-coming); Fargo, North Dakota; Richfield, Minnesota; and Daytona
Beach, Florida. In the early 1950s, Harlow characterized the climate in Daytona Beach as beautiful but the "political climate" as "anything but beautiful"

(Harlow 1977, 226). In 1954, he left Daytona Beach and spent the next 20 years working as a consultant and adviser from Connecticut to California. An editorial in the *Daytona Beach Morning Journal* (1954) described Harlow as "a dedicated man [who] believes every citizen is entitled to equal treatment and service from their City employees. He performs his duties without fear and without favor."

In this chapter, we explore what it means to lead with integrity by highlighting the careers of public administrators like Harlow. We also look at administrators who have strayed from the walk, since it is sometimes easier to understand "how to lead" by peering through the lens of "how not to lead."

Integrity

In Chapter 1, we described a person of sound moral character as one who possesses *integrity*. When applied to an organization, integrity refers to an environment characterized as wholesome—one in which respect for others transcends self-serving interests. "Organizational integrity," Lynn S. Paine (1994, 111) notes, "is based on the concept of self-governance in accordance with a set of guiding principles.... The task of ethics management is to define and give life to an organization's guiding values, to create an environment that supports ethically sound behavior, and to instill a sense of shared accountability among employees."

Ethics codes typically call for public administration professionals to demonstrate personal integrity that inspires public trust and confidence in public service. Among other things, this means that managers should be truthful and honest with others and not compromise these values for advancement, honor, or personal gain. Moreover, demonstrating personal integrity requires (1) taking personal responsibility for errors one may commit, (2) recognizing and crediting others for their work and contributions to the organization's mission, (3) guarding against any conflict of interest or its appearance, and (4) being respectful of subordinates, colleagues, and the public. A tall order to be sure, is it not?

Now consider how the International City/County Management Association (ICMA) approaches integrity, which is defined as demonstrating fairness, honesty, and ethical and legal awareness in personal and professional relationships and activities. Stated differently, the ICMA (1998) identifies three dimensions of integrity—personal, professional, and organizational—as follows:

- *Personal integrity:* Demonstrating accountability for personal actions; conducting personal relationships and activities fairly and honestly.
- *Professional integrity:* Conducting professional relationships and activities fairly, honestly, legally, and in conformance with the ICMA Code

---

Exhibit 3.1
Principles of Ethical Conduct

1. Do my best at work.
2. Avoid conflicts of interest.
3. Speak truth to power.
4. Be a good citizen.
5. Shun any private gain from public employment.
6. Act impartially.
7. Treat others the way I would like to be treated.
8. Report waste, fraud, and corruption.

Source: Stone, 2010.

---

of Ethics; requires knowledge of administrative ethics and, specifically, the ICMA Code of Ethics.

- *Organizational integrity:* Fostering ethical behavior throughout the organization through personal example, management practices, and training (requires knowledge of administrative ethics, the ability to instill accountability into operations, and the ability to communicate ethical standards and guidelines to others).

The ICMA's commitment to promoting and supporting ethical behavior is unconditional. Nonetheless, the association's extensive code (2,000 words long with a 3,200 word supplementary "Rules of Procedure for Enforcement") is sometimes perceived as "a set of rules to comply with." One friendly critic (Stone 2010) claims that the eight "Principles of Ethical Conduct" in Exhibit 3.1 are all that is needed:

J. Patrick Dobel has written extensively about public integrity. At the personal level, he asserts that "integrity covers the wholeness of our life . . . flow[ing] from the process through which individuals balance beliefs, decide on the right action, and then summon the courage and self-control to act upon those decisions" (2009, 10). Administrators, of course, are individuals who are officeholders in public (government/nonprofit) organizations. Consequently, they cannot be classified as "free agents"; the personal integrity of these administrators must be coupled with the obligations of office. Dobel (1999, 21–22) regards public integrity as a set of seven commitments:

1. Be truthfully accountable to relevant authorities and publics.
2. Address the public values of the political regime.
3. Build institutions and procedures to achieve goals.
4. Ensure fair and adequate participation of the relevant stakeholders.
5. Demand competent performance effectiveness in the execution of policy.
6. Work for efficiency in the operation of government.
7. Connect policy and program with the self-interest of the public and stakeholders in such a way that the purposes are not subverted.

These commitments are substantial and demanding, even for the most ethically well-intentioned public administrator. Thus, it is not surprising that when one scours the landscape for individuals who can and have led with integrity in private or public organizations, many leaders are encountered who have failed to lead with integrity. Such an outcome is not predestined, however. Men and women who aspire to leadership positions can *learn* to lead with integrity. This view underpins this chapter, with a primary focus on the individual as a leader who can blend and balance getting the job done with a strong dose of integrity. The famous Nike admonishment "just do it," while conveying a can-do attitude, is not sufficient. But, and there is always a "but," one's management and leadership style must be taken into consideration.

Managers as Leaders[1]

Management guru Warren G. Bennis (1993, 88–89) claims that managers and leaders are different kinds of people. Among other things, he asserts:

- "the manager does things right; the leader does the right thing"
- "the manager administers; the leader innovates"
- "the manager relies on control; the leader inspires trust"

But are they so different in the second decade of the 21st century? The answer—most likely not! Indeed, public administrators as managers are also expected to be leaders (see Terry 1995).

But there is more. Managers like to say that you must "walk the talk"—that you cannot lead a modern-day organization simply by issuing rules, policies, and standard operating procedures and controlling things. Temple Terrace, Florida's city manager, Kim Leinbach (2011), puts it this way: "Leading with integrity boils down to setting an example, practicing what you preach. . . . It's not rocket science—it's heart science." Effective leaders must demonstrate through their behavior that they believe what they say. Those who pronounce that their supervisors and street-level workers must adhere to the highest ethical standards in the conduct of their work must themselves adhere to those same standards. Leaders must be exemplars in their personal and professional lives. Easier said than done? Certainly, but it is essential. Much the same can be said about peer leadership. Middle managers or even the cops on the beat must demonstrate day in and day out their commitment to ethical behavior. Failure to do so can result only in organizations without integrity.

> "Lead by example and expect others to follow. Don't forget to regularly read your organization's ethical standards or those of the associations to which you belong—it's a rewarding practice and one that is conducive to longevity."
>
> —Kim Leinbach,
> City Manager, Temple Terrace, Florida

Fast forward to 2005, Hillsborough County, Florida, home of the Tampa Bay Buccaneers football team. The county has a long and checkered history of wrongdoing among its elected county commissioners, with three of five commissioners convicted in the mid-1980s of bribery, kickbacks, and extortion. More recently, newly elected commissioners have found themselves awash in free tickets for lush and pricey skybox seating at Buccaneer games. One commissioner explained that he accepted tickets because he couldn't otherwise afford to attend all the community events at which people would like to see him.

This form of unethical, but not illegal, leadership seems to have had a ripple effect on the more than 8,000-member county workforce in Tampa. Consider the 26-year-old after-school program leader for the Hillsborough County Parks and Recreation Department who was arrested for accepting a $150 bribe by an undercover officer. The bribe was offered in exchange for the young man's willingness to falsify the records showing that the undercover officer had performed community service hours at a county facility (Graham 2005). While it isn't clear that the commissioners' behavior motivated this young man to accept a bribe, it is not too much of a stretch to suggest that the example set at the top of the organization does have an influence on the ethical culture of the county workforce.

Elected officeholders can also serve as exemplars. Take the case of Steve Brown, mayor of Peachtree City, Georgia (pop. 31,580). Brown ran successfully for office on a platform of bringing ethical government to his community but soon found himself sitting before the Peachtree City Ethics Board accused of violating the city's ethics code. What happened? He faced a situation in

which he needed to get his daughter to summer camp and simultaneously ne-
gotiate an agreement for a local option sales tax. His assistant volunteered to
help and drove his daughter to camp—on city time. The city manager advised
the mayor that he might have committed an ethics violation by allowing his
assistant to do him a personal favor during work hours. Forty-five minutes
later, Brown realized that the city manager could be correct; embarrassed by
this ethical lapse, he took out his pen and filed an ethics complaint against
himself. After subsequent deliberation by the ethics board, it was determined
that no formal reprimand was necessary but that Brown should reimburse
the city for the assistant's time away from the office. Mayor Brown readily
complied and reimbursed the city $8.94 (Brown 2005).

Another mayor who led with integrity is Pam Iorio, who served as the
mayor of Tampa, Florida (2003–2011). When she assumed office the city was
engulfed in a housing scandal that eventually landed the city's housing chief
and top aide (also girlfriend) in a federal penitentiary. A jury found them guilty
of more than twenty-five counts of conspiracy, wire fraud, and accepting bribes
and gratuities. Eight years later she could proudly look back and say that never
once in her tenure as mayor was a question raised about the integrity of city
employees. "When I became mayor," she explains, "my staff and I not only
developed strategic goals but also defined the values of the organization . . .
integrity, excellence, teamwork, and respect" (2011, 5). "A person without an
ethical core cannot be a viable leader," she proclaimed in *Straightforward:
Ways to Live & Lead* (2011, 4). Pam Iorio walked the talk.

Some high-level managers exercise ethical leadership by helping subordinates recognize when they (the subordinates) have a lapse in ethical
judgment. Here is an example:

"We had an incident whereby a manager hung some of her colleagues
out to dry by blaming them for a problem and thereby deflecting her responsibility for a mistake. In counseling with her, I used the GFOA Code of
Ethics to explain why her conduct violated a provision in the professional
code. She recognized the problem, and there has been no recurrence
of unethical behavior" (quoted in Berman and West, 2003, 36).

Becoming an Ethical Leader

So exemplary leadership really matters, doesn't it? But what more do we know
about the leadership-ethics link? How does one become an ethical leader? An
ethical follower? Is one simply born more or less ethical? James Q. Wilson

(1993) argued almost two decades ago in his book *The Moral Sense* that all humans are born with a moral sense, an innate quality that enables us to understand and act on the difference between right and wrong. He points to how children at the very earliest age know when they are being treated fairly or unfairly. Still, even if we accept this view, we are not likely to believe that each of us has an ethical autopilot that will prevent us from straying onto the path of wrong behavior. So, there must be more.

Maybe the more has to do with how we were raised. What did we learn from our mother, father, sisters, brothers, friends? Fairness is certainly one of those ethical values that we encountered. It's also likely that we were taught the Golden Rule: to treat others the way we would like to be treated. We may even have had a parent tell us about the importance of human dignity, although maybe not in those exact words. Keep in mind that no one should be treated as a means to another person's end, and each of us is worthy and equal—two pieces of timeless advice from eighteenth-century philosopher Immanuel Kant (1785/1989). Perhaps you learned about virtues such as honesty, courage, benevolence, bravery, patience, respect, trustworthiness, and loyalty and were told to follow your heart. If practiced often enough, so the theory goes, these virtues would become so fully instilled in your being that you would no longer face the dilemmas posed by right and wrong choices. Your "habits of the heart" would help you become a virtuous person, a lofty goal that, however worthy, is never fully attained. Pursuing a life of integrity is just that.

Beware of the Utilitarian Trap

These are noble possibilities, but do they make sense in the rough-and-tumble world of the twenty-first century? Without exception, men and women of ambition are thrown into the lion's den of "getting ahead." How, then, is one to make sense of right and wrong? Enter the utilitarian. The mandate to serve the public interest is translated into making decisions that benefit the most people. As the top executive of a public agency, you might conclude that recommending an across-the-board pay raise to employees is better than a recommendation to increase the pay of a select group of employees based on performance. The organization as whole, you might rationalize, would perform worse with a large number of dissatisfied employees and only a small number of satisfied employees.

Ethics managers must not sacrifice the notion of doing the right thing by trying to satisfy too many people. The utilitarian trap is hazardous, as is the prospect of justifying an unsavory or unethical means to achieve a highly desirable result. The ends do not justify the means when seeking a goal, no matter how attractive that goal may be. This utilitarian trap is Machiavellian.

Niccolo Machiavelli (1469–1527) was an Italian political philosopher who wrote *The Prince* (1513), a slim volume that advised rulers on ways to gain power and keep it by any and all means. The term "Machiavellian" is used to describe a person who is cunning and ruthless in the pursuit of power.

A utilitarian approach is, of course, attractive, because one can calculate—however roughly—possible desirable outcomes. Thus, doing the right thing becomes an exercise in smart, and maybe lucky, calculations. But where and how does the administrator learn to do this? Through common sense? Education? Public executives typically hold master's degrees in business, public administration, or public policy; and educational institutions that award these degrees are often committed to teaching students how "to act ethically," to borrow the phrase in Standard 4.21 promulgated by the National Schools of Public Affairs and Administration. Accredited business schools are equally vociferous in this regard, although not everyone feels that such standards make a dime's worth of difference. One business school graduate put it this way: "We had classes on ethical behavior. But if you are a rotten person going into B-school, you will probably still be a rotten person when you come out" (Bellomo 2005).

The act of projecting right and wrong outcomes to ethics scenarios might seem manipulative and contrived, and it probably is wide of the mark to charge public administration educators with teaching ethics as an exercise in calculation. However, many educators believe that people can learn how to engage in a reasoning process that will more than likely result in a "right" behavior or decision. Terry Cooper, a well-known ethics scholar, is the best-known proponent of what he calls "moral reasoning." And, if the popularity of the fifth edition of his book *The Responsible Administrator* (2006a) is any indication, he is certainly not alone. At the risk of oversimplifying his argument, Cooper (2006a, 35) contends that in learning how to resolve an ethical choice, one involving right versus wrong—and sometimes, right versus right—one must develop the skill of moral imagination; that is, have the ability to produce a "movie in our minds" that takes into account the dynamics of the environment in which a choice must be made.

Are There Ethical Blind Spots?

Can it be that well-intentioned, ethically minded public managers are capable of engaging in unintended unethical behavior? Max H. Bazerman and Ann

E. Tenbrunsel, writing in *Blind Spots: Why We Fail to Do What's Right and What to Do About It* (2011), claim that human beings are often blind to their unethical behavior; that is, there is a gap between intended and actual ethical behavior that is caused by conditions and circumstances that bound our ethicality. "Bounded ethicality," they assert, "comes into play when individuals make decisions that harm others and when that harm is inconsistent with these decision makers' conscious beliefs and preferences" (5).

One explanation for ethical blind spots, or gaps between what we should do and actually do, is unawareness. That is, psychologically, "our minds are subject to bounded ethicality or cognitive limitations that can make us unaware of the moral implications of our decisions" (30). There are "aspects of everyday work life—including goals, rewards, compliance systems, and informal pressures—[that] can contribute to *ethical fading,* a process by which ethical dimensions are eliminated from a decision" (30).

Ethical blind spots can arise for yet another reason—the "want" side of yourself overpowers the "should" side. While the should side dominates pre- and post-decision making, the "want side often wins at the moment of decision" (66), so Bazerman and Tenbrunsel assert. "The want self describes the side of you that's emotional, affective, impulsive, and hot-headed. In contrast, your should self is rational, cognitive, thoughtful, and cool-headed" (66). Does this description resonate with you?

Rationalization and revisionism are other reasons why we often acquire ethical blind spots. When faced with a potential ethical choice that turns out badly, we are most likely inclined to find a reason, often directed at another person (the boss for example) or circumstance (the organization), for rationalizing the behavior. The common refrain "I didn't do anything unethical" fits easily alongside "the organization made me do it." Or, we might turn into "revisionist historians" so that our unethical actions can be hidden, at least from ourselves (Bazerman and Tenbrunsel 2011, 73).

Avoiding ethical blind spots is not an easy task. Indeed, insofar as there are built-in psychological processes that bias our decisions and how we think about ourselves, and a powerful tendency to want to be ethical no matter what, bounded ethicality is very difficult to recognize and overcome (21). Is it not so?

Leadership Styles

Leaders come in all sizes and shapes—as do their styles. Many students of leadership have been fascinated with how styles, personalities, and leader effectiveness fit together—and sometimes don't fit together. Lasthuizen (2008, 5) points out that there is a lively debate "in organizational science about leadership, its effects, and the type of leadership most likely to maximize employee performance." A secondary and often overlooked aspect of these leadership studies is the effect of ethical leadership on members of the organization as well as on the integrity of the organization as a whole.

Given the wide spectrum of leadership styles—directive, supportive, participative, delegative, achievement oriented, external, laissez-faire, inspirational, and charismatic, to name several identified by Van Wart (2008)—our interest here is limited to three particular styles: transactional, transformational, and entrepreneurial. The central question is, how do these styles match up with ethical leadership and the quest to build organizations of integrity? The reader should keep in mind that these three leadership styles are ideal types. Whether or not managers can change styles to accommodate different circumstances is an arguable proposition that is not addressed here.

Transactional Leadership

Have you ever been a member of a public organization that seems to run smoothly? Most likely you have. Of course, organizations do many different things. Some process the mail and packages and social security checks. Others provide valuable public services such as monitoring air and water pollution and overseeing permits to build shopping centers and extract minerals from the earth. Still, when an organization is efficient and effective at doing its work, that is, handling routine and sometimes nonroutine tasks, the public and members of the organization benefit. Numerous transactions take place day in and day out in organizations, public and private. And those that are very successful in handling transactions are most likely led by managers who are skillful transaction leaders.

Transactional leaders are able communicators, effective problem solvers, and task-oriented workers. However important these skills are in running the organization, they are not sufficient to ensure the organization is high performing. What could be missing? A high-performing transactional-led organization must also have leaders who understand and practice fairness, honesty, trust, and transparency. In other words, successful transactional style leadership is value driven. This is the key to leading with integrity.

Transformational Leadership

Values also underpin transformational leaders, who are often described as charismatic, inspirational, motivating visionaries, and sometimes as change agents. Have you ever been on an athletic team? If you have, you know why outstanding coaches can turn a team around when the going gets rough—they are able to motivate and inspire team members to do extraordinary things, including performing at a level that exceeds their ordinary capabilities. "Central to the conceptualization of transformational leadership is the influence that leaders exert on their followers to transcend their own self-interests and incorporate the interest of the organization and society into their goals" (Lasthuizen 2008). In other words, followers buy into the leader's message and feel empowered. The dark side of transformational leadership is that followers can become such true believers in the leader's vision and message that they become "enthusiastic sheep" (Van Wart 2008, 41).

How does one lead with integrity as a transformational leader? Is persuasion and charisma enough? Perhaps in some cases, but most likely there is more. "Leaders are authentically transformational," states Bernard M. Bass and Paul Steidimeier (1999), "when they increase awareness of what is right, good, important, and beautiful, . . . when they foster in followers higher moral maturity, and when they move followers to go beyond their self-interests for the good of the group, organization, or society." No small task, is it?

Organizations in trouble often seek out a transformational leader to make things happen. This "change agent" role has both an upside and a downside. The upside is that the change agent typically has the strong support of the appointing body, and it can be a heady experience to move the organization to a different level. However, due diligence is still required. Consider the case of Al Dunlap, a corporate CEO who enjoyed a reputation as an expert at turning a financially losing enterprise into a profit-making machine. Cutting and slashing staff with impunity earned him the nickname "Chainsaw" Al. As he moved from one struggling corporation to another, his record of success grew and caught up with him on his last assignment—to turn around the appliance manufacturer Sunbeam. In 1998, as he was promoting his book *Mean Business: How I Save Bad Companies and Make Good Companies Great* (1997), the Sunbeam Board of Directors—after much anguishing over the firm's financial well-being—decided to fire him. As it turns out, his success with Sunbeam had become suspicious, and rightly so. Under pressure to produce and sustain his reputation, he convinced Sunbeam retailers to receive and hold large inventories of Sunbeam products that on paper looked like sales. This tactic allowed him to claim that the company's bottom line was healthy. Nonetheless, this "bill and hold" approach for barbecue grills and other products amounted to little more than "cooking" the books. Chainsaw Al was shown the door. The Securities and Exchange Commission (SEC) investigated Sunbeam's management, as did the U.S. Justice Department. Dunlap agreed to pay $500,000 to shareholders to settle the SEC's charges. The Justice Department did not file any charges. However, Dunlap was banned from ever serving as an officer of a public company again. He retired to Florida and is reported to be living a comfortable life in Ocala.

Entrepreneurial Leadership

While transformational leadership inspires, entrepreneurial leadership adds value to an organization's product or output. Entrepreneurial leadership is the ability to leverage resources in a manner that "grows" the organization, not necessarily in size but in terms of the ROI (return on investment). If this sounds in some way businesslike or marketlike, it is. Heightened attention was drawn to entrepreneurial leadership with the publication of David Osborne and Ted Gaebler's best-selling book *Reinventing Government: How the Entrepreneurial Spirit Is Transforming the Public Sector* (1992). The reinvention movement swept across America with added gusto with the publication of *Creating a Government that Works Better and Costs Less: The Report of the National Performance Review* (Gore 1993) led by Vice President Al Gore.

> "Ninety-nine percent of people in business just move preexisting pieces abound the board. Entrepreneurs create. If they are very good at what they do . . . they may leave behind something that will continue after they're gone."
>
> —Peter Barton,
> Coauthor of *Not Fade Away*

High among the priorities of the newly elected Clinton administration was the creation of a government that would work better and cost less. President Clinton launched the National Performance Review in March 1993 with this announcement:

> Our goal is to make the entire federal government both less expensive and more efficient, and to change the culture of our national bureaucracy away from complacency and entitlement toward initiative and empowerment. We intend to redesign, to reinvent, to reinvigorate the entire national government. (Gore 1993, 1)

To change the culture of our national bureaucracy would require that government leaders and administrators be more risk oriented and entrepreneurial, hence the moniker *entrepreneurial leadership,* under which *customers* becomes the code word for citizens, *competition and markets* are the central ingredients in the operation of government, and bureaucrats are expected to become *enterprising workers.* Ethical leadership? No one was asked to break the law to make the government work better and cost less.

The reinvention movement, as noted in Chapter 2, in short order evolved into the new public management (NPM) school with a worldwide following. NPM is defined by the Organisation for Economic Co-operation and Development as "a new paradigm which attempts to combine modern management practices with the logic of economics while still retaining core public service values" (OECD 1998, 5). Not surprisingly, entrepreneurial leadership fits comfortably within this new paradigm.

Chapter 2 raised a number of concerns about the ethical challenges and risks of NPM-inspired entrepreneurial leadership that need not be repeated here. Rather, let's consider what it might mean to lead with integrity as an entrepreneurial leader. First, one must be able to balance the powerful and seductive drive to deliver results within the regulatory framework and processes in which the work of the organization takes place. Do you recall the famous quote attributed to legendary Green Bay Packers coach Vince Lombardi: "Winning isn't everything; it's the only thing?" Do you suppose that Coach Lombardi meant that anything goes—that the end justifies the means? Not likely. And it is worth remembering the words written by the Reverend Martin Luther King, Jr., in his "Letter from Birmingham Jail": "It is wrong to use immoral means to attain moral ends [and] it is just as wrong, or even more so, to use moral means to preserve immoral ends" (1963).

Second, entrepreneurial leaders surely practice much of what transaction and transformational leaders do—empower followers with a vision while ensuring the work of the organization is conducted in a fair-minded, honest, and transparent manner. In other words, successful entrepreneurs mix and match key qualities of transactional and transformational style management. Leading with integrity for entrepreneurial managers requires one to incorporate the best features of both leadership styles.

Leadership Success and Failure

While it might very well seem that successful leaders are people of integrity, there are many cases of successful leaders going astray. Stephen K. Bailey's (1964) dictum that "the higher a person goes on the rungs of power and authority, the more wobbly the ethical ladder" has all too often come true for many.

A Wobbly Ethical Ladder

Consider the case of the administrator of a large urban county in a southern state who climbed the ladder of success over more than 30 years to become the chief executive.[2] What happened? The county established an independent auditor who, among other things, reported that the administrator had given herself and top aides pay raises at a time when the county was experiencing significant fiscal stress with cutbacks and layoffs occurring. Moreover, the county's 8,000 employees were asked to take on more work to cope with the downsizing, a recipe for low morale and disgruntlement. The county had in place an unwritten policy to reward employees who engaged in innovative cost-saving measures, which included laying off subordinates. One of the administrator's top aides nominated her for a reward in recognition of the decision she made to lay off one of her assistant county administrators. Uncertain that she was eligible to participate in the program, she consulted the county attorney, who told her that she was indeed eligible. And so the county executive ended up accepting (some critics would say "giving") herself a $2,000 salary increase—determined by a set percentage of her $224,000 annual salary—for eliminating someone else's job. However, she failed to seek approval of the salary bump from the county commission, which was unaware of the policy to adjust her salary. The county charter specifically authorizes the commission to set the pay of the administrator.

As events unfolded, including private interchanges between the auditor and individual members of the commission, the administrator began to suspect that the auditor was "out to get her." Consequently, she ordered one of her managers to collect all e-mails involving the auditor, commission, and county attorney relevant to the pay issue. The media began to follow the story and broke the "e-mail snooping" news, as it was called. The administrator admitted that she had collected the e-mail messages but, upon second thought, decided not to read them. The commission's trust in this claim rapidly deteriorated and motivated them to place the administrator, the county attorney, and the auditor on 90 days of paid administrative leave.

As the leave period moved along, the commission struggled with "what to do"—demote the administrator, fire her and the others with or without cause, wait out an investigation by the state law enforcement agency into whether or not e-mail snooping violated the law and then decide what to do, or strike a deal with the administrator to resign. Firing the administrator without cause would let her walk with more than $500,000, according to the terms of her employment contract. Consequently, the commission and the administrator (through their lawyers) attempted to work out a settlement. As the suspension approached its end, the administrator became more determined to find an arrangement that would let her receive $550,000 or more in severance and benefits. In the meantime, there was considerable stress and distress reported in the media about the ill effects that the situation was having on employee morale, job performance, and the public's negative perception of the imbroglio. The story ends with the auditor losing his job, the administrator fired unceremoniously with cause, and the county attorney reinstated.

This case is replete with ethical breaches, most of which are obvious. Perhaps a less obvious but nonetheless egregious breach was the utter disregard for doing what was believed to be in the best interests of the community, and, of course, the consequent erosion of public trust and confidence in county government caused by the incident. While it was clearly in the best financial interests of the administrator to stay the course, did she also have an obligation to put the community interest ahead of her personal and professional interests? It would seem so. However, it is fair to say that she felt strongly that she had been victimized, especially by the auditor's reports and behavior. Her sense of fair treatment and justice was at stake along with her professional reputation; with more than three decades of county employment under her belt, she was well known in the community and had established ties with many municipal leaders and businesspeople.

The administrator in this case was held in high regard during her six-year tenure as chief executive and many years as HR director and assistant county administrator. She had gained respect and a solid reputation for promoting professional behavior among managers and employees. Moreover, while she held a master's degree in public administration from a NASPAA-accredited program that provided training "to act ethically" and was a long-standing member of professional associations (the International City/County Management Association and the American Society for Public Administration), it was still her responsibility to do the right thing.

Ethical Competency Defined

(1) Commitment to high standards of personal and professional behavior; (2) knowledge of relevant ethics codes and laws; (3) ability to engage in ethical reasoning when confronted with challenging ethical situations; (4) capacity to identify and act on public service ethics and values; and (5) willingness to promote ethical practices and behaviors in public agencies and organizations (Menzel, 2010).

This story points to two important conclusions: (1) experienced administrators can develop "ethical blind spots" that tarnish a long, successful career, and (2) the achievement of ethical competency is a lifelong pursuit that is never quite reached. This is not to suggest that the *pursuit of ethical competency* is fruitless or that one is hopelessly doomed to failure. Rather, it is to suggest that the journey is challenging but so very important.

Exemplary Leadership

No matter how wobbly the ethical ladder may become, some leaders are able to keep climbing. One such person was the former U.S. attorney general Elliot Richardson (1920–2000). Richardson became an iconic figure in U.S. history for refusing the order from President Richard M. Nixon to fire Archibald M. Cox, the special Watergate prosecutor who was determined to obtain tape recordings made surreptitiously in the White House. On October 20, 1973, Attorney General Richardson resigned rather than fire Cox. His second-in-command, William D. Ruckelshaus, also refused to fire Mr. Cox and resigned. This set of events came to be called the Saturday Night Massacre. Richardson's stand was "widely lauded as a special moment of integrity and rectitude that secured him a place in the nation's history" (Lewis 2000). In *Reflections of a Radical Moderate,* a book published several years before his death, Richardson wrote: "The more I thought about it the clearer it seemed to me that public confidence in the investigation would depend on its being independent not only in fact, but in appearance" (Richardson 1996).

Although it is not always recognized as such, the appearance standard is a very high ethical standard—one that often slips to the sidelines when an ethical choice has to be made. Mr. Richardson understood the significance of the appearance standard and had the will power and courage to abide by it. This is leading with integrity, is it not?

Another well-known contemporary figure widely acclaimed for leading with integrity was the American soldier, diplomat, and Nobel Peace Prize recipient George C. Marshall (1880–1959). Lauded for his role as army chief of staff during World War II and later as U.S. secretary of state, he is also remembered as the architect of the Marshall Plan, a postwar strategy for rebuilding and modernizing Europe. Throughout his career and life, Marshall demonstrated exceptional courage, placed the public interest before his self-interest, and earned a sterling reputation for always telling the truth. In addition, he refused to seek special treatment for his family or friends, showed consistent dedication for the welfare of others (especially the citizen-soldier), "demanded a high level of ethical conduct from everyone with whom he worked, and conducted himself in a manner that set a clear model for others to emulate" (Pops 2006, 176). "George Marshall," remarked former Secretary of State Colin L. Powell, "did not crave power or glory . . . and never confused honor with pride" (George C. Marshall Foundation 2003).

A third notable leader with integrity was Elmer B. Staats (1914–2011), who was appointed to a 15-year term as head of the General Accounting Office (GAO) by President Lyndon B. Johnson in 1966. (The GAO was renamed the U.S. Government Accountability Office in 2004.) Prior to his role as the comptroller general of the GAO—a role he singlehandedly redefined—Staats served with distinction at the Bureau of the Budget and the National Security Agency over the course of three decades. He earned his bachelor's degree in 1935 from McPherson College, Kansas, a master's degree in political science and economics from the University of Kansas the next year, and a doctoral degree in political economy from the University of Minnesota in 1939.

George Catlett Marshall

"People not only thought he was telling them the truth, he did tell them the truth. He always told me the truth when I was President of the United States."

—Harry S. Truman
from Leonard Mosley (1982, 401)

The General Accounting Office was established in 1921 as an independent agency charged with informing Congress on matters of government finance and effectiveness and serving as a check of president powers (Frederickson 1992, 218). The GAO routinely dealt with issues of fraud, waste, and criminal behavior. By 1968, the agency was heavily involved in performance auditing (conducting program evaluations).

Elmer Staats viewed his job and those who served in government as "fixing, improving, and making things work better." He assumed that civil servants meant well, were hard working and, for the most part, virtuous. Indeed, he "expected generally virtuous practices on the part of most bureaucrats" (Frederickson 1992, 225). Still, he recognized that "there is no foolproof way that you can avoid a situation where a program gets into serious trouble where fraud and waste may be involved" (223).

Leading with integrity was serious business for Elmer Staats. He was quoting as saying:

> The Comptroller General must be above reproach, cleaner than Caesar's wife. The bottom line is that the agency doesn't do anything that it wouldn't want to see in the *Washington Post* the next morning. The perception of unethical practices is almost as damaging as are actual unethical practices. . . . The main thing . . . is to make the whole organization conscious of the role that it plays, that it has to be in a position where the GAO can't be damaged by any successful charge of unethical practices. (Frederickson 1992, 235–36)

Fraud, waste, and corruption have been and are all too commonplace in America. Blowing the whistle on those who defraud the public, however, is not done easily or without consequence. Consider the case of Marie Ragghianti (1942–) who served for 14 months as the chair of the Tennessee Board of Pardons and Paroles until being fired by Governor Ray Blanton on August 3, 1977. She was accused of "gross improprieties . . . as well as demoralizing the corrections department and crippling its procedures" (Hejka-Ekins 1992, 304). Her real "crime"—she refused to acquiesce to corruption in the governor's office where clemencies were exchanged for bribes.

> "I would rather try and fail than fail to try."
> —Marie Ragghianti, cited in Cooper and Wright (1992)

It wasn't long before Ragghianti began to understand the scope of corruption at her doorstep and realized that it was not something she could combat on her own. She sought help from outside the governor's office. After contacting the FBI, she agreed to testify secretly to a grand jury investigating the bribery incidents. She then experienced "organizational retaliation for her failure to support the administration" (310). Though feeling badgered and bullied, Ragghianti refused to go along with the governor to cover up the bribery incidents. She "told the governor that she had done nothing wrong and would not resign" (311). The scandal finally broke when three top staffers with the governor's office were arrested and indicted on bribery and extortion charges. The FBI investigation revealed that over 600 pardons and clemencies had been issued during Governor Blanton's tenure (316). Although never formally charged in the scandal, he was eventually indicted on charges of selling liquor licenses, then convicted and sentenced to federal prison (Wikipedia 2011b).

Marie Ragghianti was a public servant who led with integrity. Is it not so?

Summing Up

Leading with integrity is not easy; indeed, it can be downright difficult. Oh, you say, I've always been a person with high ethical standards. Have you? Do you think of yourself as more ethical than your boss? Your fellow employees? The person sitting next to you? Your author has documented empirically in education and training sessions time after time that most of us perceive ourselves to be more ethical than those we work with, supervise, or the bosses who run any given organization. There is good news in the desire, at least, to feel as if our ethical standards are higher than those of other people. The bad news?

A sense of ethical superiority is a potential trap door through which one can plummet in the quest to lead with integrity. How so? Authenticity: Followers must genuinely believe that what you say and do is authentic. Contrived authenticity with respect to your ethics will doom you as a leader. You may be able to change and adapt your leadership style to fit varying organizational roles and workplace cultures, but you cannot do the same with your ethical standards and the perception of those standards by others.

> "Ethics has everything to do with management. . . . Ethics is as much an organizational as a personal issue. Managers who fail to provide proper leadership and to institute systems that facilitate ethical conduct share responsibility with those who conceive, execute, and knowingly benefit from corporate misdeeds."
>
> —Lynn Sharp Paine (1994),
> Harvard Business School

As this discussion of leadership styles makes clear, one can lead with integrity no matter what the style—transactional, transformational, or entrepreneurial. One of the goals of this chapter is to show that people can learn to lead with integrity, although it is not simply a matter of reading a leadership classic or taking a course. Nor does one have to be a "born leader"—whatever that may be. Rather, motivated individuals must practice, practice, practice in much the same way one aspires to leading a virtuous life rooted in honesty, benevolence, compassion, and fairness.

In its fullest sense, "leading with integrity" includes moral leadership that, as Linda A. Hill (2006, 267) puts it, "is more than avoiding ethical wrongdoing; it is about making a positive difference in others' lives and in our communities." No wobbly ladder here. Stephen K. Bailey (1964) reminds us that "the essential moral qualities of the ethical public servant are: (1) optimism; (2) courage; and (3) fairness tempered by charity."

Ethics Management Skill Building

Practicum 3.1 Blindsided: What Should You Do?[3]

Suppose you are the administrator of a wealthy, upscale county with a strong record of good governance. In fact, you have been the county administrator for 14 years and have garnered the respect and admiration of the Board of County Commissioners, good government citizen groups, and the local media. You view yourself as a person with high ethical standards and take pride in your organization's performance in getting the job done at an affordable price. You also take pride in your progressive management style, which consists of delegating responsibility to top managers whom you hold accountable.

Your county has a model code of ethics, and you trust your management team to be exemplars of respectability. You have every reason to feel comfortable with the ethical culture that pervades the 2,000-member workforce until . . . all hell breaks loose! The local newspaper publishes a story about a 55-year-old project manager in the public works department accused of accepting some $15,000 in cruises, hotel stays, gift cards, and other kickbacks from a company whose contract he helped supervise.

As the scandal unfolds, other misdeeds come to light. County supervisors are reported to "piggyback" contracts—that is, opt for the same deal another local government had with a company, thus allowing county administrators to avoid putting contracts out to bid. Procurement managers are said to have practiced "change orders," meaning a contract is bid for specific terms, only to be altered at points along the way (with extra work and pay added). The "change orders" practice would allow favored companies to come in at unrealistically low bids. Topping off the string of procurement problems is the allegation that administrators and supervisors used county issued credit cards to "break" a payment into several parts in order to stay within a $10,000 purchase limit.

As the county administrator, you are shocked to learn of these practices. You feel as if you have failed personally or been abandoned by the entire management team, in the sense that your business and personal ethics have not been translated into the culture of at least one operation.

Questions

1. What should you do?
2. Should you start cleaning house by firing a number of managers?
3. Should you write a memo to your top managers admonishing them to "fix the problems or resign"?
4. Should you accept responsibility and resign?
5. How would you "lead with integrity" under these circumstances?

Practicum 3.2 Withholding Information: When Is It Ethical or Unethical?

You are a candidate for a very competitive, high-profile city manager job. During the search process conducted by a reputable consulting search firm, you are asked: "If we conducted a thorough background check on you, would we find anything in your background which might embarrass a future employer?"

You pause for a moment as your mind flashes back to an allegation that was made about you when you were a city manager of a small community. It was alleged by two staff members of the community hospital where your wife was terminally ill that you slapped and verbally abused her.

The police investigated the allegation as did the Department of Children and Family Services (DCF). During the investigation you assert that the staff members misinterpreted a situation in which your wife was choking and you were helping her. Your wife states to the investigators that you did not abuse her. Neither the police nor the DCF investigations report that there is any physical evidence (e.g., redness on the face) that you had slapped her. Nonetheless, the investigative report is sent to the state attorney to determine whether or not to press charges. The state attorney declines to pursue the matter due to a lack of evidence. Thus, the allegation is unsubstantiated.

Decision 1: How should you reply to the question asked by the search firm? Should you or should you not disclose the incident?

Let's assume that you reason that the incident was entirely personal and was found to be unsubstantiated. Therefore, you decide to respond: "There is nothing in my background that would embarrass a future employer."

You receive an invitation to interview.

During the interview, you stress your honesty and high ethical standards.

Decision 2: Do you or do you not disclose the incident to the city's HR staff and the city commissioners?

Once more you decide not to disclose information about the incident for the same reason you did not disclose it to the search firm.

The interview goes very well. City commissioners are impressed and decide to offer you a $170,000 job contract. The local newspaper reports the story with the byline—"Ethics and experience bring Jones to the fore."

On the day the contract is to be voted on, city commissioners receive information that you were accused of slapping and verbally abusing your wife in the hospital where she was terminally ill. The commission decides to call an emergency meeting to discuss the situation. You are invited to appear before the commission and answer their questions.

Decisions 3: Do you accept the commission's invitation?

You decide "yes," as the air needs to be cleared and you need the full trust and confidence of your new bosses. During the questioning, you assert, "I haven't lied. I have not told an untruth." One commissioner asks: "Why didn't you tell us about this allegation?"

Decision 4: What do you say?

1. I forgot.
2. I didn't think anyone would find out.
3. You didn't ask me.
4. It was merely an unsubstantiated allegation, as my wife and I had a very loving relationship right up to the moment of her death.
5. Withholding information is acceptable under these very personal circumstances.
6. I thought the allegation, although untrue, would place my candidacy in jeopardy if it became public.

Outcome

The commission decides to postpone approving your contract for two weeks while they seek more background information about you. Meanwhile, you have withdrawn as a city manager finalist for several other positions and are now worried about ending up without any job.

You muse, "Am I being treated fairly by the city commission? The media? I know I haven't done anything wrong. Why am I being subjected to such scrutiny?"

Investigation Results

A three-member committee—composed of Commissioner Kent, the director of HR, and a representative of the police department—is formed and travels to the community where you served as the city manager for four years.

After visiting the community and meeting with former and current town council members, a conclusion is reached by the committee that includes your former assistant town manager, the president of the chamber of commerce, a police sergeant, and the town attorney; the committee states: "We have no concerns about his honesty or integrity." Commissioner Kent sums up his thoughts to the city commission this way: "You exercised poor judgment as a candidate who sold himself on honesty, integrity, and character, but that is not a sufficient reason to withhold the offer of a contract. Poor judgment is not an unethical act."

Decision 5: Now put on your hat as a city commissioner. How would you vote on the job offer? Would you vote for or against the candidate?

Questions

1. Is there a difference between poor judgment and committing an unethical act?
2. Is there an ethical issue facing the candidate? If so, what is it? Did he display ethical sensitivity in answering the search firm's question: "Is there anything in your background that might embarrass a future employer?"
3. Will your ability to lead with integrity be compromised if you accept the job by withholding information?
4. Is it ever "right" to withhold information? If yes, under what circumstances?

Notes

1. See Van Wart (2011) for an in-depth review of administrative leadership.
2. This case is drawn from newspaper accounts published in the *Tampa Tribune* and *St. Petersburg Times* in March–June 2010.
3. Based on an actual set of events. See Eckhart (2011).

4
Tools for Building
Organizations of Integrity

Management is doing things right; leadership is doing the right things.

—Peter F. Drucker (2004)

What are the tools available to public managers to build and sustain organizations that promote ethical behaviors and practices? How well do they work? Are some more effective than others? These are the critical questions addressed in this chapter. Ethics management tools range from soft, even symbolic, measures to more concrete measures such as ethics audits and training. No single tool will suffice to build an organization of integrity. Rather, effective ethics management requires a comprehensive approach with top-down and bottom-up commitments.

Let's begin by taking a look at ethics training—its value, scope, and type.

An Ounce of Prevention Is Worth . . .

Ethics training was a cottage industry a short while ago, but no longer. It is now a growing enterprise in both the private and public sectors. There is scarcely a large American corporation that does not conduct ethics training. And governments at all levels in the United States are spending taxpayers' dollars for ethics training, although the economic downturn of 2008–2009 slowed some program initiatives.

Ethics training is typically different from ethics education in the approaches taken and the emphasis given to laws, rules, and regulations. Normative ethics theories such as utilitarianism, principle or duty-based ethics, and virtue theory are unlikely to be discussed in ethics training. Even the concept of "moral reasoning" is unlikely to be addressed directly, although some training does employ moral reasoning exercises.

Compliance Training

One model dominates ethics training in American governments—the compliance model. It is designed to regulate employees' conduct. As Carol W. Lewis

(1991, 9) notes, this model is "a largely prescriptive, coercive, punitive, and even threatening route . . . to spur obedience to minimum standards and legal prohibitions." Harvard professor Lynn S. Paine (1994, 106) adds that the goal of a compliance-based ethics program is "to prevent, detect, and punish legal violations." This model emphasizes training in what the law says, what the rules mean, and what one needs to do to stay out of trouble. Ethics officer Alan Johnson (2011a) of Palm Beach County, Florida, describes ethics training programs as stressing "awareness and compliance among officials and public employees, and to a lesser extent, vendors and service providers to the public entity."

Law is the touchstone of public organizations. Thus, it is not surprising that the compliance model is so prominent (see Exhibit 4.1). Nor is it surprising that many public officials feel more comfortable about ethics when it involves understanding the law and following it.

Integrity Model

An alternative model is the integrity model, which fosters "an awareness of a public service ethos, ethical standards and values, plus a process of moral reasoning to inspire exemplary actions or ethical conduct. The emphasis is on the promotion of moral character with self-responsibility and moral autonomy as essential components" (Hejka-Ekins 2001, 83).

Hallmarks of an Effective Integrity Strategy

- The guiding values and commitments make sense and are clearly communicated.
- Organizational leaders are personally committed, credible, and willing to take action on the values they espouse.
- The espoused values are integrated into the normal channels of management decision making and are reflected in the organization's critical activities.
- The organization's systems and structures support and reinforce its values.
- Managers throughout the organization have the decision-making skills, knowledge, and competencies needed to make ethically sound decisions on a day-to-day basis (adapted from Paine 1994).

While there is much to be said for adopting the integrity model, perhaps a more realistic expectation is to encourage governments to combine the two models into what Carol Lewis (1991) calls the "fusion" model. Other

Exhibit 4.1   **Deterring Unethical Behavior with a Compliance Approach**

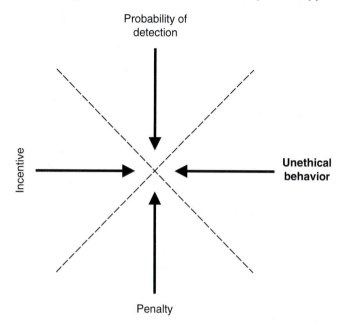

ethics experts who recommend a fusion approach are Grosenick (1995) and Truelson (1991). Truelson further argues that the fusion model should blend with the organizational culture; that is, ethics training should both influence and be influenced by the organizational culture, thus fostering a genuine and deep-seated culture of organizational integrity.

Value Added

The steady growth in ethics training at all levels of government in the United States offers prima facie evidence of its assumed effectiveness in discouraging unethical behavior and encouraging ethical behavior. The local government experience strongly suggests that training is beneficial; among the fifty states, however, it is much more problematic due to the heavy emphasis placed on a compliance approach.

A recent study of business professionals supports the view that ethics training makes a difference. Valentine and Fleischman (2004, 381) report "significant statistical support for the notion that businesspersons employed in organizations that have formalized ethics training programs have more positive perceptions of their companies' ethical context than do individuals employed in organizations that do not." They further note that employees in business organizations that have a stronger ethical context are more satisfied with their work than employees in organizations with a weak ethical context.

The results of the U.S. Office of Government Ethics (OGE) *Executive Branch Employee Ethics Survey 2000* also confirm the value of ethics training. Employees, especially supervisors, who receive more regular training than other employees have a positive perception of the ethical culture of their agencies and perceive a lower incidence of unethical behavior (U.S. Office of Government Ethics 2000). Ethics training is an important factor in building a strong ethical culture in federal agencies.

We turn next to a closer look at the scope and type of training available and make some judgments regarding the effectiveness of ethics training as a management tool, keeping in mind that the compliance model dominates training.

Scope and Type of Training

The cliché that "too much is not enough" may be an apt characterization of the size and scope of ethics strategies needed in the public sector. At the same time, there may be two overlooked issues that sometimes sideline the adoption of an effective strategy: (1) the failure of managers to appreciate and understand that ethics management is attainable, and (2) the willingness of managers to exercise the leadership needed to put ethics management strategies into place.

Should formal or informal ethics management strategies be adopted? What is the best strategy to adopt? The answer is that no single size fits all. Rather, managers need to adopt ethics management strategies—formal or informal—that fit their organization. Jonathan West and Evan Berman (2004, 189–206) studied the scope and type of training in 195 U.S. cities with populations over 50,000. They found that two of every three cities provide ethics training. New employees were the targets of the most intensive training in six of 10 cities, while the remaining four cities reported that managers are also trained. A smaller number of cities said that ethics training is mandatory.

Most municipal training focuses on the city's ethics code and/or the state's ethics law. This information typically includes knowing (1) what a conflict of interest is, (2) what "having financial interests" means in a day-to-day, practical sense, (3) the meaning of personal honesty, (4) how to address ethics complaints, and (5) due process. However, some cities go beyond these topics to include subjects such as deciding if something is unethical, coping with an ethical dilemma, evaluating ethical choices, and understanding the importance of transparency.

Live instruction, as opposed to computer-simulated or web-based instruction, is the most common method employed by ethics trainers. This method includes the use of hypothetical scenarios, realistic case materials, role playing, and lecturing. Web-based or other electronic means for delivering ethics instruction is used in fewer than 10 of every 100 cities, although there is every indication that this statistic is growing.

The most notable changes the researchers reported were in adopting a standard of conduct (up 27 percent since 1994), monitoring adherence to a code of ethics (up 26.5 percent), and requiring familiarity with the city's code of ethics (up 24.5 percent). Also noteworthy is the fact that more cities were using ethics as a criterion in hiring and promotion and mandating ethics training for all employees. And, more cities were making counselors available for assistance in dealing with ethical issues.

The study by West and Berman (2004) certainly documents that cities are moving aggressively to put into place a wide array of ethics management elements. But what is the evidence that these elements, in part or in whole, are making a difference? The researchers address this question by examining the correlates between the 16 elements of ethics management and three important organizational variables—organizational culture, labor-management relations, and employee productivity. Cities that offer ethics training report that they experience improvements in their organizational culture, better labor-management relations, and higher employee productivity. West and Berman also find positive correlations between leadership strategies and improvements in the organizational culture, better labor-management relations, and higher employee productivity. Code-based strategies, those that stress adopting a code and monitoring adherence to it, are much less likely to be associated with these three organizational variables.

Does Training Deter Unethical Behavior?

Probably, but it is difficult to gather data about something that doesn't happen—no wrongdoing. On the other hand, one can find plausible evidence of a link between the absence of ethics training and the occurrence of wrongdoing. Consider the cased of Sarasota County located on Florida's Gulf Coast, with a population 369,765 in 2009. Upscale and professionally managed for 14 years by a highly regarded administrator, the county experienced an ethical meltdown in 2011 when a mid-level manager was arrested on charges he accepted illegal gifts from a sewer repair firm. Subsequent investigations into procurement policies and practices unearthed a wide-ranging pattern of credit card abuse, contract specification deception, and bundling small jobs together for one bid that opened the door for collusion and corruption (Brady 2011).

How could such widespread collusion occur on the watch of a county administrator who garnered the respect and admiration of his elected bosses?

Had he acquired an "ethical blind spot"? Did he place too much trust and confidence in his managers to do the right thing? Did the county fail to have sound ethics policies in place? What had the county done to prepare its 2,000 plus employees for ethical challenges? The answers to these questions came in part with a report issued by the National Institute of Governmental Purchasing (NIGP). "Ethics and integrity do not stop at the procurement organization's doorway," the report noted (Brady 2011). Indeed, the report revealed that the county's human resources department published ethics guidelines "that are all encompassing and apply to all county employees, elected officials, appointees and family members [but] the county lacks an ethics training program." Nor did the county have an Intranet web link to its standards of conduct. Did unethical behavior flourish in Sarasota County as a result of too little attention paid to implementing ethics education and training programs? As the NIGP report notes: "Ethics policies are not easy to follow and encompass policies not normally encountered during the course of work."

Does ethics training make a difference? The answer would seem to be a resounding "yes."

Ethics Training in State Government

Some states provide little or no ethics training while others offer much more. State training initiatives lag behind federal and local government training. The situation, however, is not as bleak as it first appears, as a growing number of states have launched online training (see Exhibit 4.2). In 2005, New Jersey put in place an ambitious online training program for all state employees in the executive branch, and now requires employees to receive mandatory annual briefings on ethics and standards of conduct (State of New Jersey 2011).

New York State does not mandate ethics training but does offer a robust training schedule. According to the *Annual Report: 2010,* 7,022 individuals attended traditional instructor-led seminars, 333 individuals took an online training seminar, and 9,636 Internet-users utilized online training (New York State Commission on Public Integrity 2011).

A web-based training course was brought online in New York in late 2003. The course covers the fundamentals of the state's ethics laws. "Those who complete the course successfully can print out a certificate. At least two agencies have used the course as the basis for their own online training programs," comments Walter C. Ayres, director of Public Information, NYS Commission on Public Integrity (Ayres 2005; Washburn 2011). State ethics training, however, is mostly compliance oriented. And, in some instances, the training consists of little more than a superficial effort to inoculate employees against errant behavior. Illinois and California are prime examples. The state

Exhibit 4.2

Online Ethics Training in the States

State	Link
Alaska	• The Alaska Public Offices Commission provides ethics training. Ethics training is mandatory for lobbyists and employers of lobbyists. Online is an option. • The Alaska Select Committee on Legislative Ethics provides the mandatory ethics training for legislators and legislative employees. Online training consists of video and slide presentations. http://ethics.legis.state.ak.us/ethics_training.php
California	The California Attorney General's Office and Fair Political Practices Commission developed an interactive online ethics course and a noninteractive course, which is a text-only version of the online ethics course. Ethics training is mandatory and state officials must complete an ethics course within six months of hiring & every two years thereafter. http://ag.ca.gov/ethics/
Colorado	The Office of Legislative Legal Services offers an online ethics tutorial for the Colorado General Assembly. http://www.state.co.us/gov_dir/leg_dir/olls/ethics/
Connecticut	The Connecticut Office of State Ethics offers in-person training for public officials, state employees, lobbyists, and state contractors. Online training is available for public officials and state employees. http://www.dir.ct.gov/ethics/OSE%20Online%20Learning/player.html?ethicsNav=l
Florida (not accessible to general public)	The Florida Institute on Government at Florida State University offers ethics training for state employees. http://www.courses.learnsomething.com/scripts2/content.asp?r=WelcomePage&a=114&WLBS=20080730175522
Illinois (not accessible to general public)	The Office of the Executive Inspector General provides ethics training for state employees. http://www.etcc.il.gov/
Indiana (not accessible to general public)	The Indiana Office of Inspector General provides mandatory ethics training for all state officers, employees, and special state appointees. http://www.in.gov/ig/2337.htm
Massachusetts	The Massachusetts State Ethics Commission offers online training for state officials. http://db.state.ma.us/ethics/quiz_MEthics/index.asp

(continued)

Exhibit 4.2 *(continued)*

State	Link
Mississippi	The Mississippi Ethics Commission provides mandatory ethics training for all elected and appointed officials, and employees of all levels of government. The Commission posts the slides from its seminars online. http://www.ethics.state.ms.us/ethics/ethics.nsf/webpage/A_seminar_presentations?OpenDocument
Nevada	The Nevada Commission on Ethics provides ethics training. The Commission posts its slide presentations online. http://ethics.nv.gov/training.htm
New Jersey	• The State of New Jersey State Ethics Commission provides ethics training. Training is mandatory for state employees and special state officers. Online training is an option. http://www.state.nj.us/ethics/training/online/index.html • The New Jersey Legislature provides mandatory training for legislators and legislative employees. In addition to in-person training, legislators and legislative employees are required to take the online Ethics Tutorial no later than April 1 of every even-numbered year. www.njleg.state.nj.us/ethics/ethics.asp
New York	The New York State Governor's Office of Employee Relations provides online ethics training for state employees. http://www.goer.state.ny.us/train/onlinelearning/ETH/100.html
North Carolina	The North Carolina State Ethics Commission provides ethics training. The Commission posts its presentations online. http://www.in.gov/ig/2494.htm
Oklahoma	The Oklahoma Ethics Commission posts its ethics manual for state officials and state employees online. http://www.ok.gov/oec/documents/MAN08.sfi.pdf
Oregon	The Oregon Government Ethics Commission posts its ethics manual online. http://www.gspc.state.or.us/OGEC/docs/PO_Guide_2008.doc
Tennessee	The Tennessee Ethics Commission posts its publication *Guiding Principles of Ethical Conduct for Public Officials* online. http://state.tn.us/sos/tec/GuidingPrinciplesOfficials.pdf
Texas	The Texas Ethics Commission offers ethics training for state officers and executive branch employees, and the legislature and legislative employees. Online is an option. http://www.ethics.state.tx.us/main/training.htm
Washington	The Washington State Legislative Ethics Board posts its ethics manual online. http://www.leg.wa.gov/docs/Ethics-Manual.pdf
West Virginia	The West Virginia Ethics Commission posts a guide of the state's ethics act online. http://www.ethics.wv.gov/Pages/default.aspx
Wisconsin	The Wisconsin Government Accountability Board posts numerous ethics publications online. http://ethics.state.wi.us/Forms-Publications/FormsPublications.htm#Guidelines

Source: National Conference of State Legislatures, 2010, and state web sites.

of Illinois is among the newer entrants into the ethics training field and has put in place web-based training aimed at all state employees, including state college and university faculty and staff. All were trained in 2004, and by law must be retrained annually. The online ethics training program has resulted in the training of 115,000 state employees. While it may be premature to judge the effectiveness of this "inoculation" style training, it is unlikely to do more than increase awareness of the "do's" and "don'ts" in the state's ethics law.

California employs a similar approach. State officials must complete ethics training every two years. Online training consists of interactive and a noninteractive modules that cover conflicts of interest, gift limitations, misuse of public funds, bans on honoraria, post-government employment, and more. The goal, according to the California Office of the Attorney General, is not to make a state official an expert in ethics. Rather, it is to expose officials to ethics laws and their application in order to alert one to potential conflict-of-interest situations (State of California 2011). The interactive module is a full web-based audio and visual program that requires up to two hours to finish. Upon completion with a sign-off by one's agency, the participant is issued a certificate of completion, which the participant signs. The certificate is retained by the agency and is available for disclosure to the public.

In 2002, Florida designed a free online training course to reach approximately 10,000 public officials and employees in the state. Non-state employees can also register for the course with a private provider for $15 a person. In 2010, 570 individuals registered for the online training course, with 368 completing the training. Of the registrants, 18 percent were local officials and employees, 53 percent were state agency personnel, and 29 percent of the registrants were members of the Florida Bar. A total of 2,031 public officers and employees have completed the course since its inception (State of Florida Commission on Ethics 2011). These statistics suggest that Florida has a long way to go with this privatization effort to inform and educate public officials, employees, and others about ethics laws and rules.

Question: I am being considered for a job with the State of Connecticut. Am I required to sign an ethics statement?
Answer: All state employees and officials are required to abide by a Code of Ethics. Before accepting employment with the State, applicants will be given a summary of the State Code of Ethics and the hiring agency's ethics statement. Each new employee must sign a statement acknowledging receipt of such documents and agree to comply with the requirements of the state ethics laws.

How to Stay Out of Trouble: Federal Ethics Training

The OGE is the primary provider of ethics training and education materials for agencies and departments located in the executive branch. The OGE web site (www.usoge.gov/home.html) contains an impressive collection of training materials that the Education Division, a unit with seven specialists, has developed. The materials are provided in multiple formats (instructor-led, web-based, and videotapes) and cover a variety of topics to enable agency ethics officials to meet their training needs. Examples of the web-based training materials are modules dealing with the "misuse of position," "gifts between employees," "working with contractors" and "gifts from outside sources" (U.S. OGE 2005). Other government sites with computer- and web-based ethics training are identified as well. These include the U.S. Departments of Agriculture, Defense, Interior, Justice, and Treasury and the National Institutes of Health.

> "Many new leaders will not be familiar with federal laws and regulations which both authorize their actions and constrain their discretion. Simply accomplishing something may not be as easy as they expect."
> —Robert I. Cusick (2010),
> Director, U.S. Office of Government Ethics

The OGE conducts an annual conference for federal employees with ethics responsibilities, including executive branch ethics officials, inspector general officials, and representatives from state, local, and foreign governments. The 17th National Government Ethics Conference was held in Chicago in 2010 and dealt with a number of topics—confidential financial disclosure; issues in contracting out services; legal ethics; travel involving frequent-flyer benefits and premium-class accommodations; participation in professional associations; the Hatch Act and political activities of federal employees; book contracts and writing as an outside activity; how supervisors can encourage ethical behavior in the workplace; rules on job hunting and seeking post-government employment; and gifts from foreign governments. As these topics indicate, the annual conference is designed to assist federal employees sort through important hands-on issues.

The agency also offers workshops and seminars throughout the year, both in Washington, DC, and in other parts of the country. In FY 2010, the OGE delivered 54 training classes in Washington, with over 30 classes directed at the introductory level for new or inexperienced ethics officials. Topics addressed included the OGE's role in conflict-of-interest investigations, leveraging technology to improve ethics program management, and training tips.

Since 2004, the OGE has prepared annual performance and accountability reports that document in detail the accomplishments of the agency (U.S. OGE n.d.c). The *Performance and Accountability Report FY2010* (U.S. OGE 2010) focused on the agency's strategic goals and performance objectives, including the implementation of the president's Executive Order 13490, which requires full-time, noncareer presidential appointees to take an ethics pledge. The order requires each covered appointee to sign the pledge "upon becoming an appointee" (see Exhibit 4.3).

Since 1978 when the OGE was established, the executive branch of the federal government has certainly conducted a major effort to raise the ethical bar and encourage federal employees to do the right thing. Still, ethical lapses occur, as evidenced by the U.S. Air Force-Boeing air tanker scandal in 2003. This scandal involved a high-level senior civil servant, Darlene Druyun, the chief acquisition official with the Air Force, who collaborated with high-ranking Boeing executives to secure jobs for her daughter, her son-in-law, and herself in exchange for an Air Force contract to lease tankers from Boeing for a whopping $23 billion! The scandal landed Druyun in jail for nine months for violating conflict-of-interest laws. Boeing's chief financial officer, Michael M. Sears, also received jail time after he pleaded guilty to a conflict-of-interest charge for negotiating with Druyun over a Boeing job before she retired in 2002. At that time, Druyun was responsible for overseeing Pentagon contracts with Boeing (Merle 2004).

This single instance does not condemn the federal government's entire ethics education and training initiatives, but it does cast some doubt on its effectiveness at the highest levels, especially in the field of contract management.

Ethics Codes

Elected and appointed public officials typically express very positive attitudes toward codes of ethics. The conventional wisdom is that codes deter unethical acts, especially by motivated, well intended public servants. Unethical officials are likely to be unethical regardless of whether a code does or does not exist, but those who want to be ethical find a code helpful. Of course, the motivation for adopting a code is all too often a scandal or series of unethical acts.

Professional Association Codes

Professional association codes can be very helpful to public managers. Most professional organizations such as the International City/County Management Association (ICMA), the American Society for Public Administration

---

Exhibit 4.3
Executive Order 13490 Pledge

Generally, appointees must commit to:

- not accept gifts or gratuities from registered lobbyists or lobbying organizations;
- recuse, for two years, from any particular matter involving specific parties in which a former employer or client is or represents a party, if the appointee served that employer or client during the two years prior to the appointment;
- if the appointee was a registered lobbyist during the prior two years,
  * recuse, for two years after appointment, from any particular matter on which he or she lobbied during the two years prior to appointment (or any particular matter that falls within the same specific issue area);
  * not seek or accept employment with an agency or department that he or she lobbied during the prior two years;
- if the appointee is subject to the senior employee post-employment restriction in 18 U.S.C. § 207(c), to abide by such restriction for two years after termination of the appointment;
- not to lobby any covered executive branch official (as described in the Lobbying Disclosure Act) or any noncareer SES appointee for as long as President Obama is in office;
- agree that any hiring or other employment decisions will be based on the candidate's qualifications, competence, and experience.

(ASPA), the American Public Works Association (APWA), the International Personnel Management Association (IPMA), and the Government Finance Officers Association (GFOA) have ethics codes.[2] Two professional codes that receive considerable attention are the ASPA Code and the ICMA Code. The ASPA Code emphasizes aspirational values such as obey the law and serve the public (see Exhibit 4.4). The ICMA Code, which has provided guidance for practicing city and county managers for more than eight decades, is a mix of aspirational values and practical wisdom. While it admonishes managers to "be dedicated to the highest ideals of honor and integrity" to merit the respect of elected officials, employees, and the public, the code and accompanying guidelines offer specific directives about appropriate and inappropriate behavior. For example, it is inappropriate behavior for a member to endorse commercial products. Guidelines for Tenet 12 state that:

> Members should not endorse commercial products or services by agreeing to use their photograph, endorsement, or quotation in paid or other commercial advertisements, whether or not for compensation.

Managers who violate the code can be reprimanded and even expelled from ICMA. An expulsion is a serious matter that can sideline a career.

Leading with Integrity

"As a member of various professional associations, my actions are subject to multiple codes of ethics. Some, such as the ICMA Code of Ethics, provide fairly explicit interpretations that allow easy reference on a variety of situations. ICMA supplements those written guidelines by providing its members personal guidance on individual issues.

"Given the challenges that city and county managers routinely face, specific guidelines and personal guidance to members are understandable."

—Eric Johnson,
Assistant County Administrator,
Hillsborough County, Florida

Code Enforcement

Must an effective professional code be enforced? And, if so, how should it be done? The ICMA certainly advocates and practices enforcement, although it is done in a very careful and thorough manner. The ICMA goes to great lengths to ensure that allegations of wrongdoing are investigated while at the same time ensuring fairness and confidentiality. The ASPA can expel a member for a code violation but has never done so. Given the code's aspiration character and the diversity of the membership, ASPA leaders have not deemed it wise to develop the tools and procedures necessary to levy sanctions against members who stray from the code.

The ICMA's sanctions vary according to the severity of the violation. A *private censure* is issued if the violation is relatively minor. This takes the form of a letter sent to the member, the state association, and the person who made the complaint that the member has been found to have violated the code,

Exhibit 4.4
ASPA's Code of Ethics

I. Serve the Public Interest

Serve the public, beyond serving oneself. ASPA members are committed to:

1. Exercise discretionary authority to promote the public interest.
2. Oppose all forms of discrimination and harassment, and promote affirmative action.
3. Recognize and support the public's right to know the public's business.
4. Involve citizens in policy decision making.
5. Exercise compassion, benevolence, fairness, and optimism.
6. Respond to the public in ways that are complete, clear, and easy to understand.
7. Assist citizens in their dealings with government.
8. Be prepared to make decisions that may not be popular.

II. Respect the Constitution and the Law

Respect, support, and study government constitutions and laws that define responsibilities of public agencies, employees, and all citizens. ASPA members are committed to:

1. Understand and apply legislation and regulations relevant to their professional role.
2. Work to improve and change laws and policies that are counterproductive or obsolete.
3. Eliminate unlawful discrimination.
4. Prevent all forms of mismanagement of public funds by establishing and maintaining strong fiscal and management controls, and by supporting audits and investigative activities.
5. Respect and protect privileged information.
6. Encourage and facilitate legitimate dissent activities in government and protect the whistleblowing rights of public employees.

(continued)

Exhibit 4.4 *(continued)*

7. Promote constitutional principles of equality, fairness, representativeness, responsiveness, and due process in protecting citizens' rights.

III. Demonstrate Personal Integrity

Demonstrate the highest standards in all activities to inspire public confidence and trust in public service. ASPA members are committed to:

1. Maintain truthfulness and honesty and not compromise them for advancement, honor, or personal gain.
2. Ensure that others receive credit for their work and contributions.
3. Zealously guard against conflict of interest or its appearance: for example, nepotism, improper outside employment, misuse of public resources, or the acceptance of gifts.
4. Respect superiors, subordinates, colleagues, and the public.
5. Take responsibility for their own errors.
6. Conduct official acts without partisanship.

IV. Promote Ethical Organizations

Strengthen organizational capabilities to apply ethics, efficiency, and effectiveness in serving the public. ASPA members are committed to:

1. Enhance organizational capacity for open communication, creativity, and dedication.
2. Subordinate institutional loyalties to the public good.
3. Establish procedures that promote ethical behavior and hold individuals and organizations accountable for their conduct.
4. Provide organization members with an administrative means for dissent, assurance of due process, and safeguards against reprisal.
5. Promote merit principles that protect against arbitrary and capricious actions.

(continued)

Exhibit 4.4 *(continued)*

6. Promote organizational accountability through appropriate controls and procedures.
7. Encourage organizations to adopt, distribute, and periodically review a code of ethics as a living document.

V. Strive for Professional Excellence

Strengthen individual capabilities and encourage the professional development of others. ASPA members are committed to:

1. Provide support and encouragement to upgrade competence.
2. Accept as a personal duty the responsibility to keep up to date on emerging issues and potential problems.
3. Encourage others, throughout their careers, to participate in professional activities and associations.
4. Allocate time to meet with students and provide a bridge between classroom studies and the realities of public service.

Source: ASPA, 2006.

that the ICMA disapproves of such conduct, and if repeated in the future, may be cause for more serious sanctions. A *public censure* is a notification to the member, complainant, state association, and news media that a violation took place and that the ICMA strongly disapproves of such conduct. Additionally, a notification is sent to the local governing body to "protect the public against unethical conduct in local government." The next level of seriousness is a *revocation* of the member's privileges. Finally, the most severe sanction is a *prohibition* against reinstatement of membership. In other words, the member is expelled permanently (ICMA 2005).

The permanent expulsion of a member from the ICMA occurs only under the most compelling and clearly warranted circumstances. In December 2010, for example, the ICMA executive board took such action against Robert Rizzo, the former city manager of Bell, California. Bell's citizens voted in 2011 to recall the mayor and four other council members (Gorman, 2011). That same year, the former city manager was indicted and charged with more than 50 counts of fraud, falsification of records, and conflicts of interest. He pleaded not guilty (Dobuzinskis, 2011). (See Chapter 5 for more details regarding the shocking abuse and wrongdoing in Bell.)

> The board found that Mr. Rizzo personally benefited from misuse of city funds; failed in his fiduciary responsibility to ensure that public funds were legally and properly used for the public's benefit; did not fully and accurately disclose his compensation in a transparent manner; and failed in his obligation to ensure that city matters were transparent and fully communicated to the council and public. (ICMA 2010)

How Do Managers Use a Code?

Some exhort members of the organization to adhere to a professional code by encouraging them to join associations such as the ASPA or ICMA or GFOA or IPMA. Others demonstrate through their own behavior that they walk the talk. Still others go so far as to require subordinates to endorse their code publicly. For example, here is what one city manager claims:

> I require managers to sign their professional codes and to hang them on their office wall, and I list the values that are most important to me on a plaque on my wall, as well. (Berman and West 2003, 36)

Leading with Integrity

"In roles as a mentor and as the chief executive and advisor to elected and appointed boards and councils, I have found that the commitment to lead with integrity requires the willingness to define and live by clear principles and values in order to build trust and the willingness for others to follow.

"Relying upon the expertise and advice of others requires the ability to also admit one's own mistakes and limitations and to seek and accept the thoughts and ideas of others. Having the flexibility to reach identified goals through a variety of paths can help build that trust and the credibility needed for sustained success."

—Martin P. Black,
AICP, ICMA-CM, former city manager, Venice, Florida

Requiring members of the organization to sign and display a code does not always produce desirable results. Consider an example from the private sector—the Boeing Company. Boeing suffered a string of corporate scandals in the early 2000s that motivated the company to bring CEO Harry C. Stonecipher out of retirement to restore Boeing's reputation. One of his first steps was to require Boeing's top managers and 160,000 employees to sign the company's code of ethical conduct. He also signed the code. Alas, he was forced to resign a mere 15 months after taking the wheel because of a sexual tryst with a female executive officer. The board of directors concluded that while a personal consensual affair is a private matter, Stonecipher's extramarital affair had become a management and public relations issue severe enough to dismiss him. The chairman of the board, Louis E. Platt, said that having an affair in and of itself was not a violation of Boeing's code of conduct (Wayne 2005). However, the one-page code states that "employees will not engage in conduct or activity that may raise questions as to the company's honesty, impartiality, or reputation or otherwise cause embarrassment to the company" (The Boeing Company 1/26/2004). The code further states that integrity must underlie all company relationships, including those with and among employees. Mr. Stonecipher's actions, Platt asserted, embarrassed Boeing and compromised his "ability to lead going forward" (Wayne 2005).

Local Government Codes of Ethics

Local government codes of ethics are often covered by state statutes or incorporated in local ordinances—but not always. Pinellas County, Florida, for example, adopted a "Statement of Ethics" (see Exhibit 4.5) that emphasizes the aspirational values of right behavior rather than the "follow the rules or else" mentality that many law-derived codes espouse.

Across Tampa Bay from Pinellas County, another large, urban county—Hillsborough County—adopted a more detailed statement of ethics in 2005 (Hillsborough County, Florida 2005). The ethics statement contains five key elements (see Exhibit 4.6) along with 17 sub-elements. Notice how much more detailed the Hillsborough statement is than that of Pinellas County, with the emphasis placed on the individual as illustrated by the "I will" statements. Which code do you feel will work the best—the brief aspirational code of Pinellas County or the more detailed code of Hillsborough County?

Most local government do not have stand-alone codes. The typical rationale is that the state's ethics laws cover employees, so it is not necessary to have a local code, although this is not always the case. New York's ethics laws, for example, do not cover local governments.

Local governments that do draft a local code often find the drafting process as important as the final product itself. Mountain View, California, for example, developed a code from the "bottom up," a process that involved more than 150 employees from all city departments (Duggan and Woodhouse 2011). Former city manager Kevin Duggan and deputy city manager Kevin Woodhouse assert that a bottom-up approach "can proceed successfully and efficiently alongside

---

Exhibit 4.5
Pinellas County Statement of Ethics

We, the employees of Pinellas County, as providers of public service; and, in order to inspire confidence and trust, are committed to the highest standards of personal integrity, honesty and competence.

To This End We Will:

• Provide open and accessible government, giving courteous, responsive service to all citizens equally.
• Accept only authorized compensation for the performance of our duties and respectfully decline any offers of gifts or gratuities from those with whom we do business.
• Disclose or report any actual or perceived conflicts of interest.
• Comply with all laws and regulations applicable to the County and impartially apply them to everyone.
• Neither apply nor accept improper influences, favoritism and personal bias.
• Use County funds and resources efficiently, including materials, equipment and our time.
• Respect and protect the privileged information to which we have access in the course of our duties, never using it to stir controversy, to harm others or for private gain.

Source: Pinellas County, Florida, n.d.

---

all of the other priority demands of an organization" (2011, 10). Of course, if a code is not viewed as a living document, it may become little more than a nicely framed ornament that adorns an office wall.

Code Implementation

How can a code be more than words on a piece of paper? Administrators, especially at the highest organizational level, must demonstrate their commitment to the values and principles contained in the code. One approach toward doing this is for top managers to conduct special sessions on the code, including sessions for newly hired employees. A study of employees in one

Exhibit 4.6
Hillsborough County: Statement of Ethics

As a Hillsborough County employee:

In order to fulfill my role as a public servant, I will adhere to legal, professional and trade rules and standards. I will demonstrate and be dedicated to the highest ideals of honor and integrity in all public and personal relationships to merit the respect, trust and confidence of government officials, other public officials, employees, and the public.

1. Responsibility
   A. I will be sensitive and responsive to the rights of the public and their changing needs.
   B. I will strive to provide the highest quality of performance and service.
   C. I will exercise prudence and integrity in the management of funds in my custody and in all financial transactions.
2. Employee Development
   A. I will devote my time, skills and energies to achieving excellence in my job and my department both independently and in cooperation with other professionals.
   B. I will abide by approved practices and recommended standards for my line of work.
3. Professional Integrity—Information
   A. I will not knowingly sign, make any oral or written statement or report which contains any misstatement or which omits any material fact.
   B. I will respect and protect privileged information as I respect the right of citizens to access public records and public meetings.
   C. I will be sensitive and responsive to inquiries from public officials, the public and the media, within the framework of Hillsborough County policy.
4. Personal Integrity—Relationships
   A. I will strive to exhibit respect and trust in the affairs and interests of Hillsborough County government.

(continued)

Exhibit 4.6 *(continued)*

    B. I will not knowingly be a party to, condone or conceal any illegal or improper activity.

    C. I will respect the rights, responsibilities and integrity of fellow employees and customers with whom I work and associate.

    D. I will manage all matters of supervision within the scope of my authority so that fairness and impartiality govern my decisions.

    E. I will promote equal employment opportunities, and shall oppose any discrimination, harassment or other unfair practices.

5. Conflict of Interest

    A. I will perform my duties without favor.

    B. I will refrain from engaging in any outside matters of financial or personal interest incompatible with the impartial and objective performance of my duties.

    C. I will not, directly or indirectly, seek or accept personal gain which would influence, or appear to influence, the conduct of my official duties.

    D. I will not use public property or resources for personal or political gain.

Source: Hillsborough County, Florida, 2005.

---

high-tech organization found that sessions delivered on the ethical code of conduct by high-ranking executives had an enduring impact (Adam and Rachman-Moore 2004). Such sessions can "leave an unforgettable impression about the importance assigned to ethics in the workplace" (2004, 239).

Codes should be regarded as living documents that are integrated into the fabric of the organizational culture. Ethics managers who take pride in their professional code of ethics by displaying it in the work environment are taking an important step in cultivating an ethical culture.

Why Codes Succeed or Fail

Hard evidence that a code of ethics deters unethical behavior and encourages ethical behavior is difficult to find in the scholarly literature. Studies along these lines have been carried out primarily in the field of business administration, and the results are mixed. Nonetheless, the fact that nearly nine of every ten Fortune Global 200 companies have a business code of ethics certainly suggests that top management believes codes make a difference. A recent study by Muel Kaptein (2011) examines several factors thought important in determining the impact of a code on unethical behavior. His research assessed (1) the presence of a code, (2) the content of the code, (3) the frequency and (4) quality of the communication activities surrounding the code, and the extent to which (5) senior management as well as local management were committed to the code. Their study sample consisted of 3,075 adults working for organizations in the United States that employ at least 200 people.

Which of the five factors identified above mattered the most? The mere presence of a code absent the other four factors was insignificant in deterring unethical behavior. Similar results were found when the frequency of communication was added to the model. The results changed dramatically, however, when the other three factors are added to the model. The one factor that had the greatest impact on reducing unethical behavior in the workplace was the suffusion of the code's values by senior and local management throughout the organization . In other words, the effort and commitment by top management to embed the code in the organization's culture was a major factor in building an organization of integrity.

Another way to assess a code's effectiveness is offered by Stuart C. Gilman (2005), a practitioner-scholar who has written extensively on this subject. Here are his explanations for why some codes succeed and others fail: Successful codes must have clear behavior objectives. The behaviors you want to encourage and discourage should be spelled out. Successful codes must fit with the mission of the agency; a tax collection agency, for example, must be respectful but firm. "They must demand honesty from not only public servants but from the public as well" (61). Codes that are successful must have pragmatic goals; codes that promise too much are not likely to succeed. Codes that promise to end corruption are promising too much—nothing will end corruption, Gilman asserts. We can only hope to control it so it has the least impact on citizens. Finally, successful codes must be supported by feedback. "Aggregate data such as the number of administrative actions taken or successful prosecutions not only helps administrators understand the effect of their program, but it also provides insights as to changes or necessary resource reallocations that might be necessary" (63).

Exhibit 4.7 contains a code of ethics for the city employees of Mountain View, California. You can "test" Gilman's recommendations by answering the following questions: (1) Does the code have clear behavior objectives?

Exhibit 4.7
Mountain View, California, Employee Code of Ethics

As a City employee, I will be guided by prudent judgment and personal responsibility, whether serving the public or working with colleagues, and my decisions and actions will be made according to the following Ethical Principles:

- I will uphold the City's policies in a transparent and consistent manner at all times.
- I will make unbiased decisions and use my authority fairly and responsibly.
- I will act with honesty and be an advocate for an environment that promotes public trust.
- I will not use City resources or my position for personal gain.
- I will be mindful of how my actions may be perceived by others and avoid conflicts of interest.

These Ethical Principles serve as guidance and work in concert with:

The City's Mission Statement:

The City of Mountain View provides quality services and facilities that meet the needs of a caring and diverse community in a financially responsible manner.

The City's Organizational Values:

Provide exceptional service, act with integrity and treat others with respect.

---

(2) Does it fit well with the city's mission statement? (3) Does the code have pragmatic goals? (4) Does the code promise too much or too little?

Most codes fail because they raise unrealistic expectations or try to control too much. Codes that require excessive reporting and tracking can produce cynicism within the organization and among the public. The pursuit of absolute integrity can be a fool's quest if the result is organizational ineffectiveness. A shift in political leadership can also bring a working code to its knees. "It is not uncommon for new political leaders to either de-emphasize ethics programs or to criticize them as being ineffective" (Gilman 2005, 65). Finally, codes can fail if there is no commitment to public service or simply become out of date. Changes in technology, the legal structure, or the organizational culture often necessitate a re-examination of the code of ethics.

Oaths

Oaths signed by employees are also used to encourage ethical behavior and can be a key element in an integrity or fusion model. Oaths are challenging to adopt because they are difficult to frame in a manner that public officials find agreeable. Public service oaths such as those shown in Exhibit 4.8 are widely used in the federal government, and some states and local governments have developed their own version of an oath. Consider the oath for the Unified Government of Wyandotte County and Kansas City, Kansas. It requires elected and appointed officials, including employees on the front lines of service delivery, to swear (with their signature) that they will support the U.S. Constitution and the State of Kansas's Constitution and abide by the provisions of the Code of Ethics of the Unified Government.

A similar local government oath was adopted in Salt Lake County, Utah, in 2004. In response to several scandals, county reformers put into place the oath shown in Exhibit 4.9. Notice that the oath applies to all persons employed by the county, including elected and nonelected officials. Notice also that all officials and employees are required only to "read and review" the oath—nothing more.

Some scholars believe that oaths have lost much of their value in the modern age. Stephen L. Carter (1997, 108), for example, claims, "In the cynicism of our age, nobody assumes that simply because an individual swears by God to tell the truth that the person is telling the truth. . . . An oath . . . is seen as a silly little formality, like the stamping of a passport." It might be recalled that President Bill Clinton was impeached by the House of Representatives in 1998 largely because of lying under oath. (A trial in the Senate did not convict him of the charges.) Other scholars take a different view of oaths. Gilman (2006) puts it this way:

> I take a slightly less cynical view of oaths and their impact. I have been in a position to really watch them work, and work the way they are supposed to. To suggest this occurs all of the time would be silly. But I have watched the mighty fall, most notably Mr. Edwin Meese III, former U.S. Attorney General in the Reagan Administration, and Mr. John Sununu, former White House Chief of Staff under President George H.W. Bush, because of ethics

Exhibit 4.8
Public Service Oaths

U.S. Presidential Oath of Office

Since George Washington first said the words on April 30, 1789, as prompted by Robert Livingston, Chancellor of the State of New York, every President of the United States has repeated the following simple presidential oath of office as part of the inauguration ceremony:

I do solemnly swear (or affirm) that I will faithfully execute the Office of President of the United States, and will to the best of my ability, preserve, protect and defend the Constitution of the United States.

Source: Constitution of the United States, Article II, Section 1, 1787.

U.S. Senator Oath of Office

I do solemnly swear (or affirm) that I will support and defend the Constitution of the United States against all enemies, foreign and domestic; that I will bear true faith and allegiance to the same; that I take this obligation freely, without any mental reservation or purpose of evasion; and that I will well and faithfully discharge the duties of the office on which I am about to enter: So help me God.

Source: U.S. Senate, 1884.

The Athenian Oath

The Athenian Oath was recited by the citizens of Athens, Greece, over 2,000 years ago. It is frequently referenced by civic leaders in modern times as a timeless code of civic responsibility.

We will never bring disgrace on this our City by an act of dishonesty or cowardice. We will fight for the ideals and Sacred Things of the City both alone and with many. We will revere and obey the City's laws, and will do our best to incite a like reverence and respect in those above us who are prone to annul them or set them at naught. We will strive unceasingly to quicken the public's sense of civic duty. Thus, in all these ways, we will transmit this City not only, not less, but greater and more beautiful than it was transmitted to us.

Source: National League of Cities, 2010.

Exhibit 4.9
Salt Lake County, Utah, Code of Ordinances:
County Ethics Code

Ethics Statement: All county elected officials, appointed officers, deputies and employees, in the employment of Salt Lake County, before commencing the duties of their respective offices, shall read and review the following *ethics* statement:

Employees of Salt Lake County support, obey and defend the Constitution of the United States, the Constitution of the State of Utah, the laws of the State of Utah, and the ordinances of Salt Lake County, to the best of their abilities and will always strive to meet the highest ethical standards implicit in their employment and in the furtherance of the best public interest.

Source: Salt Lake County, Utah, 2011.

---

violations. Each was ultimately allowed to resign because the violations were tied to their oath of office.

Oaths, especially those tied to a code of ethics, are not common in state and local governance. John A. Rohr, a highly respected ethicist, takes strong objection to this oversight. He contends it is the oath of office that defines the public servant as a professional (see Exhibit 4.10 for an example). In his classic *To Run a Constitution: The Legitimacy of the Administrative State* (1986, 192), Rohr asserts:

> The oath to uphold the Constitution can then be seen not simply as a pledge to obey but also as an initiation into a community of disciplined discourse, aimed at discovering, renewing, adapting, and applying the fundamental principles that support our public order. The task is to see the oath more as an act of civility than submission.

LeRoy F. Harlow (1914–1995), a highly respected city manager and government consultant, believed an oath is far more than words on a piece of paper or uttered during a swearing-in ceremony. In *Servants of All* (1981), he contends that "all elected, appointed, or employed public servants, whether

---

Exhibit 4.10
Oath of Office for Employment in the U.S. Postal Service

Before entering upon their duties and before receiving any salary, all officers and employees of the Postal Service shall take and subscribe the following oath or affirmation:

"I, _____, do solemnly swear (or affirm) that I will support and defend the Constitution of the United States against all enemies, foreign and domestic; that I will bear true faith and allegiance to the same; that I take this obligation freely, without any mental reservation or purpose of evasion; and that I will well and faithfully discharge the duties of the office on which I am about to enter."

Source: U.S. Department of Justice, 2005.

---

full-time or part-time," should be required to take an oath of honor. The result "may reestablish character in the public service [and] may divert and lessen the stream of governmental corruption that has come close to inundating us all" (323). Harlow readily admitted that no sworn oath would stop a public officeholder bent on violating the public trust; nonetheless, an oath may be the moral crutch that many leaders and followers who straddle the ethical fence may need to strengthen their "resolve to perform their duties regardless of personal consequence" (323). Although Harlow's comments were made 30 years ago, they resonate loudly in 2011. Is it not so?

A Public Servant's Oath of Honor

"I hereby swear (or affirm) that during my service with (name of agency) I will not (or I did not) lie, cheat, steal, or illegally favor one citizen or group of citizens over another (nor tolerate any public officer or employee who does)" (Harlow, 1981, 322).

The point here is that oaths provide officials with the legitimacy and empowerment to carry out their duties in a manner that is both ethically and morally sound. This approach contrasts significantly with the "follow the rules" method that many codes become when transformed into law-like documents.

Ethics Audits

A proactive tool for building organizations of integrity is the ethics audit. Although not widely employed, an ethics audit can serve as a very useful tool. It has been described as an "appraisal activity, the purpose being to determine if changes need to be made in the climate, environment, codes, and the enforcement of ethics policies" (Wiley 1995). An ethics audit is not an accounting or financial management audit. By way of example, the New York State comptroller recently completed an audit of the accounting and expenditures of a Long Island school district and found that the former district superintendent and the assistant superintendent for business had, for eight years, plundered the district's treasury of $11.2 million (Lambert 2005). This affluent school district had a stellar record for graduating students who went on to top universities. Perhaps this is the reason why the school board, the treasurer, and the external accounting firm hired by the school district failed to exercise adequate oversight. Failed oversight is, in itself, unethical.

But why are audits uncommon? There are several reasons. First, it can be threatening if presented as an effort to root out wrongdoing; furthermore, when done for the first time, it raises anxiety levels and questions about why it is needed. After all, don't most public employees believe they are ethical and work in an ethical organization? Perhaps. Second, audits are uncommon because they need to be comprehensive in both the information solicited and the members of the organization covered. It can be challenging in terms of the time and effort required, which, in turn, places a demand on the agency's budget. Third, employees and managers might not be convinced of the confidentiality of the audit, especially in states with strong laws that require public officials to conduct all business in an open, transparent manner, sometimes referred to in the "sunshine" The reasons for not carrying out an audit should be weighed carefully in light of the organizational pay-offs they provide: increased productivity, greater worker satisfaction, lower turnover rates of personnel, and the building of public trust and confidence in the agency.

There are other important reasons to conduct an ethics audit. First, it can identify gaps in policies and procedures, including gaps in the need to increase awareness of areas of potential ethical risk (McAuliffe 2002). Second, another plus for conducting an audit occurs if the agency contracts with an outside party, such as a university institute, to carry it out. An internal, agency-conducted audit is automatically suspect and unlikely to be viewed as trustworthy by employees. A more transparent, university-conducted audit benefits agency officials through "ethical conversations, opportunity for critical reflection, and the support that could be offered to staff with no professional qualifications" (2002, 4).

An ethics audit might also include an assessment of occupational risk or vulnerability. Some organizational work is inherently vulnerable to ethical abuse if not criminal wrongdoing; for example, work that involves the handling and processing of finances, purchasing and contracting, conducting inspections, and enforcing rules and regulations are high risk, especially for workers whose ethical compass is subpar in the first place. A systematic assessment of the ethical risk factor of work is a necessary first step in putting into place appropriate accountability and transparency mechanisms. It is also a valuable step in identifying ethical training priorities.

Local Government Audits

To illustrate further what an ethics audit might entail, consider the audits conducted in a city and a county in Florida. The city had a population of 67,000 and a council-manager form of government. The county, with a population of 850,000 and a commission-administrator form of government, was situated on Florida's Gulf Coast. Both governments have a history of stability with appointed city/county managers who typically serve for many years.

Questionnaires were sent to randomly selected samples of employees from each government. The surveys were made available to employees within their workplace. A postage-paid return envelope with the university identified as the recipient was also provided. Two hundred sixty-five ($N = 265$) city employees returned usable questionnaires for a response rate of 53 percent. Four hundred sixty-five county employees ($N = 465$) returned usable questionnaires for a response rate of 62 percent.

Both samples were drawn from alphabetized payroll lists using a fixed interval selection method. All participants were informed that their participation was voluntary and all responses would be treated confidentially. Cover letters from the city manager, the chief personnel officer of the county, and the principal investigator (a faculty member at a local university) explained the purpose of the study and assured anonymity. To provide additional anonymity, participants were not identified by sex, race, or work unit.

All major organizational subunits (police, fire, and so on) in the city participated in the study. The county study population included all employees under the county administrator's jurisdiction, the supervisor of elections, the property appraiser's office, and the clerk of the circuit courts. Employees under the appointing authority of the sheriff did not participate.

Each respondent was asked to provide information about the ethical climate of his or her organization. This approach assumed that the respondent could perform as a reasonably objective observer. A measurement type such as this does not focus on whether the respondent believes he or she behaves ethically, nor does it emphasize whether the respondent sees the ethical climate as good or bad (Victor and Cullen 1988). The questionnaire elicited *descriptions* of, rather than feelings toward, the ethical climate (see Exhibit 4.11).

Statistical analysis found that a strong ethical climate is associated with the values of efficiency, effectiveness, quality, excellence, and teamwork. Indeed, the city results showed that the ethical climate was the single most important influence on organizational performance, suggesting that the aforementioned values are strongly reinforced by a strong ethical climate. These findings challenge the conventional wisdom that ethics and high performance are incompatible.

Also challenged is the conventional wisdom that bureaucratic environments, with their emphasis on hierarchy and rule following, are incompatible with a strong commitment to organizational ethics. Indeed, the study's results support the opposite view; that is, procedural emphases—in combination with other variables in the workplace—may actually reinforce an ethical workplace. Although limited to two local governments in a single state, the results are provocative in light of the attention given to the "evils" of hierarchy. Could it be that the defining, if not essential, characteristics of ethical public organizations are order, authority, and rules? Or, is it conceivable that hierarchy and rule following merely reinforce the prevailing ethical climate, regardless of how strong or weak it may be?

U.S. Office of Government Ethics

In 2000 the U.S. Office of Government Ethics (OGE) conducted an audit known as the *Executive Branch Employee Ethics Survey 2000*. The audit was an effort by the OGE to determine how well the federal program was working. Was it making a difference? A rigorous sampling methodology along with a sophisticated statistical analysis was employed to survey respondents and assess responses. Overall, the audit revealed three important findings: (1) ethics training encourages employees to take a positive view of ethics in their agency; (2) unethical behavior is perceived as infrequent by federal employees; and (3) "supervisors play a critical role in promoting and maintaining an ethical culture" (7). How the OGE has used these findings, however, is not clear. Nor has the agency conducted a follow-up survey.

The United Nations Organizational Integrity Survey

The United Nations contracted with a management consultant in 2004 to conduct an integrity survey of all UN staff and leaders in the Secretariat—a population of 18,035. A total of 6,086 (33 percent) returned the questionnaire. The purpose of the survey was "to measure both attitudes and perceptions

---

Exhibit 4.11
Ethics Climate Survey Items

1. It is not unusual for members of my department to accept small gifts for performing their duties.
2. Some members of my department use their position for private gain.
3. Members of my department have misused their position to influence the hiring of their relatives and friends.
4. My supervisor encourages employees to act in an ethical manner.
5. Managers in my department have high ethical standards.
6. The people in my department demonstrate high standards of personal integrity.
7. There are serious ethical problems in my department.
8. Members of my department sometimes leak information that benefits persons who do business with the city.
9. My superiors set a good example of ethical behavior.

Source: Menzel, 1993, 197.

---

about integrity among UN staff" (United Nations 2004, 5). What did the results show? The final report notes,

> Staff care most about what they see others doing and saying. Organizational integrity is about: eliminating discrepancies in what leaders and supervisors say and do; living the UN's vision, mission and values while limiting political and cultural influences; doing the right things even when it's inconvenient, uncomfortable or without precedent; demonstrating the value of integrity by rewarding those who do while disciplining those who do not. (2004, 9)

The findings indicated that staffers were very satisfied with their work and committed to the organization's goals, but many were reluctant to become whistleblowers or report misconduct. "Staff members feel unprotected from reprisals for reporting violations of the codes of conduct" (11). Not surprisingly, staff personnel were uncomfortable about approaching their managers with ethical concerns, and many did not feel that their supervisors and colleagues regularly discussed ethical issues arising in the workplace (ASPA 2004).

In November 2005, the then UN secretary-general Kofi Annan used the audit findings as the basis for a proposal to the General Assembly to establish an Ethics Office. The proposal was favorably received and the office became a reality on January 1, 2006. The primary objective of the UN Ethics Office is "to assist the Secretary-General in ensuring that all staff members observe and perform their functions in consistency with the highest standards of integrity . . . through:

(a) fostering a culture of ethics, transparency and accountability;
(b) developing and disseminating standards for appropriate professional conduct;
(c) providing leadership, management and oversight of the United Nations ethics infrastructure." (United Nations General Assembly 2005, A/60/568)

The United Nations ethics audit, although meritorious, illustrates the limitations of an audit. For example, the UN director of elections, Carina Perelli, was dismissed from her post in December 2005 because of accusations of sexual harassment and abuse of authority. A management review (not an ethics audit) of her office conducted earlier in the year "faulted her for an abusive style of leadership and favoritism and said she had created an atmosphere where 'sexual innuendo is part of the "fabric" of the division'" (Hoge 2005). Ms. Perelli was unceremoniously escorted from the UN Headquarters in New York and told "she would no longer be permitted to enter the building unless she had a scheduled appointment to discuss her appeal" (A23).

When Serious Wrongdoing Turns Up

An ethics auditor may discover serious incidents of wrongdoing, especially when interviews rather than mail surveys are employed to collect information about the ethics climate. If these incidents are of sufficient scale and severity to be potentially criminal in nature, such as that in the Long Island school district, what are the auditors to do? The answer is straightforward: They must report their suspicions and findings to the appropriate legal authorities. However, the line between criminal acts and unethical acts is sometimes difficult to discern. Auditors must be convinced that an unethical act has a very high probability of being unlawful while at the same time being very careful to not assume the role of a prosecutor.

Although objectivity is at a premium in conducting an audit, administrators "must recognize that an assessment of this nature involves considerable subjective judgment" (Reamer 2000, 364). Nonetheless, an ethics audit, whether done by a third party such as a consultant or university, is a valuable tool that can be drawn on to foster integrity in the workplace.

Human Resources Management

Personnel decisions—hiring, evaluating, promoting, and firing—are essential features of all organizations. Should the ethical behavior of an employee be considered in these decisions? Should only "honest" people be hired? Promoted? Hiring and promoting honest people is no easy task. How does an agency know if a person is honest? Should a lie-detector test be used? Or an integrity test? Or a fitness of character test? And, even if we could determine if a person is honest or of high moral character, can we presume that these qualities will persist over the years of employment? Not necessarily, given what we know about the moral challenges facing individuals in complex, modern organizations of the twenty-first century.

Stephen J. Bonczek, a city manager with many years' experience in different localities and states—Michigan, Florida, Texas, and Pennsylvania—is a strong advocate of raising the ethical awareness of employees through hiring, evaluation, and promotion. He is equally adamant about installing an ethical consciousness in the organization through the use of codes, audits, committees, and weekly staff meetings. "It is advantageous," he claims, "to use weekly staff meetings to review all discussions and decisions for ethical implications. When a potential problem is identified, a staff member can be assigned to clarify the issue and develop a strategy for resolving it at the next meeting" (Bonczek 1998, 78).

Hiring Practices

Screening of a job applicant for her ethical judgment is, of course, challenging. One approach that can be taken during the interview is to ask the candidate to respond to hypothetical situations. Here are several examples. Mary Jane Hirt, the former city manager of two Pittsburgh communities, recommends this scenario: "You are the assistant manager in a community and have just been informed by a council member that council intended to fire the town manager at the next public meeting. The council member asked whether you are interested in being considered for the manager's position. What is your response? Do you warn the manager that s/he is about to be fired?" (Hirt 2003).

Ann Hess with the City of Boston asks a specific question during the interview process by posing a hypothetical situation. "When I interview staff for the City Council (one staff; fourteen bosses), I try to gauge an applicant's understanding of the need to be confidential while respecting divergent interests across bosses" (Hess 2003). She presents the candidate with this scenario:

> You as a Central Staff member are asked to compile some research for one councilor. Another councilor comes to you with a request for information on the same issue, but the councilor has a different position on the issue. Part I: How do you comply with each person's request? Part II: The first councilor comes back to you and asks who else is working on the issue and what else you have produced for them. What do you say?
>
> I usually give the applicant five minutes to draft some informal comments and responses and then we talk about it. I look for how they come to the decision—while there's no specific right answer, better candidates will discuss wanting to know level of confidentiality in advance, providing both sides of the story to both councilors with focus on the particular position they are advocating, the inability to disclose who else they are doing research for, and how they present that fact to the requesting councilor with respect and understanding.

Scenarios like these can be helpful in screening job applicants, but more probing may be needed as well. To query applicants about their personal lives—have you ever stolen anything, lied, cheated—can be a tricky matter. Of course, there is also the possibility of prying too deeply into one's private affairs when taking this approach. Considerable care and caution needs to be exercised.

Annual Evaluations

Putting an ethics component into annual evaluations is a daunting task but one that many managers find useful. While it's challenging to incorporate an ethics criterion into evaluation, it would not be difficult to require employees to complete an ethics education or training course before being promoted. Mayor Steve Brown (2005) of Peachtree City, Georgia, urges local governments to "create a study course on ethics that has to be completed in order to be eligible for promotion." The U.S. Department of Defense Acquisition Workforce requires ethics training annually but does not mandate it as a condition for promotion. "To be a DoD Program Manager or Contracting Officer," Keith McAllister (2005) notes, "one must be certified to an appropriate level. Certification as a Program Manager includes a series of formal classes (continuous learning credit). . . . The DoD spends significant public resources annually. It is imperative that those resources be used in a manner consistent with public expectations and trust—hence the embedded ethics training."

The Value of a Hotline

"Regardless of the number of legally sufficient referrals through the hotline, it serves as a safety valve for public discontent with government. Whether it's a call regarding a rude employee, or allegations of significant abuse in public contracts or procurement, it provides an avenue that the citizen or public employee can turn to.

"During office hours, our hotline is answered by a member of our staff. After hours, the caller can leave a message. We acknowledge receipt of all hotline calls that are identified. On many occasions, even if the facts do not allege an ethics code violation, we can refer the caller to an appropriate agency to handle their concerns.

"Sometimes just 'blowing a little steam' has a beneficial effect on the caller. In these cases, there is a palpable benefit to the public regardless of the outcome. While an ethics hotline is important, it serves as only one cog in the wheel of an effective program created to foster an increase in ethics awareness and compliance."

—Alan Johnson (2011b),
Ethics Officer, Palm Beach County

One approach that might be taken to incorporate an ethics component in an employee's annual evaluation is to place a checkbox on the evaluation form. The checkbox could read: "Employee treats others with respect and dignity." As simplistic as this solution might be, it would certainly make every employee sensitive to the fact that he or she will be held ethically accountable once a year. And, if multiplied over hundreds or perhaps thousands of employees, what a difference it could make.

Ethics Counselors

Another tool for ethics management is the ethics counselor. An example is a clinical psychologist working as a federal employee in a U.S. Department of Veterans Affairs Medical Center. She is chairperson of the hospital ethics committee and coordinator of the employee assistance program (EAP). Her committee members function as consultants when people confront dilemmas and wish to discuss them. Issues like these reach her as an EAP counselor when someone is attempting to resolve an ethical issue between a superior and a subordinate; for example, they may come to her to discuss the incident and seek advice. A VA-wide National Center for Ethics in Health Care provides formal and informal consultation, as well. If the psychologist has a thorny issue come up in the Hospital Ethics Advisory Committee and wishes to get an outside perspective, she can call the National Center to get ethics advice.

The Department of Veterans Affairs Medical Center also has a monthly hotline teleconference where issues are discussed (for example, the Pope's declaration on patients in a persistent vegetative state, or whether gifts or meals provided by vendors can be accepted by service providers). Most of these issues deal with clinical or organizational ethics, and the consultants represent a variety of disciplines, including medicine, nursing, social work, psychology, law, and chaplaincy (West 2005).

Human resources management can be drawn on to promote ethics and integrity in governance. This discussion has demonstrated the many possibilities that lend themselves to this task. The failure by officials to include human resources management in their ethics management arsenal will limit the ability of the most dedicated, well-intentioned leader to build an organization of integrity.

Hotlines

The most famous hotline in history is the one that connects the red phones in Washington, DC, and Moscow, a Cold War relic perhaps. Fortunately, the Washington-Moscow hotline has had little use. Not so with other hotlines in widespread use in many organizations and governments. Tracking down fraud and waste is not an easy task, but fraud hotlines can be crucial in solving such cases. Ethics hotlines are typically dedicated to allegations involving violations of an ethics code. Sometimes, however, the same line is used for both purposes—tracking fraud and code violations. Consider the cases of Jacksonville and Palm Beach County, Florida.

Jacksonville Hotline

In August 2007, Mayor John Peyton directed the city's ethics officer to implement a confidential telephone hotline for the discovery of waste, fraud, and ethics violations. Later in the year, the city council authorized the Ethics Commission to receive hotline calls for reporting offenses under the local ethics code. A single telephone hotline number was used for all calls.

The results for the period August 2007–May 2011 show that 395 calls were made with 59 cases opened for further review and all but six closed. Many calls (30 percent) involved citizen education, as some complaints were based on a misunderstanding of the law or the facts. The ethics officer was able to clear up these issues quickly. Other calls came from city employees concerned about hiring relatives or allegations about employees receiving gifts (for example, football tickets). The ethics officer, Carla Miller (2011a), feels strongly that the educational benefits of hotlines are significant, as is the prospect of deterring intentional or unintentional wrongdoing by city employees.

Local Government Ethics Hotline Effectiveness

- Anonymity for the caller
- Documentation for oversight and transparency
- Well-trained staff that can distinguish various legal and ethical issues and put them in a local context
- Effective working relationship between the ethics office and other bodies such as the General Counsel and the Inspector General
- Dedicated line that is not part of the city phone system
- Fairness in handling complaints made about employees and elected officials
- 24/7/365 access (Miller 2011a).

Setting up a hotline is not without fiscal cost. In the case of Jacksonville, however, the ethics officer estimates that the cost savings far outweighed her $75,000 yearly part-time salary. She says the city saved somewhere between $579,483 and $938,527 as a result of the withdrawal and rebidding of several contracts (Miller 2011a).

Characteristics of Ethics Hotlines: Business Model

- Toll free—Ensures ease of access to all employees.
- Accessible internationally—Provides employees at global organizations with access to the ethics office.
- Advertised widely—Demonstrates organizational commitment to ethics.
- Assures anonymity—Prevents employees from fearing repercussions. (Corporate Leadership Council, 2003)

Palm Beach County Hotline

Ethics reform in Palm Beach County, launched in 2010 (see Chapter 6 for more details), included the establishment of an ethics hotline and the use of e-mail to receive and process attributed and anonymous information. Alan

Johnson, Palm Beach's ethics officer, views the value of an ethics hotline as going far beyond investigating tips and allegations of government wrongdoing. "Training programs," he contends, "stress awareness and compliance among officials and public employees, and to a lesser extent, vendors and service providers to the public entity. Outreach is a critical step in the ethics process and includes the publication and maintenance of a viable hotline" (2011b).

Summing Up

Public administrators must use all the ethics management tools available to them to put into place a comprehensive and integrated program. Still, it is reasonable to ask whether some tools are more effective than others. One study of a private-sector organization provides help in answering this question. Adam and Rachman-Moore (2004) examined several methods used to implement a code of conduct. Among others, they assessed three tools discussed in this chapter—managerial leadership, the means of enforcement, and ethics training. What did they find? First, they found that training was more important than either managerial leadership or the means of enforcement. Second, the surprise finding was that the means of enforcement—that is, signing an oath, providing performance evaluations, and so forth—were the least important in influencing employees "to behave in accordance with organizational ethical rules." This result is contrary to the "common view that organizational enforcement mechanisms are of prime importance as control mechanisms and are considered to effectively impact on the conduct of employees" (Adam and Rachman-Moore 2004, 238).

As this chapter has shown, many tools can be drawn on to cultivate an ethical culture in public organizations. However, no one tool is the single most effective. Ethics managers must use all the tools at their disposal.

Ethics Management Skill Building

Practicum 4.1. Ethics and Performance Evaluations

Your city workforce has been experiencing a rash of ethical lapses. It seems as if nearly everyone from the janitorial staff to the department managers to the deputy directors has had an ethics miscue over the past year. As the director of human resources, you feel strongly that it is time to put an ethics component in the annual evaluation of hourly workers and managerial/professional employees. You realize, of course, that your boss must agree, and you begin to think about how you will make the case to evaluate the ethical behavior of employees.

Why not collect information from cities like yours to identify what others are doing? After a few weeks of telephone calls and e-mails, you discover that very little is being done, but you do find one municipality that has an ethics component in the annual evaluation of the city manager, the city clerk, and the city attorney. The evaluation instrument asks the evaluator to rate the city manager/clerk/attorney as "Excellent," "Fully Satisfactory," "Satisfactory," or "Unsatisfactory" in response to the statement: "Conducts self in accordance with the ethical standards of the office of Charter Officer."

Disappointed by what you learn, you decide to form a committee to draft language that could be placed on the form to evaluate professional/management personnel. You decide to do the same thing with the hourly employees' evaluation language, but at a later date. The committee takes their assignment to heart and produces the following set of evaluative statements:

A. Demonstrates an ethical approach in the discharge of duties.
B. Displays ethical behavior—promotes an environment that is open, fair, tolerant, trustful and respectful. Values public interest over self-interest and is accountable.
C. Clearly understands and communicates ethical practices, policies, and goals relevant to the community.
D. Shows respect for the views of others, takes pride in work products, places public interest over own self-interest.
E. Demonstrates integrity in all aspects of work.
F. Adheres to the city's ethics code.
G. Demonstrates a clear ability to identify, evaluate, and resolve issues related to ethics.
H. Demonstrates sound ethical judgment and encourages ethical behavior in others.
I. Complies with rules and laws defined by city Personnel Manual and professional standards and conducts self with integrity while avoiding undue influence.
J. Displays proper attitude toward organizational transparency and has sufficient knowledge of city's ethical standards.
K. Demonstrates ethical judgment as defined by the city code of ethics or applicable professional standards.

Questions

1. Which of these 11 statements do you like the best? Like the least? Why?

2. Rank three of the eleven evaluative statements as your first, second, and third choices, with the first being the most important.
3. Would the list differ in any significant manner for hourly employees?
4. In forming the committee to draft language that will appear on the performance evaluation, what should be the key criteria for membership?
5. Do you anticipate resistance from the workforce about including an ethics component in the annual evaluation? Why or why not?
6. Do you believe that the ethical performance of an employee can be evaluated fairly and accurately? Why or why not?
7. What do you say to persuade your boss that the city should place your preferred statement on the annual performance evaluation form for managerial/professional staff?

Practicum 4.2. Ethics Training for the Trainer

Your urban county government has nearly 10,000 employees who are responsible for streets, sewers, water, solid waste pickup and disposal, and an array of social services such as assisting homeless people and curbing drug abuse. As the head of the county's Division of Training, it is your job to provide a range of training exercises that fits the needs of a diverse workforce. Some training, for example, helps frontline employees deal with angry people. Other training involves following proper procedures when a citizen complains about an employee or a public service.

The county administrator who recently attended an ethics program conducted by her professional association returned with a great deal of enthusiasm for establishing a comprehensive ethics training program for all 10,000 county employees. Recognizing that the training division does not have trainers with this expertise but knowing that you have a strong background in this area, she asks you to put into place a "train the trainer" initiative.

You immediately call your staff of six trainers together to discuss the situation. The staff is somewhat uncertain and uneasy about taking on this responsibility. In fact, one of your trainers pipes up and says, "Adults can't be taught ethics. People learn ethics from their mother or father or church or wherever. It's a waste of county time and money to take this on. You should go back to the county administrator and respectfully tell her to forget it."

Questions

1. How would you respond to your staff member? Would you tell him he's totally off base—that acquiring ethics is a lifelong endeavor?

2. If you and the staff agree with the trainer who spoke up, how would you approach the county administrator? Would you say that the training staff feels strongly that a countywide ethics training program will not be successful? Or, would you tell her that the training staff does not feel that they can teach adults ethics but will go through the motions anyway?

3. Would you say to the administrator that we could teach compliance with ethics ordinances and state law but nothing more? How would you defend this assertion?

Notes

1. Some material in this chapter is drawn from Menzel 2005b.

2. For a broad overview of professional associations that serve public administrators, see Haynes and Gazley 2011.

5

Ethics Management in American Cities and Counties

I think we're probably just too comfortable out here to do our civic duty.

—Neil Morgan, former columnist for the *San Diego Union-Tribune*, commenting on corruption in San Diego, 2005

The U.S. Census Bureau reports that there are 19,492 cities and villages in the United States and 3,033 counties (U.S. Census Bureau 2009). Cities and counties are legal artifacts of the states; local governments have no U.S. constitutional standing in the same manner as states do. Their powers and authority are set by state laws and constitutions. Counties do not exist in every state; Rhode Island and Connecticut do not have counties. In 48 states, however, America's 3,000 plus counties occupy an unusual niche in the American federal system. They are a hybrid government, with both state and local government characteristics. They have responsibility for many state functions such as maintaining vital records on births and deaths, marriage and divorce, property transactions, taxation, and so forth. At the same time, counties, especially the more urban counties, provide numerous services such as public safety, emergency medical services, solid waste collection and disposal, road repair, parks and recreation, and more.

Many county governments are highly fragmented with independently elected "row" (also referred to as constitutional) officers such as sheriff, tax collector, property appraiser, clerk, and others sharing power. Even more fragmentation can be found in highly urbanized counties that have many municipalities. Cook County, Illinois, for example, consists of 133 municipalities including the City of Chicago. The most densely populated county in Florida, Pinellas County, has 24 municipalities. Farther south, Miami-Dade County includes 34 cities.

More than two dozen counties are consolidated with a city government, such as Jacksonville-Duval County; Honolulu, Hawaii; Indianapolis-Marion County; Miami-Dade; and New Orleans-Orleans County. Thus, the challenges of coordinating and managing cities and counties are as huge as the challenges to building and sustaining organizations of integrity.

This chapter provides an overview of ethics management in American cities and counties. Chapter 6, which follows, offers an in-depth look at ethics management in action in selected cities and counties.

Ethics and Integrity Past

Historically, American cities and counties are known for their lack of ethics and integrity in carrying out the people's business. Courthouse gangs and city hall bosses once ruled a vast number of cities and counties by handing out jobs, contracts, and other favors to friends and political cronies. Senator George Washington Plunkitt of New York City's Tammany Hall fame once proudly proclaimed, "I seen my opportunities and took 'em!" Indeed he did, becoming a millionaire in his lifetime as a power broker. Corrupt local officials still roam the corridors, although not as freely as in the past. Monmouth County (New Jersey) is a prime example. Eleven officials, including three mayors, were arrested in early 2005 on federal corruption or money laundering charges as a result of an FBI sting (Smothers 2005).

On the West Coast, San Diego has had its share of troubles. In 2005, two councilmen were convicted of extortion, wire fraud, and conspiracy. They were charged with accepting money from a strip club owner and his lobbyist in exchange for efforts to repeal a ban on touching between dancers and patrons (Gustafson 2006). Scandal enveloped San Diego's pension board as well, whose members were charged with increasing benefits while underfunding the program. Financial irregularities prompted the then mayor Dick Murphy to resign in mid-2005, only seven months into his second term.

Still, times change, and so do cities and counties. Both are increasingly adopting the tools and practices needed for improved ethical governance. In San Diego in 2006, for example, newly elected Mayor Jerry Sanders moved promptly to establish an Office of Ethics and Integrity to work alongside the city's Ethics Commission. The new office enforces standards of conduct and provides ethics training for the city's nearly 11,000 employees who work in departments under the mayor. The mission of the office is to strengthen "the City's ethical climate so that honor is cherished, personal integrity and ethical courage are the cultural norms, and all employees are supported and encouraged to use their judgment and initiative in the conduct of ethical practices in the workplace" (City of San Diego, California 2007).

Ethics Management and Local Governance

Ethics management in and among local governments is even more varied than that which is found at the state and national levels. Among America's cities/

counties, some have impressive ethics management programs: to name a few, King County (Seattle, Washington), Miami-Dade (Florida), Anne Arundel (Annapolis, Maryland), and Cook County (Chicago, Illinois) have local ethics commissions armed with substantial investigatory powers. The city of Los Angeles has one of the most comprehensive programs in the United States. Jacksonville also has a proactive program with an ethics code that touts "aspirational goals for the conduct of city employees" (City of Jacksonville, Florida, n.d.b).

Other cities—for example, New York City—have ethics codes and agencies to enforce them, although the primary emphasis is placed on managing financial conflicts of interest. Some cities, such as St. Petersburg, Florida (pop. 245,314), do not have a separate ethics commission but do have an ethics investigatory process. Under these circumstances, when a violation is alleged, city council members put on their hats as members of an ethics commission to investigate the allegations and render a ruling. Unlike many cities, St. Petersburg has an *appearance standard* in its code of ethics for city employees.

An *appearance standard* is a very high standard. It requires an employee to behave in a way that a reasonable person would consider ethical. In other words, an appearance of unethical behavior is as unwelcome as an actual occurrence of unethical behavior.

Agency rules that define acceptable behaviors for employees are commonplace among local governments. In Kansas City, Missouri, for example, the ethics handbook issued to all employees asserts that it is unacceptable behavior to spend several hours a week on city time downloading Internet information on a relative's medical condition (Rabin 2003, 466). In California, local governments typically place restrictions on employees receiving gifts, benefits, or using one's position to "induce or coerce any person to provide, directly or indirectly, anything of value which shall accrue to the private advantage, benefit, or economic gain of the City Official or his or her immediate family" (City of San Diego, California 2002). In the California town of Los Gatos, administrative regulations are very restrictive. For example, one rule states that "no employee shall accept money or other consideration or favor from anyone other than the town for any reason" (Simmons, Roland, and Kelly-DeWitt 1998).

Smaller municipalities are even less likely to devote resources to ethics and integrity in governance—and some experts contend that this is a significant deficiency. Mark Davis, executive director of the New York City Conflicts of

Interest Board, asserts that contrary to what many people think, "small municipalities are most in need of ethics boards, because in small municipalities conflicts of interest are absolutely unavoidable" (1999, 408).

Not all small communities are without ethics management initiatives, however. The town of Highland, Indiana, a community of 23,727 people located 20 minutes from Chicago, is an example. In 2005, the city adopted an ethics ordinance that applies to all officials, elected and appointed, and the employee workforce. It proudly proclaims that all elected and appointed officials, employees, volunteers, and others who participate in the business of the town of Highland are required to subscribe to its "Ethics Code of Values." They are expected to "understand how it applies to their specific responsibilities and practice these core values in their work. Because we value the public's confidence and trust in our services and its decision makers, our character and behaviors must meet the most demanding ethical standards and demonstrate the highest levels of achievement in following this code" (Town of Highland, Indiana 2005).

Some small communities have joined arms and resources to promote ethical governance. In Northwest Indiana, for example, five communities in 2005, including Whiting, formed the Shared Ethics Advisory Commission, adopted a common ethics code, and began ethics training for municipal employees and elected officials. "The Shared Ethics Advisory Commission," states Calvin Bellamy, president, "is an all-volunteer agency created by an inter-local agreement among five Lake County communities—Crown Point, Highland, Munster, Schererville and Whiting. . . . We are not an adjudicatory body. Judgment on specific cases is left to each community or law-enforcement officials. Our mission is to provide training on ethical issues facing municipal employees in their day-to-day experience. We have developed a Shared Ethics Code, which sets out broad principles of ethical conduct. We then make those broad principles more concrete and specific through commission-designed training programs" (Bellamy 2010).

Wanted: Ethics Management I

In Bell, California, a mostly Hispanic working-class town of 38,000 residents located 10 miles southeast of downtown Los Angeles, the city manager for FY 2009–2010 collected a salary of $666,733 plus benefits ($543,750) for a total payout of $1,210,483. The assistant deputy city manager pulled down $578,203. The police chief collected $428,370, and some city council members raked in nearly $100,000 (Nagourney and Cathcart, 2010).

Is there something wrong with this picture? Astonishing? Scandalous? Shameful? Just plain wrong?

Special Districts and Authorities

While cities and counties are recognizable local governments, there are thousands (an estimated 37,381, according to the U.S. Census Bureau) of special districts that provide a wide variety of public services (airports, buses, housing, taxation, lighting, water conservation, and the like). Yet, they are mostly out of ethical sight, since many do not have elected boards or officials. Special districts are often referred to as "invisible governments." Larger special districts usually have a code of conduct (Berman and West 2012) but few have launched comprehensive ethics management initiatives.

One notable exception is the Los Angeles County Metropolitan Transportation Authority, with an impressive program directed by a chief ethics officer and six colleagues in a separate ethics department and a budget of $800,000. The ethics staff "educates and advises employees, board members, contractors and the public about ethics rules and maintains the records concerning lobbyist reports and employee statements of economic interest disclosures" (Council of Governmental Ethics Laws 2004). LA MTA has issued three ethics codes—an 11-page code for the 13-member board of directors, a six-page code for contractors, and a 10-page code for the authority's 10,000 employees (Los Angeles County Metropolitan Transportation Authority 2011).

The New York City Transit Authority also has issued a code of ethics that "established a 'zero-tolerance policy' toward employees who receive gifts from companies and individuals conducting business with the authority" (Chan 2005). Additionally, it has published a Vendors Code of Ethics that prohibits vendors from giving gifts or contingent fees to authority employees, spells out negotiating rules for a vendor who might want to hire an authority employee, limits the ability of former employees to appear before the Transit Authority, and obligates vendors to report any solicitation of gifts by transit employees (Metropolitan Transit Authority [MTA] 2009). The authority adopted the code after a string of ethical lapses occurred. Fourteen high-level managers were charged by the New York Ethics Commission with accepting gifts from companies and individuals who do business with the authority. The commission also charged the president, Lawrence G. Reuter, with accepting improper gifts. He admitted that he had accepted $633 in gifts from companies that do business with the authority and reached a settlement with the commission to pay a fine of $1,200 (Chan 2005). The New York State Ethics Commission awarded the Theodore Roosevelt Ethics Award to the MTA in 2007 in recognition of its outstanding record in promoting and building an organization of integrity.

Even though special districts are often out of the public eye, it is quite clear that they have their share of ethical problems. In fact, California became so concerned about ethical issues in special districts and other local governments in 2005 that the legislature passed Assembly Bill 1234, requiring all local agencies—officers and employees—to receive at least two hours of training in general ethics principles and ethics laws relevant to their public service. Moreover, every official is required to receive at least two hours training every two years thereafter (California Fair Political Practices Commission 2011).

City-County Ethics Programs

As shown in Exhibit 5.1, some city/county ethics agencies operate with few employees and few resources (for example, the Denver Board of Ethics) while others (such as those in Los Angeles, New York, and San Francisco) have a sizable staff and a respectable budget. And, while most agencies have jurisdiction over elected officials, some do not. Programmatic responsibilities are more consistent across units. Nearly all provide advisory opinions and some type of ethics training. Most are authorized to investigate alleged ethics violations at their own initiative (see Exhibit 5.2). It is difficult, however, to assess the variance in activity levels as shown in the number of advisory opinions issued and investigations conducted. While some agencies appear to be quite active, others are less so. The differences are a result of several factors that include variation in local ordinances, resources, personnel orientation, and culture of the community.

Filing and Investigating a Complaint

An ethics complaint filed against a public official, elected or appointed, is a serious matter for the accused official, even if it is eventually dismissed. The filing of a malicious complaint can be tempting for a citizen who wishes to "get even" with a public official or for a person who wishes to seek a political advantage. Consequently, cities and counties are careful about investigating a complaint unless there is persuasive evidence that a violation has occurred.

The handling of a complaint involves a series of steps and stages. The process conducted in Miami-Dade County is illustrative (see Exhibit 5.3). First, a written, notarized complaint must be filed by a citizen. Second, the commission staff examines the complaint to assist the commission in determining if it is "legally sufficient"—that is, relevant to the city's ethics ordinance. A complaint such as "city council member Jones interferes with the work of the city manager" would not be legally sufficient. An example of a legally sufficient complaint would be if a council member voted for the purchase of a parcel of land that was owned by his spouse. Third, if the complaint *is* found to be legally sufficient, then the commission must rule on whether or not "probable cause" exists. That is, is there sufficient reason and evidence to believe that a violation has occurred? If the commission finds there is no probable cause, then the complaint is dismissed.

Exhibit 5.1

Selected Cities and Counties with Ethics Management Programs

	Operating size		Jurisdiction over . . .		
	Budget	# employees	Elected officials	Appointed officials	Employees
Cities					
Atlanta	$346,317	3	yes	yes	yes
Chicago	$580,000	7	yes	yes	yes
Denver	$102,500	1	yes	yes	yes
Honolulu*	$270,690	3	yes	yes	yes
Jacksonville*	$99,000	1	yes	yes	yes
Los Angeles	$2,160,000	21	yes	yes	yes
New York City*	$2,022,327	20	yes	yes	yes
Philadelphia*	$810,000	8	yes	yes	yes
San Diego	$897,000	6	yes	yes	yes
San Francisco*	$9,500,000	18	yes	yes	yes
Seattle	$611,000	6	yes	yes	yes
Counties					
Anne Arundel, MD	$150,000	2	yes	yes	yes
Cook, IL	$150,000	3	yes	yes	yes
King, WA	$200,459	1	yes	yes	yes
Miami-Dade, FL*	$2,200,000	17	yes	yes	yes
New Castle, DE	$217,690	1	yes	yes	yes

Source: COGEL, 2010, and agency web sites.
*City/county consolidated.

However, if a finding of probable cause is rendered, then a public hearing is scheduled before the ethics commission. Evidence and arguments presented at the public hearing are the basis for the commission's ruling on either a finding of a violation or a finding of no violation.

Georgia's Certified Cities of Ethics

The Georgia Municipal Association (GMA) initiated an innovative, voluntary program in 1999, encouraging each of Georgia's 531 cities and towns to seek certification as a "City of Ethics." As of May 2011, 219 cities had received this designation. Jim Higdon, the Georgia Municipal Association (GMA) executive director, explains that this "indicates that cities in Georgia are committed to honest, ethical government" and wish to earn and maintain the public's trust in government (GMA 2009a).

What does a city have to do to qualify as a "Certified City of Ethics?" It must (1) adopt a resolution subscribing to specific ethics principles, and (2) adopt an ethics ordinance. The resolution must embrace five ethics principles recommended by a GMA task force of public and private sector leaders.

Exhibit 5.2

Advisory Opinions, Investigations, and Training in Selected Cities and Counties (2010)

	Advisory opinions		Investigations		
	Authority to issue	# per year	Authority on own initiative	# per year	Training required
Los Angeles Ethics Commission	Yes	n/r	Yes	n/r	Yes
Oakland Public Ethics Commission	Yes	4–5	Yes	20	Yes
San Diego Ethics Commission	Yes	5–10	No	80–100	Yes
San Francisco Ethics Commission	Yes	n/r	Yes	28	Yes
Denver Board of Ethics	Yes	500	No	33	Yes
Jacksonville Ethics Commission	Yes	100	Yes	20	Yes
Tampa Ethics Commission	Yes	n/r	Yes	n/r	Yes
Miami-Dade Commission on Ethics & Public Trust	Yes	215	Yes	80 in 2004	Yes
Atlanta Board of Ethics	Yes	5	Yes	10	No
Honolulu Ethics Commission	Yes	5–10	Yes	91	Yes
Philadelphia Board of Ethics	Yes	20	Yes	20	Yes
Chicago Board of Ethics	Yes	65	Yes	135	Yes
Minneapolis Ethical Practices Board	Yes	1	No	45–60	Yes
Cook County Board of Ethics, IL	Yes	8	Yes	6	Yes
Anne Arundel County Ethics Commission, MD	Yes	75	Yes	5–15	No
Buffalo Board of Ethics	Yes	0	Yes	1–2	No
New York City Conflicts of Interest Board	Yes	484	Yes	132	No
Seattle Ethics & Elections Commission	Yes	2	Yes	50	No
King County Board of Ethics, WA	Yes	n/a	Yes	n/r	Yes

Source: COGEL, 2010, and agency web sites.
n/r = not reported in COGEL (2010); n/a = not available.

The five ethics principles recommended by the Georgia Municipal Association (2009a):

- Serve others, not ourselves.
- Use resources with efficiency and economy.
- Treat all people fairly.
- Use the power of our position for the well-being of our constituents.
- Create an environment of honesty, openness, and integrity.

Exhibit 5.3   **Citizen Complaint Process in Miami-Dade County**

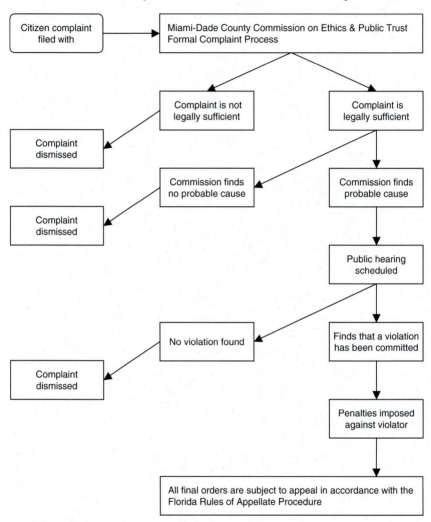

The GMA Board requires that the ethics ordinance "contain definitions, an enumeration of permissible and impermissible activities by elected officials, due process procedures for elected officials charged with a violation of the ordinance and punishment provisions for those elected officials found in violation of the ordinance" (GMA 2009a). Some Georgia cities have given their ethics boards the power to fine offenders, although there is some uncertainty about whether such sanctions are beyond the legal authority of the board. The GMA contends that while "this punishment might seem obvious and even fitting given that the ethics board polices conflicts of interest and misappropriation," it may be the more prudent position for a board of ethics to provide for public reprimands (GMA 2010, 44).

To help small and large cities develop a resolution and ordinance, the GMA has made available a sample resolution and recommends that municipalities fashion an ethics ordinance that best fits their community (GMA 2009b). City leaders are advised to consult the model provided by the International Municipal Lawyers Association and their handbook *Ethics in Government: Charting the Right Course,* which is available online at the GMA web site (see GMA 2010). Once a municipality passes an ethics resolution and ordinance, it submits these documents to the GMA for review and approval by the executive committee of the GMA City Attorneys Section. When certified as a City of Ethics, a municipality receives "a plaque and a logo which can be incorporated into city stationery, road signs and other materials at the city's discretion" (GMA 2009a).

Once a city receives certification is it forever? The answer is "no." In 2009, the GMA instituted a requirement that recertification is necessary every four years and approved a new sample ordinance. (See GMA 2009b for the URL to get a copy of the ordinance.)

The GMA also recognizes organizations of ethics that can include counties, special districts, or nonprofits. Three counties (Paulding, Cobb, and Jackson) and five organizations are certified, two of which are the Central Savannah River Area Regional Commission and the Newton County Water & Sewage Authority. The GMA's designation of an organization of ethics "is limited to organizations who have as their mission enhancing the quality of life, the provision of public services or economic development within their community" (GMA 2009a). Other criteria stipulate that an organization of ethics must be committed to serving the public interest as a nonprofit authority or instrumentality created by the Georgia General Assembly or a local government.

The Georgia Municipal Association's Certified City of Ethics program is a creative, innovative effort to promote ethics and integrity in local governance. Indeed, the popularity of the program is reflected by the 219 cities that have received this designation. Moreover, this statistic is testimony to the commitment that city officials have in strengthening local governance. But are these steps—a resolution and an ordinance—sufficient? Perhaps, but there are other challenges that must be met to put into place a truly effective, comprehensive ethics management program. One such step is building a strong ethical culture throughout city departments. Moreover, while the adoption of an ethics code and ordinance is meritorious, there are no assurances that this step alone will prevent unethical behavior. Nonetheless, the GMA ethics handbook puts the matter plainly: "Establishing a code that deals with ethics violations up front provides notice to officials as to what kinds of behavior will be allowed within the municipality" (GMA 2010, 49).

Challenges to Ethical Governance in Cities and Counties

Five challenges must be overcome to bring about ethical governance in cities and counties. First, city and county leaders must *acknowledge* that ethics and integrity in governance are important. This challenge may appear rather obvious, almost a given. But many local government officials and others presume that since cities and counties are often subject to state ethics laws, there is no need to be especially attuned to ethics and integrity. State ethics laws typically cover nepotism, conflicts of interest, and financial disclosure. In short, most states have enacted ethics laws that are minimal in their coverage and consequences. Thus, if cities and counties do not set ethical standards higher than the state requires, they are already on the low road to ethics and integrity. Cities and counties need to move beyond the standards established by state laws in order to be responsive to citizen expectations and meet the demands of modern professional management.

Leading with Integrity

"Every organization needs an honest and credible leader that establishes ethical standards and then reinforces them."
—former mayor of Tampa Pam Iorio in
Straightforward: Ways to Live & Lead (2011, 38)

The second challenge is to *recognize* that ethics and integrity in local governance are not limited to a single organization or a single category of employees. American counties in particular, with few exceptions, are loosely coupled collections of organizations with many different kinds of employees, administrators, and elected officials. This hydra-headed reality means that a piecemeal approach to ethical governance is not likely to succeed. It is not sufficient to put forward a code of ethics or training or orientation program that covers only one of a county's many units (such as the administrative staff, the clerk's office, the sheriff's office, the auditor's office, the assessor's office, or the property appraiser's office). Employees, appointed professional administrators, and elected officials must be included in a comprehensive approach to ethics. This approach also ensures equal treatment of all those who work in county government, regardless of position and power.

Effective Ethics Reform

"Even well-meaning elected officials will lack the political will to self-police without a significant level of public pressure. Politicians will pay attention to their constituents. Therefore, the most effective ethics programs emerge from, and thrive within, a process in partnership with the people.

"In many cases a local ethics initiative begins with a series of events that create a grassroots movement to attack the current spate of corruption in the system. After the current problems are addressed, there is a danger that outrage will dissipate and public attention will go elsewhere.

"Ethics reform is a long-term project that requires continued attention. In turn, sustained public involvement requires an effective outreach effort as well as the responsiveness of the ethics entity. Without outreach and public input, and an equally robust response, an ethics commission is no more than a glorified code enforcement board."

—Alan Johnson (2011b),
Ethics Officer, Palm Beach County

The third challenge is to *commit* sufficient resources to building and sustaining integrity in local governance. Neither city nor county governments are in the business of producing ethical governance. Rather, they are producers of valuable public services ranging from those mandated by the state—taxation, property assessment, roads, and vital statistics—to those services demanded by citizens—for example, parks and recreation, marinas, golf courses, solid waste collection and disposal, and air and water quality management. These goods and services consume the vast majority of local revenues. Moreover, these service needs and demands compete with one another for vital resources, and there is typically never sufficient funding in a city or county budget to meet all of the services that are needed or desired. In other words, local officials can and often do feel that spending scarce tax dollars on ethics and integrity is a low priority when funds for vital services are in real or imagined short supply. This view, of course, ignores the distressing reality that corruption is a major cause of a waste of resources.

The fourth challenge is to *avoid* a narrow rules and regulations approach to ethics in local governance. Remember the old saying, "there ought to be a law!" Problems, this old bromide suggests, can be best dealt with by passing a law to correct errant behavior. Laws, ordinances, codes, and new or stricter personnel policies are too often viewed as quick fixes or solutions to problems that occur. Cities and counties that move along this path and do nothing more are engaging in "feel good ethics." A comprehensive management strategy that fosters ethical governance demands more than a new ordinance or a revised personnel manual. What is required is an integration of standards into all aspects of management and policy, as well as unquestionable leadership commitment to the new culture of invigorated ethics standards.

Wanted: Ethics Management II

In Bell, California, a state audit found that tens of millions of dollars were funneled to noncompetitive bids by companies owned by city employees. The audit reported that the city manager "had complete control and discretion over how city funds were to be used" (Chiang 2010).

Steve Cooley, the district attorney of Los Angeles, described the situation as "corruption on steroids" (Gottlieb et al. 2010).

California State controller John Chiang added that the city's "General Fund was run like a petty cash drawer" (California State Controller's Office, 2010).

The fifth challenge is to *learn* from ethics failures. Governance is a people-driven enterprise. Yes, technology, machinery, and more are the tools needed to carry out the work of governance, but human beings still make the important decisions day in and day out, and these decisions have a direct effect on the lives of residents. Human beings have ethical lapses—sometimes egregious and other times minor or modest. These failures are part and parcel of modern organizational life. Cities and counties that are truly committed to building and sustaining ethical governance must be able to learn from failures and scandal and commit to corrective actions. Public officials must have an open mind and learn from ethics failures. Scandal might trigger ethics reform, but if reform measures simply become standard operating procedures, little can be achieved in effecting genuine change. Organizations that do not learn do not grow and do not become agents for building integrity in local governance.

Meeting the Challenges

What more should local government leaders do to meet the challenge of ethical governance? Above all, they must commit themselves to a comprehensive strategy, and they must stay the course. An ethics summit or other forum could be arranged as a first step in recognizing that ethics and integrity in governance are important. Additionally, a code of ethics and/or a statement of principles should be adopted that applies to all employees, elected and appointed. At the county level, this group of employees should include all agencies, including the constitutional officers. The development of a code and/or statement of principles should strike a balance between ethical aspirations and the practical reality of day-to-day work.

Management should emphasize training and employee development programs. Employees in all types of organizations are vulnerable to ethical lapses. A continuous, ongoing training program—one that is stitched into the daily work and culture of city and county governance—tends to amplify the message that ethics matters. Managers must provide organizational members with clear guidelines for proper behavior, an unambiguous explanation of the ramifications of an ethical lapse, and practical tips on how to make ethics behavior an ordinary work habit.

An ethics audit could be equally valuable, perhaps invaluable as a benchmark for tracking changes in the organizational culture. An audit, whether based on a survey of employees or an assessment of occupational vulnerability, should be conducted periodically. City manager Steve Bonczek (1998) strongly supports the use of an audit to let employees know the positive as well as the negative effects of their behavior.

Government leaders must advocate and embrace transparency in the work of national, state, and city-county offices and agencies. Sunshine laws that require open meetings to let the public view the decision making of elected officials and whistleblowing ordinances can contribute to transparency, but are often insufficient. Top officials must encourage subordinates to carry out their work with full disclosure, citizen access, and a tolerance for competing claims.

Summing Up

Is ethical local governance achievable? Without question. Indeed, many local governments, as evidenced by the 219 communities in Georgia, embrace ethics and integrity in governance. But this trend must extend across the country to ensure that democracy, justice, and the pursuit of happiness are more than just hollow words. Local governance is, after all, the bedrock upon which the American experiment with democracy rests. Is it not so?

Ethics Management Skill Building

Practicum 5.1. Ethics Challenges in Disasters

On August 29, 2005, Hurricane Katrina made landfall near New Orleans, Louisiana. A day or two later, the levees protecting the city (New Orleans actually sits below sea level) were breeched; water spewed into the streets and residences, flooding nearly all of the city, with some water levels reaching 18 to 20 feet. As conditions worsened, law and order broke down. Looters sacked stores and gangs roamed the streets. The New Orleans police force of 1,500 was overwhelmed by the lawlessness. Scores of police officers were cut off by the storm and floodwaters, and as many as 500 others either walked off of their posts in the days after the storm or otherwise couldn't be accounted for. Many officers experienced high levels of stress and distress—the rising floodwaters endangered their lives, as well as the lives of their loved ones, and some became targets of angry residents and mob violence, in some cases dodging sniper bullets as they rescued victims. The city's police superintendent put it this way: "I had officers in boats who were being shot at as they were pulling people out of the water." Two officers committed suicide (Treaster and Desantis 2005).

Questions

1. Assume you are the New Orleans chief of police. What explanations do you have for the failure of some police officers to carry out their duties? Was this an ethical failure of the individuals? The NOPD? Something else?
2. How would you deal with the stress experienced by NOPD officers? Raise their pay? Hire counselors? Send them to Las Vegas for a five-day vacation? Give them time off to visit relatives? None of the above?
3. What would you do to discourage desertions by police officers in the event of a disaster? Would you launch a major ethics training program? Emphasize a code of ethics? Hire a consultant to assess the organization's culture? Nothing, as this is a matter of duty?

Practicum 5.2. Decisions, Decisions, Decisions!

In any large organization, people make many decisions day in and day out. In this practicum, you are asked to make decisions in three different roles: a professional with expertise in beach restoration (the beach guru), the supervisor of the beach guru, and the chief administrative officer. The setting is an urban county renowned for its world-class beaches, memorable sunny vacations, and baseball spring training. Let's name this fictitious county Stingray.

Laura—The Beach Guru

You were hired by the county of Stingray seven years ago and charged with securing funds annually to replace depleted beach sand. You find that you are quite entrepreneurial and able to acquire millions of dollars for projects that earn you glowing performance reviews. Your achievements become widely recognized at home and in neighboring states. Ahaa, you say to yourself, perhaps I should set up my own consulting firm with the proviso that I would not do any work that is in competition for money that Stingray County might secure.

Decision: Should you move forward? Why or why not?

You decide to approach your supervisor about your interest in creating a consulting firm and recognize that your work might present a real or perceived conflict of interest. You don't want to lose your $76,000 county job.

Decision: As the supervisor, would you sign off on Laura's request to do consulting work? Why or why not?

You call Laura into the office to get answers to questions that would help you decide what to do. What kinds of questions would you ask her? Might one of them be: "Will you work for other cities and counties in this state?" Laura's answers seem satisfactory so you decide to have it put in her contract that she will not work on projects that compete for funds with the county, including other cities or counties in the state. A sign-off on a conflict of interest form is also standard policy, so you include that in her personnel file as well.

Decision: As the county administrator, you learn that Laura has done consulting work with a neighboring county and sought a contract in Texas that competed with Stingray County for beach renourishment funds. What should you do?

You decide to review Laura's performance ratings and learn that she has an exemplary work history, including perfect scores on the ethics portion of the evaluation over the past two years.

Questions

1. Given her performance evaluations, should you call her in your office and perhaps warn her that she will be fired if she breeches her contract once more?
2. Should you simply tell her that she has gone over the line and fire her?
3. What should you do?

6

Local Government Ethics
Management in Action

Tampa is a microcosm of America and reflects our country in the
twenty-first century. Diverse culturally and racially, Tampa is a big
city with a small town nature that welcomes newcomers.

—Tampa Mayor Pam Iorio (2003–2011)

This chapter examines ethics management in "action" in three cities (Tampa, Chicago, and New York City); four counties (Palm Beach County, Florida; King County, Washington; Salt Lake County, Utah; and Cook County, Illinois); and two consolidated governments (the Unified Government of Wyandotte County and Kansas City, Kansas; and Jacksonville-Duval County, Florida). These cities and counties were chosen because of their variation in ethics management styles, practices, and innovativeness.

Tampa, Florida: Progress in Slow Motion?

Nearly every municipality that has begun to put into place sound ethics management practices has faced difficulty along the way, and most have been moved to action by a scandal. The City of Tampa, Florida, is among the newcomers to scandal-driven ethics reform. The embarrassment that triggered ethics reform in Tampa began in 2001, with a romantic relationship between the city housing chief, Steven LaBrake, and his top aide, Lynne McCarter, who had moved rapidly through the city ranks. The housing chief and his aide built a 4,200-square-foot home for a bargain-basement price of $105,000. Adding more suspicion to the situation, the builder had received more than $1 million in housing contracts through the city's housing department.

Along the way, the city under the then mayor Dick Greco began an investigation of LaBrake's handling of his office and, in October 2001, placed LaBrake on a 90-day paid administrative leave pending the resolution of criminal charges. The following month, the Florida Ethics Commission reported that LaBrake did not violate state ethics laws. Later that same month, however, the commission repudiated the report, saying that the information submitted by the city and Mayor Greco was unreliable.

A year later, the LaBrakes (LaBrake and McCarter wed in 2002) and several others were indicted on fraud and corruption charges. The accusations eventually landed the couple in court where the builder confessed to bribing the city housing chief. The LaBrakes were tried in 2003 and found guilty on more than 25 counts of conspiracy, wire fraud, and accepting bribes and gratuities. LaBrake was sentenced to five years in a federal penitentiary; McCarter received three years and five months. The developer was handed a five-year probationary sentence.

> "What strikes me about the LaBrakes' situation is that they were part of the culture that permeates Tampa government, where you do me a favor and I'll do you a favor, even though it violates the public trust."
> —U.S. District Judge Richard A. Lazzara,
> who sentenced the LaBrakes (Testerman 2005)

Tampa's Ethics Code

The housing scandal motivated the city council to deliberate on the wisdom of an ethics code that would guide the behavior of its 4,800 employees. In March 2003 a new mayor—one known as a strong advocate of integrity in city governance—was elected. Eight months later the city promulgated its first ever code of ethics. Not surprisingly, the code includes a prohibition on "fraternization." That is, no employee or officer shall appoint, employ, advance, or recommend for any position "any individual with whom they have a close personal relationship" (City of Tampa, Florida 2003d). The enforcement of this prohibition is another matter and will most likely be resolved at some future date in a court of law.

Ethics Commission

The code of ethics also created a five-member ethics commission made up of faculty members from two local universities, two citizens appointed by the chief judge of the Thirteenth Judicial Circuit, and one member (who has held elective office at the local level) appointed by the mayor. One university appointee is a faculty member who is knowledgeable in the field of legal ethics; the other appointee is a faculty member who specializes in ethics more broadly defined. Ethics commissioners are appointed for staggered four-year terms and are precluded from partisan political activity or employment by the city.

The commission is empowered to "review, interpret, render advisory opinions and letters of instruction and enforce" the code (City of Tampa, Florida, 2003b). Advisory opinions must be requested in writing, and the facts may be real or hypothetical. If an advisory opinion is rendered, it is binding on the conduct of the person who sought the opinion. A written, sworn complaint by a citizen submitted to the city ethics officer initiates the enforcement process. The complaint is then delivered to the commission for a preliminary investigation. If the commission finds "probable cause" that the code has been violated, it must notify in writing both the complainant and the alleged violator (City of Tampa, Florida, 2003c). A public hearing may or may not be called, depending on the circumstances. If the commission finds that a violation has occurred, it then recommends to the appropriate body—agency head, city council, mayor—that "appropriate action for correction or rectification of that conduct" be taken (City of Tampa, Florida, 2003f). The Commission has no enforcement power; that is, it cannot impose a disciplinary action on a code violator. Disciplinary measures can range from a verbal admonishment to censure, suspension, or removal from office.

Code Implementation

According to Tampa's new code and its rules of implementation, the Department of Human Resources is designated as the Ethics Office, and the HR director is the city's designated city officer. The Ethics Office is charged with overseeing the code's implementation. The ethics officer is assigned the task of developing education and training programs for city officers and employees. Moreover, the ethics officer is expected to "serve as the liaison between the ethics commission and the officers and employees of the city" (City of Tampa, Florida 2003a). Each city department has an ethics liaison who assists the ethics officer in the formulation of ethics-awareness training sessions, conferences, and seminars.

Ethics education and training are required of all elected officials; they must attend an ethics-in-government program within 90 days of taking office. Newly appointed employees must participate in an ethics training program within six months of their first day of employment. The code also mandates that current employees be trained as soon as practicable. There is no requirement that elected officers or employees attend an ethics-in-government program on a continuing basis. Nor are there whistleblowing provisions in the code to protect city employees. This measure was omitted because it was seen as unnecessary, since city employees are protected by Florida's whistleblower law.

A review of the *Ethics Commission 2010 Annual Report* (City of Tampa, Florida 2010) suggests that the Ethics Commission has not had much business: only one ethics complaint was received, zero advisory opinions were rendered, and no appeals of disapproval of noncity employment were made. The commission held three meetings in 2010. Is this progress in slow motion? Possibly, although it may reflect the deterrence power of the newly established Ethics Commission. It may also be the case that Mayor Pam Iorio (2003–2011) has "led with integrity" over the past eight years.

Tampa is moving forward with its effort "to elevate the level of ethics in local government, to provide honest and responsible service to the citizens, and to maintain the confidence and trust of the public that this government serves" (City of Tampa, Florida 2003e). Still, the city is pursuing a limited, reactive form of ethics management. This approach parallels those taken in so many other cities—know what constitutes acceptable behavior to stay out of trouble and know the consequences of getting in trouble. Of course, there is no substitute for the power of mayoral leadership that exemplifies ethical behavior.

City of Chicago: In Pursuit of Compliance?

Historically, ethical governance and Chicago have not gone hand in hand. The "city of big shoulders," with its industrial, blue-collar past and hard-nosed machine politics often meant votes and more were for sale. While this reputation has receded in recent years, problems remain. In 2004, a bribery case involving the city's trucking contracts grew into a full-scale federal investigation of political patronage and influence. Twenty-three persons were convicted by mid-2005. Eight of Mayor Richard M. Daley's cabinet members and other top officials either resigned or were fired as a result of accusations that they rigged hiring tests to ensure jobs for campaign workers (Wilgoren 2005).

Ethics Ordinance and the Board of Ethics

City efforts to prevent wrongdoing actually began in earnest in Chicago with the creation of an "independent City agency to administer and enforce the City's Governmental Ethics and Campaign Financing Ordinances. These laws were adopted by City Council in 1987 to help ensure that City officials and employees perform their public responsibilities impartially and do not use their public positions for private gain, and to foster public confidence in the integrity of City government." The seven members of the board of ethics are appointed by the mayor and confirmed by city council. They can be removed only for cause and with the written approval of remaining board members. A seven-member professional staff works with the board (City of Chicago, Illinois 2010).

Board programs include education and training, advice and guidance, regulation, and financial disclosure.

Ethics Training

The Governmental Ethics Ordinance sets forth an ambitious educational requirement that all 50 aldermen, aldermanic staff, and senior executive service employees attend ethics training every four years (City of Chicago, Illinois 2011). The ordinance also requires all new employees attend an ethics training program within 120 days of entering service and once again every four years afterward. Those who fail to attend are subject to a $500 fine. About 3,800 officials and employees, or approximately 10 percent of the workforce, are covered by this training requirement in the Governmental Ethics Ordinance. During the 2008–2009 year, the Board conducted 25 classes for the 503 city employees and officials who were required to attend. Online training is offered as well. As of July 31, 2009, approximately 24,250 city employees and aldermen had completed the online training program.

Mandatory Ethics Training in Chicago

Since calendar year 2006, the Governmental Ethics Ordinance has required all aldermen and full-time city employees to complete, each year, an ethics training program designed by the board. More than 90 percent of the city's workforce completes this requirement through online programs developed and administered by the board. The rest complete their training through a DVD based on this online program. The board completely revises the program each year (City of Chicago Board of Ethics, 2009).

Like the U.S. federal government, each agency in Chicago has a designated ethics officer (DEO) who serves as the primary liaison with the board of ethics and assists agency employees in understanding and complying with the Governmental Ethics Ordinance.

Advice

The board's advice and guidance program consists of two categories of assistance: inquiries and cases. An *inquiry* is a request for information or professional advice in which the inquiring person does not ask for a written response. In FY 2008–2009, the board handled 5,350 inquires. A *case* is a written complaint or a request for an opinion. The board approved oral or issued written advice in 32 cases, dismissed or referred 20 complaints, and issued 168 reports regarding determinations or recommendations from concluded investigations. The subject matter of the inquiries and cases are shown in Exhibit 6.1. Financial interest disclosure, gifts, and lobbying are the subjects most often addressed by inquiries and complaints.

Investigation and Enforcement

Regulation and enforcement activities encompass campaign financing, financial disclosure, registration of lobbyists, and investigations, complaints, and preliminary inquiries. The Campaign Financing Ordinance limits the amount of money that can be contributed to an individual seeking elected city office—especially contributions from lobbyists. Between 9,000 and 12,000 employees and officials are required to file statements of financial interest with the board each spring. Failure to file a financial disclosure can result in a fine. Lobbyists are required to register with the board and pay a $200 fee to do so. They must reveal the names of their clients and report all lobbying-related compensation and expenditures. As of July 31, 2009, 613 lobbyists were registered in Chicago compared to nearly 400 in 2004 (Chicago Board of Ethics *Annual Report 2008–09,* 18). More than 1,000 clients were represented by lobbyists. The board of ethics maintains a list of registered lobbyists and their clients on its web site at www.cityofchicago.org/city/en/depts/ethics.html.

The board also has considerable authority to investigate alleged wrongdoing. Unlike most boards, it can initiate an investigation on its own. However, this authority is limited in the case of a complaint against an alderman. A complaint of an alleged violation of the Governmental Ethics Ordinance by an alderman must be signed and sworn to gain authorization to initiate an investigation. The board also has subpoena power. All investigations are treated as confidential.

For the most recent reporting year, 2008–2009, the board received 20 written complaints. The executive director dismissed 11 for lack of jurisdiction (they raised issues outside the scope of the Governmental Ethics or Campaign Financing Ordinances), and nine others because they failed to provide reasonable cause for the board to commence an investigation. However, in eight cases, the complainant or complaint was referred to other investigative agencies—two to the Office of Inspector General and Office of Compliance and six to the heads of the departments for which the employees worked.

Ethics management in the City of Chicago is legalistic in its orientation, with substantial authority granted to the board of ethics to launch investigations and ensure compliance with the Governmental Ethics Ordinance. This

Exhibit 6.1

Chicago Board of Ethics Inquiries, 2007–2009, year ending July 31

	2007	2008	2009
Outside employment	107	94	62
Post-employment	304	97	128
Gifts/travel/honoraria	102	332	283
Lobbying activity/disclosure	439	584	702
Conflicts/improper influence	38	46	41
Employment of relatives/domestic partners	13	53	44
Financial interest disclosure	2,396	3,135	2,999

Source: City of Chicago Board of Ethics, 2009.

is indeed impressive for city government, but like many city- and state-level counterparts, such an approach is a "compliance" strategy (City of Chicago, Illinois 2010).

New York City: Taking Ethics Management Seriously?

The "Big Apple" also has a history of scandal and corruption that few cities can rival. It has an equally long record of reform intended to prevent wrongdoing. Anechiarico and Jacobs (1996), in their account of "the pursuit of absolute integrity," cite four periods in which corruption and reform waxed and waned in New York City and across the nation. The three decades between 1870 and 1900 came to be called the *spoils* or *patronage* period, when big city political machines reached their height.

From 1900 to 1933, in a period known as the *Progressive Era,* an unparalleled effort was made to root out corruption in New York through the complete reformation of the city's political system. The rise of nonpolitical, merit-driven civil service, along with nonpartisan elections, was central to making government more effective, if not more ethical. The separation of politics from administration was the key to achieving these goals, so Progressives argued. In the years that followed, from 1933 to 1970, the *science of administration* came to the fore, with an emphasis on organizational efficiency and economy. Embedded in scientific administration was the view that bureaucratic corruption could not be controlled internally by the bureaucrats themselves. External controls were needed in the form of auditing and investigatory agencies.

The fourth period, spanning from 1970 to the 1990s, experienced a hardening of the comprehensive surveillance and investigation strategies that were sown in the previous period. Anechiarico and Jacobs label this the "panoptic" era, one in which public employees are "akin to probationers in the criminal justice system" (1996, 24). The end result is an ethics management system run amok. The pursuit of absolute integrity, a system in which everyone is presumed guilty of some wrongdoing, turned New York City into an ungovernable enterprise. Corruption control of this nature results in ineffective governance, according to Anechiarico and Jacobs. However, not everyone agrees with their assessment.

Panoptic is a term used to describe a prison in which the architecture features a control tower at the center of a circular cell house. Thus, the cells, inmates, and staff would be completely visible to the watcher (Anechiarico and Jacobs, 1996, 24).

Let's take a closer look at the specific measures taken by New York City to combat corruption and promote ethical governance. The starting point was the establishment in 1959 of a board of ethics, an advisory body that was created along with the city's first code of ethics. A *New York Times* front-page story on August 21, 1959, proclaimed boldly that a strict city code had been passed by the board of estimate after two years of deliberation. On September 3, 1959, Mayor Robert F. Wagner signed the ethics ordinance into law (Bennett 1959b). The code, the *New York Times* reported, would cover 225,000 officials and employees, holding them to rigid standards of conduct (Bennett 1959a). Several months later, in January 1960, Mayor Wagner swore in the city's new five-man board of ethics and charged it with administering "the finest Code of Ethics of its kind in the United States" (Bennett 1960). The principal author of the 1959 code, S. Stanley Kreutzer, described this landmark event in the following way:

> City administrations change, but the fundamental concepts of ethics as written into law are ageless because they have inherent in them the object of government in our Republic—to be fair to the people who serve and who are served by our municipality. (McFadden 2005)

Conflicts of Interest Board

Three decades and, regrettably, a number of scandals later, good government reformers called for a major overhaul of New York City's government. Charter amendments were passed that, among other things, replaced the board of ethics with the Conflicts of Interest Board (COIB) in 1990. The new board's powers were expanded significantly. No longer an advisory body only, the renamed board was empowered to impose fines of up to $10,000 per violation. In 2010, a voter-approved recommendation by the Charter Revision Commission increased the maximum civil penalty to $25,000. The COIB does not have the authority or power to conduct investigations. This power is lodged in the city's Department of Investigations.

> "When you are dealing with 300,000 city employees, there are going to be some who are crooks and very smart crooks—they're New Yorkers—and others who are incompetent. . . . I still believe that public service is the noblest of professions when done honestly and done well. Most people in government are honest and competent."
> —Edward I. Koch (2010),
> Mayor of New York City, 1978–1989

The five members of the board are appointed by the mayor, subject to the advice and consent of the city council, and serve staggered six-year terms. A staff of 20 with a budget of more than $2 million tends to the board's daily business. While the emphasis is placed on conflicts of interest such as accepting gifts, moonlighting (working full-time for the city and also part-time elsewhere), and ownership in firms doing business with the city, the ethics law (Chapter 68) also covers post-city employment, disclosure of confidential information, political activities, and relationships between employees and supervisors. A separate city whistleblowing law offers protection for employees who report possible ethical violations.

The COIB is an independent agency, subject only to budgetary constraints imposed by the mayor and city council. Any citizen can file a written complaint that triggers an assessment by the staff. In 2010, the COIB received 523 new complaints, with 76 disposed that imposed fines amounting to $145,850. If the board finds probable cause to believe that a public servant has violated the ethics law, it is empowered to direct the Department of Investigation to conduct an investigation. Further steps include the possibility of a confidential hearing in which the accused official may defend himself or herself.

The COIB also issues advisory opinions requested by an employee or supervisor. Opinions are disclosed to the public without the disclosure of the identity of the person requesting the opinion. In 2010, the COIB received 599 written requests for advice and more than 3,200 telephone requests. Other duties include overseeing the city's financial disclosure law and providing training programs.

Charter changes in 2010 mandated that city employees receive conflict-of-interest training offered by the COIB staff that conducted 279 classes attended by employees from 37 agencies. The COIB offers vendor training as well.

Ethics management in New York City is a substantial enterprise that also involves a web site and media outreach, online training, an annual seminar on ethics in New York City government, and visits by international delegations. In 2010, board staff met with officials from Fujian, Tianjin, Dalian, and Jiangsu, China, as well as a delegation from Slovakia, at the request either of the U.S. State Department or the delegation organizers themselves (City of New York Conflicts of Interest Board 2010). Does New York City take ethics management seriously? You decide.

Palm Beach County, Florida: Progressive in Ethical Matters?

Located 70 miles north of Miami on the Atlantic seaboard, Palm Beach County is home to more than 1.3 million residents, making it the third-largest county in Florida. Fifty-five percent of the residents reside in one of the county's 38 municipalities. The Florida Marlins and St. Louis Cardinals hold their spring training camps in Palm Beach County. With 150 private and public golf courses, the county is often referred to as "the Golf Capital of the World."

Palm Beach County is a charter county led by a seven-member elected commission that appoints a professional county administrator to oversee day-to-day affairs. The administrator manages an annual budget of approximately $4 billion and oversees some 6,100 county employees in more than 30 departments, divisions, and offices. As a charter county, Palm Beach is granted home rule powers to engage in self-governance, although bound by the laws of Florida. As a professionally governed county, it would seem to be on the high road of ethics management. Alas, this has not been so in recent years, with three commissioners serving jail time for corruption.

Corruption issues also surfaced in the city of West Palm Beach, landing two elected officials in federal prisons in 2006–2007. And, more recently (2011), seven current and former city and county officials were arrested on charges of public corruption—racketeering, money laundering, and unlawful compensation. Has the reputation of Palm Beach County deteriorated to the point that some citizens refer to the county as "Corruption County?" And, if it has, what should be done to put the county back on the high road of ethical governance?

Turning Back a Crisis of Confidence in Good Governance

In early 2009, the Palm Beach County state attorney Michael McAuliffe convened a grand jury to investigate county governance and public corruption. The grand jury concluded that a "culture of corruption" engulfed the county—land deals, bond underwriting arrangements, conflicts of interest, and gifts and gratuities became impossible to ignore. The grand jury called for significant reform:

> The Grand Jury finds that a fundamental need exists for an entity within the Palm Beach County governmental structure with meaningful independence from the governing body to be an effective "watchdog" for the citizens of Palm Beach County. The need for effective oversight of county governance is real and change is necessary (McAuliffe, Zacks, and Johnson 2009).

Two months later, the county commission recommended the creation of the Office of Inspector General and an independent Palm Beach County Commission on Ethics. In December 2009, ethics reform shifted into high gear with the proposal of a new ethics code that would provide for tougher lobbying registration and reporting; greater disclosure of potential conflicts of interest; and punishment of ethics violators with public reprimands, employee removal, and a fine of up to $500. The Palm Beach County Commission on Ethics is empowered to issue advisory opinions and investigate local cases of suspected violations (Reid 2009). Other reform measures call for tighter rules on gifts that county employees can receive and additional ethics training for employees and officials.

In July 2010, the Palm Beach County Commission on Ethics—a five-person body whose members are expected to have an "outstanding reputation for integrity, responsibility and commitment to serving the community" (Palm Beach County, Florida 2009)—went to work. The newly appointed executive director, Alan Johnson, says the commission hit the ground running: "We want to be a commission with teeth and not only a force processing complaints, but a force bringing ethics to the forefront" (Abramson 2010).

"Palm Beach County has recently seen three county commissioners as well as two commissioners from a principal municipality sent to prison for crimes involving official corruption. The 'pay to play' attitude of the last decade has resulted in our being derisively referred to as 'corruption county.'

"A strong code of ethics along with vigorous enforcement, training, and public outreach has been put in place to raise the level of ethics, in perception as well as reality."

—Alan Johnson (2011b),
Ethics Officer, Palm Beach County

Voters in November 2010 approved a referendum expanding the county's ethics code jurisdiction to all 38 municipalities The countywide training includes live sessions for each municipality, along with online video and DVD training for those unable to attend. All county and municipal officials and employees will be required to sign an acknowledgment of training.

"Training is ongoing, and in my opinion," writes executive director Johnson "our most important function. The county has roughly 6,000 employees, 1,000 volunteer board members, and seven elected officials. The 38 municipalities have approximately 9,000 full- and part-time employees, 1,800 advisory board members, and 194 elected officials. All our advisory opinions are posted on our web site, and we are in the process of creating a search engine so that the public can easily search by terms" (Johnson 2011b).

"Any person may file a complaint with the Commission on Ethics regarding a violation of the code of ethics, lobbyist registration or post-employment ordinances. Complaints must be in writing . . . allege a violation of the ordinances . . . be based substantially upon personal knowledge and be signed under oath or affirmation by the complaining person" (Palm Beach County 2011). The commission's executive director, the state attorney, and the inspector general also have the power to initiate a complaint.

Is Palm Beach County progressive in ethical matters? You decide.

King County, Washington: A Unique Division of Labor?

Among America's 3,033 counties with policies and procedures for dealing with unethical conduct, King County (Seattle) in the State of Washington might have the oldest. The county enacted a code of ethics in 1972 in response to corruption. In its original form, the code focused on conflicts of interest, placed restrictions on business transactions between former members of the county council and sitting council members, and required financial disclosure statements by commissioners and senior county managers. A three-member appointed ethics board was established to enforce the code. In its initial 17 years of existence, "the board held only one major public hearing [and] very few county employees knew of the code's existence" (Dobel 1993, 164).

After still another series of scandals erupted in 1986–1987, the code and its enforcement were further strengthened. A new ethics code went into effect in 1990, which, unlike its predecessor, presented "a positive vision of public service" and emphasized its role in building legitimacy and respect for government as well as its support for independent judgment and public trust (171). The revised code was accompanied by the establishment of an ombudsman's office and a full-time ethics administrator who reports directly to the county council and the board of ethics. The revision also increased the board's membership from three to five members.

Board of Ethics

In 1994, the board began an intensive education and training program to familiarize county employees with the code and "provide them with the decision-making skills necessary to resolve routine ethics issues within the workplace" (King County Board of Ethics 2009). How effective has the King County ethics program been over the past decade? A true measure of its impact is difficult to discern, but some output data are available (see Exhibit 6.2).

The King County Board of Ethics has not conducted an ethics audit or carried out an organizational survey to measure the ethical climate of county agencies. However, it initiated an ethical awareness campaign in 2003 that included, among other things, the development of a voluntary survey quiz. In 2010, the board conducted its seventh annual quiz online. Over 2,000 employees participated voluntarily in the quiz. The online interactive survey sought "to determine the extent to which employees understand basic provisions of the Code of Ethics, and the quality of the employee's experience and effectiveness of the contact when seeking information from the ethics office" (King County Board of Ethics *Annual Report 2010b,* 14).

So, what did the board learn from the quiz? Their findings include the following:

- Employee participation remains consistent and indicates a significant level of interest in county ethics.
- Employees demonstrate a solid, basic understanding of the King County Code of Ethics based on the high percentage of correct responses.
- The Ethics Help Line is a "go to" resource to help employees make ethical decisions and discuss concerns.
- Ethics office customer service—including timeliness and courtesy—rated high for callers (King County Board of Ethics 2010a).

Office of Ombudsman

The King County Ombudsman Office was established in 1968, when county voters approved the Home Rule Charter. The ethics code revisions of 1990 reassigned the responsibility for ethics code violations from the ethics board to the ombudsman. Alleged violations of the county's whistleblowing ordinance are also under the authority of the ombudsman, as are complaints about the administrative conduct of executive branch employees.

The office is staffed with four professionally trained ombudsmen, including the ombudsman-director and a support staff of two. The ombudsman cannot initiate investigations under the ethics code but does have subpoena

---

Exhibit 6.2
Ethics Training in King County, Washington

- In 2004, over 2,220 employees, including board and commission members, received ethics training. Fifty-eight percent were new employees. New employees are required to sign a statement that they have received a copy of the summary of the ethics code. Ethics training is mandatory for supervisors every eighteen months. In 2005, 688 supervisors and their deputies received ethics training.
- Post-employment provisions were amended in 2004, banning for one year a former employee from becoming a contractor or subcontractor on any county action for which he or she had responsibility as a county employee.
- From 1991 through 2005, the board issued 149 advisory opinions and 746 staff informational responses (written responses to employee inquiries on situations where the code and advisory opinions have already been applied to an analogous issue).
- In 2005, statements of financial disclosure were filed by 2,411 elected officials and employees and approximately 300 contractors and vendors.

Sources: King County Board of Ethics, 2005, 2006.

---

power to compel sworn testimony and retrieve records or material relevant to an investigation. If the ombudsman finds reasonable cause for a violation of the code of ethics, the respondent may appeal the ruling to the board of ethics. The civil penalty for a violation by one of King County's more than 13,000 officers or employees can range from a slap on the wrist or suspension without pay for one month to termination of employment. The criminal penalty includes payment of a fine not to exceed $1,000 or imprisonment in the county jail not to exceed 90 days, or both. The ombudsman can recommend disciplinary action but cannot compel an agency to take disciplinary measures. The board of ethics is equally lacking in enforcement authority. "The employee's management makes the ultimate determination as to whether disciplinary action will be implemented" (Conquergood 2005).

The *Ombudsman 2009 Annual Report* shows that the county's ombudsman's office received 2,742 citizen contacts, 84 contacts by county employees, and 21 cases from other county offices (King County, Washington 2010). There were

55 completed investigations of complaints alleging violations of the ethics code and retaliation for reporting improper governmental action protected under the whistleblowing code. Five formal ethics complaints were made against county employees, with one case being found a violation. The *2009 Annual Report* states that "the small number of formal ethics complaints may be due to a high level of awareness resulting from outreach efforts by the Board of Ethics, and publicity from the Ombudsman's past ethics findings" (2010, 10).

King County may be the only county in the United States that divides the responsibility for ethics management between a board of ethics staffed by one professional and a much larger Ombudsman office. The ombudsman's duties, of course, encompass far more than dealing with complaints of unethical behavior.

Is this the "best" approach to ethics management? You decide.

Salt Lake County, Utah: Fits and Starts?

Reform measures to foster ethical governance in Salt Lake County, Utah, were launched in 2004 in response to a scandal in which the county's mayor at the time, Nancy Workman, was forced from office. She had been accused of a felony—misusing public funds. Court documents alleged that Mayor Workman had misused health department funds to hire bookkeepers at a Boys and Girls Club where her daughter was the chief financial officer. The scandal set in motion a call for ethics reform. The county council set to wrangling about specific measures and failed to come up with a coherent proposal. Then, the deputy mayor, standing in for Mayor Workman, put together a set of proposals for consideration as a whole. Democratic mayoral candidate Peter Corroon (then mayor-elect) offered a similar list of proposals, with some additions.

Salt Lake County is a mayor-council form of government with a nine-member council, three of whom are elected at-large (by the entire county). All elections are partisan. There is one elected constitutional officer district attorney and seven independently elected statutory officers—assessor, auditor, clerk, recorder, sheriff, surveyor, and treasurer.

Many, but not all, of the proposals have been adopted (see Exhibit 6.3). They include:

1. adopting an ethics statement that all county officials and employees must read and review before taking office;

2. requiring ethics training for all county officials and employees every two years;
3. encouraging county officials to hold open records and meetings consistent with state statutes and county ordinances;
4. requiring the disclosure of outside interests and conflicts of interest;
5. placing strict limits on employees from accepting or soliciting gifts, honoraria, or requests for employment;
6. banning for one year county officials and employees from directly communicating, for compensation, with their former county agency for the purpose of influencing any matter pending before that county agency;
7. prohibiting the appointment or hiring of a relative to any county position except for seasonal employment;
8. prohibiting officers and employees from engaging in political activities, including the solicitation of political contributions, during the hours of employment;
9. prohibiting employees from using county resources in connection with any political activity (Salt Lake County, Utah 2011);
10. requiring lobbyists to register with the county and disclose lobbyist's clients (Anderson 2011).

> Employees of Salt Lake County support, obey, and defend the Constitution of the United States, the Constitution of the State of Utah, the laws of the State of Utah, and the ordinances of Salt Lake County, to the best of their abilities and will always strive to meet the highest ethical standards implicit in their employment and in the furtherance of the best public interest (Salt Lake County, Utah 2011).

These measures have put Salt Lake County on a steady ethics management path. No significant ethics issues have surfaced since 2004. The reform measures acknowledge that ethics and integrity in governance are important and require the commitment of county resources to building a strong ethical climate. While they take a legalistic approach to ethical governance, they recognize that this approach is not sufficient—thus the requirement for ethics training for all officials and employees.

Salt Lake County appears to have learned from ethical failure, but have they learned enough? A proposal to create an ethics commission, while discussed several times since 2004, is yet to become a reality. Gavin Anderson (2011), deputy district attorney, notes: "I think the potential cost has been the discouraging factor."

Exhibit 6.3

Chapter 2.07—Salt Lake County Ethics Code

Sections:

2.07.010—Ethics statement.
2.07.020—Employee training.
2.07.030—Government in the sunshine.
2.07.201—Conflicts of interest.
2.07.203—Definitions.
2.07.204—Gifts.
2.07.205—Gifts and the procurement process.
2.07.206—Honoraria.
2.07.207—Exceptions.
2.07.208—Restrictions on post-county employment.
2.07.209—Nepotism.
2.07.401—Political activities of employees.
2.07.402—Prohibitions on political use of county resources.

Source: Salt Lake County, Utah, 2011.

Has Salt Lake County embraced comprehensive ethical reform? Apparently not. Will the reform measures introduced to date instill a vibrant ethical culture in Salt Lake County governance? Maybe; maybe not. Time will tell.

Cook County, Illinois: A Work in Progress?

Cook County is the fourth-largest populated county in the United States with more than 5 million residents, 2.9 million of whom reside within the city limits of Chicago, the county seat. In addition to Chicago, some 132 municipalities also call Cook County home. The county is governed by a 17-member board of county commissioners, and an at-large elected (commissioner) county president who serves as the board's chief executive officer. Other independently elected county officials include the assessor, the board of review commissioners, the county clerk, the clerk of the circuit court, the recorder of deeds, the sheriff, the state's attorney, and the treasurer.

Like the city, the county has not enjoyed a reputation for ethics and integrity. Stories of patronage, political payoffs, and other skullduggery are legendary. Among the more infamous events was the FBI's Operation Greylord, an undercover operation in the 1980s that brought to justice 17 county judges, 48 lawyers, eight policemen, 10 deputy sheriffs, eight court officials, and one state legislator for receiving or giving bribes (FBI 2004). More recently, in May 2010, four suburban public servants were arrested in "Operation Cookie Jar" for setting up a company to receive payments from a suburban park district in which they worked (Wojciechowski 2010).

By 1993, the county recognized the need for an ethics infrastructure by adopting Ethics Ordinance 04–0–18, which has been amended three times over the past several decades—most recently in 2004. The Ethics Ordinance covers gifts and proper disclosure of gifts, conflicts of interest, improper influence, dual employment, confidential information, campaign contributions, nepotism, political activity, post-employment, and use of county-owned property. The 2004 amendment brought the county into line with the 2003 Illinois State Officials and Employees Ethics Act. It also reinstates the board of ethics' authority to initiate investigations and mandates ethics education of senior administrative staff and elected officials.

The board is composed of five members appointed by the president of the Cook County Board of Commissioners, with the advice and consent of the county board. The board of ethics is under the jurisdiction of the president's office and is responsible for implementing and enforcing the Ethics Ordinance (93–0–29). Staff performs this responsibility by investigating complaints, issuing advisory opinions, and conducting employee training seminars. Monthly public meetings are held to discuss cases and issues brought to its attention (Cook County, Illinois 2011a, 2011b).

Advisory Opinions

City employees, contractors, and officials and candidates for office can obtain *advisory opinions* based on real or hypothetical situations from the board. Citizens cannot make a request for an opinion unless they have personal or direct involvement in the subject matter of the request. This provision eliminates the possibility of a citizen acting on hearsay or a media story. The name of the person making a request, as well as any person named in the request, remains confidential. Advisory opinions are made public, although the names of the individuals involved are not disclosed.

Investigations

A written complaint is required to initiate an investigation into alleged wrongdoing. The executive director then decides if there is reasonable cause to initiate an investigation. Once reasonable cause is determined, the investigation, which could include interviews and the issuance of subpoenas, commences. The board may call for a hearing if it deems it helpful to the investigation. Upon finding a violation, a report is prepared and presented to the person who is the subject of the complaint and to appropriate officials or administrators. Disciplinary recommendations are also forwarded to the president or another county official.

This ethics infrastructure—ordinance, board, advisory opinions, investigation—has put Cook County on a footing for deterring and reacting to wrongdoing. However, there are gaps in the county's ethics management strategy, especially in transparency. For example, no annual reports or statistical information are made available on the county's web site. Also, while the advisory function of the board of ethics is impressive, the confidentiality blanket makes it difficult for the public to know what is happening.

Is ethics management in Cook County a work in progress? You decide.

Unified Government of Wyandotte County and Kansas City, Kansas: Marching to a Different Drummer?

In 1997, the voters of Wyandotte County (pop. 157,091) and Kansas City (pop. 146,866) voted overwhelmingly in favor of consolidation. As the population figures indicate, the vast majority of Wyandotte County residents live in Kansas City proper. Motivating the reformers was the widespread view that both city and county governments were corrupt. The Unified Government (UG) replaced the seven-member city council and three-member county commission with an 11-member board of commissioners, with the eleventh member elected countywide as the mayor. The mayor has veto power, can vote in the event of a tie on the commission, and appoints the county administrator with the consent of the commission.

Ethics Commission

The 1997 governmental reform created a five-member ethics commission with an appointed part-time ethics administrator. The commission and the administrator are completely independent of the UG. The commission members are appointed by the administrative judge of Wyandotte County District Court, and the ethics administrator is appointed by the legislative auditor. The UG contracted with the University of Kansas to serve as the ethics administrator. Professor H. George Frederickson, a well-known ethics specialist and scholar, was appointed the administrator.

The UG adopted a code of ethics by ordinance (Number 0–25–98) on May 21, 1998. The code covers all UG elected officials and employees. The topics covered include conflicts of interest, gift solicitation and acceptance, post-employment, gratuities, nepotism, political activities, and whistleblowing. Alleged violations of the code are investigated by the ethics administrator when directed by the commission to do so. The commission may subpoena documents and witnesses and render a decision regarding a violation. Once a violation is determined, the administrator is empowered to recommend corrective action to the legislative auditor in the form of a censure. Such corrective action can include recommendations for demotion or other administrative measures and/or referring the matter to the district attorney if there is reasonable belief that a crime has been committed. The ethics administrator is also authorized to render advisory opinions when requested in writing. Opinions when rendered are binding. A popular confidential ethics hotline is an additional tool employed by the ethics administrator to provide UG "officials and employees with a reliable source of advice on ethical dilemmas" (Manske and Frederickson 2004). The hotline also serves as a medium for reporting allegations of wrongdoing.

Ethics Training

The ethics administrator is also responsible for ethics training for all UG officials and the 2,200 employees. Training is mandatory for new employees and newly elected officials within one year of assuming their position. Moreover, all employees and elected officials must undergo "refresher" ethics training once every three years. While the training emphasizes the UG Code of Ethics, it goes beyond the typical, narrow "gotcha" approach. The ethics administrator and a colleague describe the curriculum for the ethics education program as

> carefully constructed to facilitate meaningful instruction in ethical conduct. The formal language of the code of ethics has been restated in an easy-to-understand format, and ethical-dilemma cases have been developed to present clear—yet challenging—vehicles through which practical application may be enhanced. (Manske and Frederickson 2004, 20)

The continuing education of officials and employees emphasizes topical, in-depth analysis of current ethical issues. "Employees," Manske and Frederickson (20) assert, "do not simply relearn the previous lessons."

An additional innovative aspect of the strategy adopted by the UG is the ethics pledge and oath. The pledge contains ten items that, when signed by the official and/or employee, signifies his or her commitment to honor the pledge. It obligates the employee to treating his or her office as a public trust—a true Jeffersonian legacy. The oath is a brief signatory statement:

> I do solemnly swear that I will support the Constitution of the United States and the Constitution of the State of Kansas, and faithfully discharge the duties of _____, and to abide by and adhere to the provisions of the

Code of Ethics of the Unified Government of Wyandotte County–Kansas City, Kansas. So help me God.

Although it may be premature to pass judgment on the success of the strategy adopted by the Unified Government of Wyandotte County, the indicators are very positive. County Administrator Dennis Hays claims:

Since the consolidation of governments in 1997, the public's trust and confidence in the government have increased dramatically. I am proud that there has been no public wrongdoing; however, should something arise, with the proactive avoidance through the ethics program, a swift and unbiased judgment will be made. (Manske and Frederickson 2004, 21)

And former Kansas lieutenant governor Gary Sherrer says:

Throughout my public life and private life, I have never been part of such a dramatic political, social, and economical change as what has occurred in Wyandotte County. While ethics alone would not have produced all that has been achieved, all that has been achieved would not have been accomplished without the strong emphasis on ethical behavior. (Manske and Frederickson 2004, 22)

The secret of a sound local government ethics program, according to Manske and Frederickson (22), rests on an integrated approach that contains four essential elements:

1. independence and autonomy, which, in the case of the UG, is completely outside of the government;
2. confidentiality in the treatment of allegations and investigations;
3. trust by citizens, officials, employees, and unions that the administrators of the ethics program are approachable, fair, just, and reasonable; and
4. the promotion of good and honest local government rather than a "gotcha" approach to dealing with misconduct.

Professor Frederickson served as the Wyandotte County ethics officer for ten years. Here's what he says about ethics reform in the UG: "The ethics program is doing fairly well, following the format established at the time of the city/county consolidation. The new jurisdiction continues to flourish economically and to be increasingly seen as an honest jurisdiction" (Frederickson 2011).

Is the unified government marching to a different drummer? You decide.

Jacksonville-Duval County, Florida: National Leader?

Duval County (pop. 817,480) merged with the Jacksonville, Florida (pop. 735,617), government in 1968. The merger was triggered by political corruption and scandal involving a city commissioner indicted by a Duval County grand jury for accepting bribes to influence city purchases of mechanical equipment. The new consolidated City of Jacksonville government coexists alongside four municipalities that were not included in the consolidation.

The charter set forth a code of ethics (Article 20) that applied to all officers and employees of the new government, including the Duval County board of public instruction. The key components addressed in the code include (1) conflicts of interest, among them the improper disclosure of confidential information to advance the financial interest of an officer or others, (2) financial disclosure of interest in any contract or matter pending before the consolidated government, (3) prohibition of use of public property for personal benefit, and (4) employee participation in political campaigns disallowed during duty hours.

The seven-member elected civil service board was designated as the board of ethics and charged with enforcing the code. The board of ethics could issue advisory opinions, hear and investigate complaints alleging violations of the code, subpoena witnesses, administer oaths, and take testimony. An officer or employee found guilty of violating the code could be reprimanded, suspended, reduced in rank, or removed from office. The board could not remove an elected official, however; this power was reserved for the city council. After only a few years in operation, however, the ethics provisions were taken out of the Charter and the Ethics Board was disbanded in the early 1970s.

This minimalist "gotcha" approach in Jacksonville did not produce much in the way of ethical governance. In the early 1980s, city hall corruption once more became the focus of a federal investigation. Further mischief in the late 1980s resulted in the state's attorney convening a grand jury to investigate wrongdoing. Several years later, the state's attorney was elected mayor on a platform of ethics reform. Thus, in the mid-1990s, a committee of lawyers hammered out a new ethics code that was enacted in June 1999. The authors asserted that the new code would "position Jacksonville to be a national leader in governmental ethics" (City of Jacksonville, Florida 1999). Highlights of the code follow:

- The establishment of aspirational goals for the conduct of city employees. The development of ethics in city government, the code states, must be more than the "avoidance of criminal behavior. It is a commitment for public servants to take individual responsibility in creating a government that has the trust and respect of its citizens" (CityEthics.org 2006). City employees "are considered stewards of the public's trust and should aspire to the highest level of integrity and character" (City of Jacksonville, Florida 2009).

- The creation of an ethics officer who has responsibility for encouraging compliance with the code, coordinating ethics training, and developing citywide programs for achieving the aspirational goals (see Exhibit 6.4). A former federal prosecutor served as the voluntary ethics officer until 2007, when the appointment became part-time with compensation set at $75,000.
- The initiation of ethics training for city employees and an "Ethics in Government Program" for elected officials.
- The restructuring of the City of Jacksonville Ethics Commission into a quasi-independent nine-member body with term limits, and the expansion of its role "in monitoring compliance with training requirements and financial and gift disclosure reporting requirements."

Ethics training is a high priority in Jacksonville's consolidated government. All new employees are trained on the first day of employment. "We also train existing employees monthly through our departmental ethics officers," says ethics officer Carla Miller (2005). "We pick a topic, like campaign laws, discuss it in our departmental ethics officer meetings," and then the ethics officers get it out to their staff. The Jacksonville Ethics Commission Annual *Compliance Report 2004* notes that the training department offered two ethics classes, one on "Character Counts" and the other an "Introduction to Ethics." Additionally, a seminar on "Ethics in Public Service" was presented by well-known ethics expert Michael Josephson of the Josephson Institute of Ethics.

Enforcement of the code of ethics is the responsibility of the ethics commission, and while the commission has wide latitude to investigate possible violations of the standard of conduct for city officers and employees, it has no authority to levy penalties. "The ethics commission," Miller asserts, "was not given power to handle specific violations—only to investigate generally and recommend legislation to city council" (2005). As the Internal Operating Rules of the Jacksonville Ethics Commission state, the commission "is not vested with the authority to determine whether specific violations have occurred for purposes of entering sanctions or penalties." Who, then, has this authority? The answer is the state attorney. How many code violations has the state attorney handled over the past five years? None. Does this mean that the new code, with its emphasis on aspirational goals, is working well? Perhaps. The consolidated government does appear to be on the road to strong ethics management, but it can get bumpy.

Indeed, the 19-member Jacksonville City Council members found themselves under intense public scrutiny in 2007, when the *Florida Times Union*

Exhibit 6.4
Jacksonville Ethics Officer's Responsibilities

- Conduct periodic meetings with the department director, senior management, and employee groups to discuss or provide advice on ethics issues.
- Conduct a review of and disseminate within his or her department the appropriate city and department policies and regulations that relate to the Code of Ethics for employees.
- Assist the city ethics officer(s) in the formulation of ethics awareness training sessions, conferences, and seminars that are developed for and presented to department employees.
- Assist the department head in the development of an overall internal ethics plan.
- Report compliance with the ethics code to the city ethics officer(s).
- Make recommendations for improvement in training to the city ethics officer.
- Accomplish such other duties as are delegated by the city ethics officer(s), including conducting investigations or complaints as authorized by the city ethics officer(s).

Source: City of Jacksonville, Florida, n.d.a.

---

published a story raising serious questions about council members meeting clandestinely outside of Florida's "Sunshine Law" (Kormanik 2007). A second story by the *Times Union* published two months later delved into the awarding of no-bid contracts (Palka 2007). These stories sparked public outcry that motivated State Attorney Harry L. Shorstein to convene a grand jury whose charge was to investigate whether "(1) Jacksonville's City Council members failed to comply with Florida's Sunshine Laws, and (2) the city of Jacksonville failed to ensure transparency and fairness in local procurement practices" (Shorstein and Schulz 2008).

The grand jury's investigation lasted six months, with the presentment released on January 17, 2008. Although the investigation found no violations of law, it did find much amiss with the way in which the city council conducted itself and the lack of transparency in procurement. Katie Dearing, vice chairwoman of Jacksonville's Ethics Commission, declared that Jacksonville "suffered a setback in recent months wherein the public's perception is that ethics and 'doing the right thing' are not priorities for those in local government" (Shorstein and Schulz 2008).

In an attempt to get in front of the problems, Mayor John Peyton issued Executive Order No. 07–09 in August 2007, creating the position of inspector general, whose "principal objective is to promote ethics, honesty and efficiency in government and to promote the public's trust in government" (City of Jacksonville, Florida 2007). The mayor also formally established the position of Ethics Officer and charged this office with eliminating even the appearance of impropriety. The inspector general and the ethics officer were expected to work alongside each other. Both were housed in the mayor's office, although they were assured of operational autonomy. The inspector general's web site states, "the Mayor will not prevent, impair or prohibit the Inspector General from initializing, carrying out or completing any audit, investigation or review" (City of Jacksonville, Florida n.d.c).

More reform took place in the summer and autumn of 2011when the council approved ordinances that provided the Ethics Commission with more autonomy (Patterson 2011), eliminated the Office of Inspector General, and created the Office of Ethics, Compliance and Oversight (OECO). The new office is charged with the responsibility of coordinating and handling

> citywide ethics training, compliance, and oversight issues. In furtherance of the above, the Office shall ensure the investigation of all situations involving fraud, waste, corruption and conflicts of interest by city officials and employees, and to staff the Jacksonville Ethics Commission. The organization and administration of the office shall be independent to assure that no external interference or influence adversely affects the independence and objectivity of the office.

These ethics management initiatives have put the City of Jacksonville on a forward-looking path toward recognizing that ethical governance requires more than laws and penalties. Ethics officer Carla Miller, who also served as the first chair of the revitalized board of ethics, notes that "it is easy enough to lecture people about the laws in existence, but much harder to instruct on the basics of ethics and ways to develop an ethical culture" (2005).

Is ethics management in Jacksonville a national leader? You decide.

Summing Up

Several key themes identified in Chapter 1 have been illustrated here in Chapter 6. First, scandal is the trigger that motivated ethics management initiatives in many local governments. Scandals that plagued Tampa, Chicago, New York

City, King County, Jacksonville, Miami-Dade County, Cook County, Palm Beach County, and Salt Lake County motivated public officials to take corrective action. Second, ethics management strategies vary a great deal among the local governments examined here. Nearly all share a strong legal compliance orientation; there are exceptions, however, with the Unified Government of Wyandotte County and Kansas City, Kansas, being the most notable.

Ethics Management Skill Building

Practicum 6.1. What to Do?

Imagine that you are the county sheriff in a large (1 million), urban, high-growth county where you have served as a popular elected county sheriff for 20 years. To your dismay, you are informed that one of your sergeants, who has served the county for many years, has been charged with 129 counts of falsification of official documents, 144 counts of failure to follow standard operating procedures, and conduct unbecoming a member of the sheriff's office—charges made by your internal affairs investigators. The deputy, as it turns out, coordinates all the work at the port authority and is in a position to log off-duty assignments for himself at the port that far exceed regular workweek hours. The investigators charge that the sergeant knowingly cooked the books and overrode computer programs to prevent others from knowing what he did.

The sergeant's supervisor wants him suspended for 30 days and reduced to the rank of deputy. The disciplinary review board wants him fired. You are about to retire and don't need to worry about being reelected. The allegations against the sergeant have been published in the local newspaper.

Questions

1. What would you do with the sergeant? Would you put a letter of reprimand in his personnel file? Ban him from working any off-duty assignments? Suspend him? Reduce his rank? Fire him?
2. How would you size up the implications of your decision for the morale of the uniformed officers under your command?
3. What are the implications for the ethical climate of your organization?

Practicum 6.2. An Ethics Audit for Your Agency?

You have decided that an ethics audit for your agency is needed. There have been no serious incidents of unethical behavior, but you are not sure that agency personnel are paying enough attention to ethical issues. In addition, there is some evidence that most of your middle-level managers are complacent about promoting proper behavior. Ethics issues are never discussed during staff meetings. It just seems as if ethics doesn't matter that much to most managers. An ethics audit, you believe, will get people in touch with their own ethics and exert a positive influence on the agency's culture of "getting the job done."

Now, you say to yourself, where am I going to find an ethics auditor? And, what do I really want an auditor to do? You know that an ethics audit can't be done on the cheap, so the first task is to estimate the costs of conducting an audit; this will not be possible in-house because you do not have staff who are sufficiently familiar with an audit to properly estimate the cost. An RFP (request for proposal) will get the job done, you muse.

You decide to ask the director of the Human Resources Division to develop the RFP. As you are talking with him, he asks: "How should I state the objective of the RFP?" What exactly is it that we want an ethics auditor to do? Do we want the auditor to investigate the (un)ethical behavior of all employees? Some employees—say, frontline workers—and not others? Is there a timeline for the completion of the work? Is there a limit on how much we should budget given that our agency employees 500 people?

Questions

1. How would you reply to the director of the Human Resources Division?
2. What should be the key components of an RFP?
3. What guidance should you provide the auditor about releasing the results of the audit?

Note

1. This chapter draws in part from Menzel (2006).

7
Ethics Management in the States

I have embarrassed myself, my family and many people who have
expressed faith in me in the last 25 years. As I look back over the
years, I see that I had lost sight of my ethical judgment.

—Former Connecticut governor John G. Rowland (Yardley and Stowe 2005)

The American states have taken a number of measures to strengthen ethics
and integrity in governance, although there is considerable variation among
them. Some states do a great deal; others do very little. New York passed
the first major ethics law in 1954. Other states have moved more slowly in
launching ethics reform initiatives, with many doing so in the 1970s on the
heels of the Watergate scandal. This chapter opens with a wide lens view of
ethics management in the American states by focusing attention on the executive, legislative, and judiciary branches of government, and it closes with an
in-depth look at three states—Florida, Illinois, and New York.

State Ethics Laws

The Better Government Association (BGA), a Chicago-based civic watchdog
group, compiles a 50-state Integrity Index (see Exhibit 7.1) based on the extent
to which the states have adopted laws dealing with freedom of information,
whistleblowing, campaign finance, open meetings, and financial conflicts of
interest. In 2008, five states—New Jersey, Rhode Island, Hawaii, Washington,
and Louisiana—received the best overall scores, while Montana, Tennessee,
Alabama, Vermont, and South Dakota, respectively, were ranked the bottom
five. Some states performed much better than others in a relative sense, yet
the best state—New Jersey—still fell far short of high performance as measured on a scale of 0–100. The worse state, South Dakota, received a zero
mark for freedom of information and low scores for whistleblower protection,
campaign finance, open meetings, and conflict of interest. The reader should
keep in mind that the Integrity Index is based on the strength of laws in five
areas; it does not measure ethical or unethical behavior. For example, while
New Jersey enjoys the highest score for freedom of information, there are no
assurances that the law is not broken consistently.

Exhibit 7.1

Better Government Integrity Index, 2008 and 2002
(States ranked by 2008 Index from highest to lowest)

The 2008 index represents combined scores on laws dealing with Freedom of Information, Whistleblower Protection, Campaign Finance, Open Meetings, and Conflicts of Interest. The 2002 index did not include Open Meetings; it had Gifts-Trips-Honoraria. This difference explains in part why a state that is ranked high in 2008 may have been ranked low in 2002 and vice versa.

	2008	2002		2008	2002
New Jersey	1	12	Iowa	26	43
Rhode Island	2	2	Georgia	27	26
Hawaii	3	4	Kentucky	28	3
Washington	4	11	Indiana	29	34
Louisiana	5	46	South Carolina	30	7
Nebraska	6	6	Ohio	31	14
Texas	7	9	Maine	33	24
Arkansas	8	31	Nevada	34	30
Maryland	9	10	North Dakota	34	39
Colorado	10	16	Utah	36	27
Arizona	11	20	New York	36	29
West Virginia	12	8	Virginia	38	28
Illinois	13	41	Mississippi	39	33
Connecticut	14	13	Alaska	40	23
Minnesota	15	17	New Hampshire	41	36
Florida	16	18	New Mexico	42	48
Wisconsin	17	1	Delaware	43	38
Kansas	18	21	Idaho	44	42
California	19	5	Wyoming	45	37
Massachusetts	20	15	Montana	46	45
Oklahoma	21	25	Tennessee	47	44
Oregon	22	19	Alabama	48	47
Missouri	22	35	Vermont	49	49
North Carolina	23	22	South Dakota	50	50
Michigan	24	32			
Pennsylvania	25	40			

As already suggested, states differ widely in the content and coverage of ethics laws, although all states provide some protection from retaliation for employees who blow the whistle on government fraud, waste, or abuse of power. (See Exhibits 7.2 and 7.3 for subject matter coverage in selected states.) All 50 states also require lobbyists to file disclosure reports that identify persons seeking to influence legislation, as well as the expenditures made by lobbyists. Gift restrictions on legislators vary substantially, with some states limiting the monetary value of gifts at $3 while other states allow gifts valued as much as $500. Thirty-seven states have campaign finance contribution limits, with 27 of them placing restrictions

Exhibit 7.2

Operating Size and Jurisdiction of Ethics Commissions in California, Florida, New York, and Texas

	Operating size		Jurisdiction over . . .		
	Budget	# employees	Legislators	State elected officials	Local government employees
California	$8.2 mil	80	Yes	Yes	Yes
Florida	$2.4 mil	21	Yes	Yes	Yes
New York	$4.3 mil	50	No	Yes	No
Texas	$1.9 mil	37	Yes	Yes	Yes

Source: COGEL, 2010.

Exhibit 7.3

Advisory Opinions, Investigations, and Training in California, Florida, New York, and Texas

	Advisory opinions		Investigations		Training required
	Authority to issue	# per year	Authority on own initiative	# per year	
California	Yes	200–300	Yes	511	Yes
Florida	Yes	25	No	n/r	No
New York	Yes	5–10	Yes	60–70	No
Texas	Yes	4	Yes	374	No

Source: COGEL, 2010.
n/r = not reported.

on the contributions that legislators can receive from lobbyists. Restrictions on former legislators from lobbying are in place in 26 states, with 19 states restricting former legislators from lobbying for one year after leaving office and six states imposing a two-year ban on this revolving door. Some states prohibit legislators from receiving honoraria if offered in connection with a legislator's official duties (State of Connecticut General Assembly 2004).

Ethics Commissions and Boards

The principal agency for overseeing a state's ethics laws is a commission or board. These boards generally act as regulatory watchdogs. Thirty-six states have an ethics commission or board that administers and enforces ethics codes and rules for public officials, state employees, and lobbyists. Louisiana was the first state to establish an independent ethics commission in 1964. The commissions vary enormously in size and capacity, with some states (for example, Montana) having a single commissioner and other states (such as West Virginia) having 12 commissioners. Budgets vary from as little as $5,000 in Michigan to $7 million in California. State ethics laws typically cover local government employees, although not all do. These agencies can issue advisory opinions, provide training and information regarding the state's ethics laws, and adjudicate allegations of unethical behavior. The more powerful agencies can initiate investigations, subpoena witnesses, and levy civil fines. Decisions reached by ethics commissions are subject to judicial review.

Effectiveness

How effective are state ethics laws and their regulatory commissions? It is not easy to determine, as the evidence is sparse and somewhat anecdotal in nature. Complicating matters further during these challenging economic times, some states are cutting back on their budgets for ethics agencies. The Florida Commission on Ethics, for example, has had its funding reduced by $352,000 since fiscal year 2007–2008 (State of Florida Commission on Ethics 2011). Moreover, the legalistic and rule-driven approach taken by most states emphasizes ethics management as a legal process; thus, training, for example, turns mostly around interpretations of the law—what the law says and what can happen to those who break the law. And, of course, state ethics regulatory commissions and agencies are mindful of the need for due process in all rulings.

A handful of studies have attempted to assess the effectiveness of state ethics laws and agencies. Among them is Smith's (2003) study of Connecticut, Florida, and New York. These states have established commissions that, as ethics watchdogs, take as their primary mission the enforcement of ethics laws. All were created as a result of scandal, with the Connecticut and Florida ethics commissions established in 1978 and 1977, respectively. The New York State Ethics Commission was created in 1987. All issue advisory opinions, provide training, and conduct investigations, although the Florida Commission cannot initiate investigations on its own nor can it directly levy civil penalties; it can recommend penalties but needs an executive order to implement a recommendation. Smith concludes that "ethics commissions play a positive role in the states" (293). "Enforcement actions," he asserts, "send a message to violators or would-be violators to be mindful of ethics transgressions" and therefore function as an effective deterrent.

Other investigators are not so confident. Herrmann (1997) contends that ethics commissions face serious problems. They are not effective regulatory agencies and need to be empowered with adequate funding, greater operating autonomy, and vigorous enforcement authority. He describes commissions as houses built with bricks without mortar—that is, agencies with weak organizational structures. Mackenzie (2002) claims that the enactment of numerous ethics laws and ordinances—federal, state, and local—have tried to make government scandalproof, but there is little evidence that this approach has succeeded. Indeed, he goes so far as to suggest that "some ethics deregulation will improve the overall quality of the public service and of government performance with no discernable impact on public integrity" (164–165). Williams's (1996) study of the Florida Commission on Ethics also lends little support to the contention that ethics agencies are effective. He found that the commission (1) is weak in education and training initiatives to aid public officials' understanding of a state's ethics laws and rules; (2) is totally reactive in responding to complaints, and (3) does little to improve the ethical climate of Florida. Williams suggests that commission practices may actually detract from the ethical climate in the state.

> What should be done to strengthen state ethics commissions? Robert W. Smith (2003, 293–294), who has conducted in-depth research on New York, Florida, and Connecticut, makes a number of recommendations to improve the functioning of state ethics commissions. They include:
>
> - Removing any partisan considerations for determining who serves on the commission.
> - Enhancing the education and training function of commissions.
> - Providing for independent investigatory power.
> - Empowering commissions to impose substantial fines.
> - Providing adequate base-level funding.
> - Providing for a uniform ethics structure, not a fragmented structure.
> - Expanding the discretion of commissions to interpret how the law should be applied in certain circumstances.

Governors

The ethics problems facing state governments are not insignificant and all too often cross over into the criminal domain. The youngest governor in Connecticut history when elected to office in 1994 at age 37, John G. Rowland (R), was sentenced in March 2005 to one year and one day in federal prison for accepting $107,000 in gifts from people doing business with the state and not paying taxes on them. Mr. Rowland resigned in July 2003, halfway through his third term in office. In Illinois in 2001, Republican Governor George Ryan chose not to seek reelection after one term in office as a result of the "licenses-for-sale" scandal. The scandal involved bribes paid to state officials to issue commercial drivers' licenses. The bribe money was laundered into Governor Ryan's 1998 campaign for governor. Federal investigators brought indictments against 79 persons and secured convictions of 75 of them, including Ryan. After a lengthy, complex trial lasting more than five months, the former governor was found guilty of 18 felony charges that ranged from racketeering conspiracy to mail fraud, tax fraud, and making false statements to the Federal Bureau of Investigations (Davey and Ruethling 2006). Former Governor Ryan will be released from the federal penitentiary in Terra Haute, Indiana, on July 4, 2013.

Perhaps the most sensational, highly publicized case involving gubernatorial corruption belongs to Illinois Democrat Rod Blagojevich, who succeeded George Ryan in 2002. Mr. Blagojevich, the first Democrat to win the Illinois governor's seat in 25 years, campaigned on a platform of government reform, including ethics reform. Seven years later (2009), he became the first governor in Illinois to be impeached (House vote 114–1) and removed (Senate vote 59–0) from office for abuse of power and corruption. Most controversial was his effort to "sell" the U.S. Senate seat once held by President Obama.

"I'm going to keep this Senate option for me a real possibility, you know, and therefore I can drive a hard bargain. You hear what I'm saying. And if I don't get what I want and I'm not satisfied with it, then I'll just take the Senate seat myself."
—Former Illinois governor Rod R. Blagojevich (Davey 2008)

Following his removal from office, Mr. Blagojevich was indicted by a federal grand jury on racketeering and charged with 16 felonies, including racketeering conspiracy, wire fraud, extortion conspiracy, attempted extortion, and making false statements to federal agents. The trial in the summer of 2010 resulted in a hung jury on 23 out of 24 counts against him with a single guilty finding of lying to federal agents. Federal prosecutors called for a second trial in May-June 2011; this time, Mr. Blagojevich was not so fortunate. He was convicted on 17 of 20 counts, including the charge that he conspired to sell the U.S. Senate seat held by Barack Obama. The jury forewoman, a retired church employee from the Chicago suburbs, put it this way: "There's a lot of bargaining that goes on behind the scenes . . . but I think in the instances when it is someone representing the people, it crosses the line." After about six weeks of testimony, she added, "I told my husband that if he was running for politics, he would probably have to find a new wife" (Davey and Fitzsimmons 2011).

Not every governor who has ethics lapses is subject to criminal proceedings. Governor Bob Taft (R) of Ohio failed to report 52 gifts, including golf outings, hockey tickets, and meals, on his annual financial disclosure reports from 1998 to 2004. The gifts amounted to nearly $6,000. Under Ohio law, gifts worth more than $75 must be reported. Governor Taft admitted that he had failed to disclose the gifts. A judge ordered him to pay $4,000 in fines and write a letter of apology to the people of Ohio (Dao 2005). Another governor, James McGreevey (D-New Jersey), was forced out of office in 2004 as a result of an adulterous affair with a former aide, a man who was given special employment consideration by the governor as an adviser to the New Jersey Office of Homeland Security.

New York's former governor, David A. Paterson, found himself on a wobbly ethical ladder when he, two members of his staff, his son, and his son's friend attended the first game of the 2009 World Series at Yankee Stadium. An investigation by the New York Commission on Public Integrity found reasonable evidence that he had misused his official position to solicit and secure free tickets. The Governor testified that he attended the World Series game in his official capacity and always intended to pay for the tickets of his son and his son's friend. Subsequent testimony by his staff refuted the governor's testimony. Furthermore, information from e-mail exchanges, along with an independent handwriting expert's assessment of a check written to cover the cost of the tickets, led the commission to conclude that the governor had given false testimony and knew that his conduct was unlawful. On December 20, 2010, the Commission levied a fine of $62,125, which included $2,125 for the value of the tickets and $60,000 for violating several provisions of the state's Public Officers Law. Michael Cherkasky, the chairman of the commission, wrote: "The moral and ethical tone of any organization is set at the top. Unfortunately the Governor set a totally inappropriate tone by his dishonest and unethical conduct" (NYS Commission on Public Integrity 2010a).

One governor who set the moral and ethical tone of his administration on day one was Florida's Charlie Crist. Upon taking office in January 2007, Governor Crist issued Executive Order Number 07–01.

An excerpt from former Florida governor Charlie Crist's Executive Order 07–01

I hereby direct the immediate adoption and implementation of a Code of Ethics by the Office of the Governor. This Code of Ethics applies to all employees within the Office of the Governor, as well as the secretaries, deputy secretaries, and chiefs of staff of all executive agencies under my purview.

I further direct the immediate adoption and implementation of a Code of Personal Responsibility by the Office of the Governor. The Code of Personal Responsibility applies to all employees within the Office of the Governor and sets forth clear standards and procedures regarding appropriate conduct in the workplace.

State Legislators

Members of the 50 state legislatures, like governors and members of Congress, are subject to ethical lapses. Indeed, some critics assert that legislative ethics is an oxymoron. Certainly, there is no shortage of lobbyists in Tallahassee, Albany, Springfield, or Sacramento—all seeking to influence lawmakers legally but all too often unethically. Campaign contributions flow freely from the clients of lobbyists, and conflicts of interest are a constant peril. Most efforts to curb unethical behavior among state legislators in the pre-Watergate period focused on enacting antibribery laws.

States began tightening their ethics laws following the Watergate scandal, an ethical meltdown that drove a sitting president from office. "Eleven states that had not enacted any laws regulating legislative conflicts of interest before 1972 took decisive action during the short period from 1973 to 1976" (Rosenson 2005, 91). Other states—North Carolina and Texas—strengthened their bribery statutes, and still others—California, Minnesota, and Wisconsin—added financial disclosure to their ethical restrictions. Eight states, including Florida and Kansas, set up independent ethics commissions to monitor legislators' financial disclosures and investigate allegations of wrongdoing (91). By 1996, three dozen states had taken steps to strengthen their legislative ethics laws.

A handful of states have been aggressive in enacting restrictive ethics laws. Beth A. Rosenson, writing in *The Shadowlands of Conduct: Ethics and State Politics* (2005) points to California, New Jersey, and Illinois as placing "substantive restrictions on legislators' activities, including limits on lawyer-legislators' appearances before state agencies, limits on gifts, limits on legislators becoming lobbyists after leaving office, and mandatory financial disclosure" (65). And in 2005, the Republican-controlled Florida legislature enacted what is probably the most restrictive gift law in the nation: Effective January 1, 2006, "no lobbyist or principal shall make, directly or indirectly, and no member or employee of the Legislature shall knowingly accept, directly or indirectly, any expenditure" (Section 112.313 of the Florida Statutes).

The devil, of course, is always in the details. Consequently, the legislative leadership drafted "Interim Lobbying Guidelines for the House and Senate" (Lee and Bense 2006). The guidelines advise that, among other things, a legislator cannot accept a subscription to a newspaper or periodical that is paid for by a lobbyist or a client, free health screening by an association that is a principal, payment for travel expenses to deliver a speech, or a drink at a bar without verifying that the person picking up the tab is not a lobbyist or a client of one. The law does permit a lobbyist or principal to buy a legislator a meal if the legislator "contemporaneously provides equal or greater consideration."

So, if a lobbyist puts out $50 for a legislator's dinner but the legislator buys a $75 bottle of wine, all is well.

The law exempts political fundraising. A legislator can accept food or drink paid for by a lobbyist or principal who sponsors a fundraising event. Moreover, the law does not prohibit expenditures made by lobbyists or principals to influence legislative action through oral or written communication. Nor are local legislative bodies—city councils and county commissions—covered by the gift-ban law.

Investigations of alleged ethics violations by members of a state legislature are typically handled by a standing legislative ethics committee. Every state except Colorado and Connecticut has a standing legislative ethics committee. In Colorado and Connecticut, a committee is appointed by the speaker of the House and the Senate president when a complaint is lodged against a lawmaker (Rosenson 2005, 114). Ethics commissions in states where they exist may also be involved if the complaint alleges a violation of state law.

State Judiciary

State judges are not subject to the U.S. Code of Conduct, but each state has a judicial commission that deals with complaints of judicial misconduct, with most commissions established in the past 30 years (Wex n.d.). Judicial commissions typically have the power to sanction a judge and to require a judge to retire or resign. Commission findings are almost always appealable to state courts.

State judges are selected in a variety of ways—partisan election, nonpartisan election, appointment and then reelection on a ballot that permits citizens to vote to retain or not retain the judge, and merit selection by appointment or with a commission. Eight states (including Illinois and Kansas) select judges through partisan elections, 13 (including California and Florida) choose judges through nonpartisan election, 15 states (including Massachusetts and Utah) use merit selection with a nominating committee, nine states (including South Carolina) choose judges through merit selection combined with other methods, and two states (New Jersey and Virginia) authorize the governor and/or legislature to select judges (Public Broadcasting Service 2005).

The kaleidoscope of selection methods and accountability mechanisms poses its own ethical challenges in the states. Consider the case of Judge John Renke III, a Florida circuit court judge. In 2002, then-candidate Renke defeated two others vying for a seat on the Pasco-Pinellas circuit court. The election was very competitive, with Renke accused of nine counts of campaign misconduct. The Florida Judicial Qualifications Commission (JQC) heard the case in 2005 and ruled that Renke brought disrepute to the judiciary as a result of his misconduct. The misconduct included an illegal contribution of $95,800 from his father. The commission recommended a public reprimand and a $40,000 fine but not removal from office. Evidence collected by the commission indicated that Judge Renke had done an excellent job as a circuit court judge, presiding mostly over domestic cases (Jenkins 2005).

The Florida Supreme Court concluded that the JQC-recommended sanctions were not severe enough for the violations documented. Consequently, the court ruled that Judge Renke be removed from the bench. "He is presently unfit to hold office and . . . removal from the bench is the only appropriate sanction in this case" (The Supreme Court of Florida 2006, 1).

Judges who break the law pose a special challenge for judicial ethics. Ohio Supreme Court justice Alice Robie Resnick, for example, was convicted of drunken driving and therefore charged with violating the state's judicial code of conduct. Canon 2 of the Ohio code states that "A Judge Shall Respect and Comply with the Law and Shall Act at All Times in a Manner That Promotes Public Confidence in the Integrity and Impartiality of the Judiciary" (The Supreme Court of Ohio 1997). A 13-member panel of state appellate judges heard her case and decided that Justice Resnick had indeed violated Canon 2. The panel publicly reprimanded her for professional misconduct. No other discipline, such as suspending her law license or removing her from the bench, was recommended.

Some states are especially lax about judges receiving gifts and favors. In Pennsylvania, for example, judges (including those holding the highest posts) can receive gifts as long as they are reported. Exceptions are judges at the grassroots level. Neither Philadelphia's traffic court judges nor Pennsylvania's 546 magisterial district judges are allowed to accept gifts and favors. Much criticism has been directed at Pennsylvania's Chief Justice Ronald Castille, who has received and reported gifts of dinners, event tickets, golf outings, and plane rides from law firms and businessmen (*New York Times* 2010a). No evidence, however, has surfaced to indicate that Justice Castille has shown favoritism in his decisions. Should disclosure be the final say? Does the acceptance of gifts and favors, regardless of who gave them to whom or when, create a public perception of biased judicial decision making?

In the remainder of this chapter, we take a close look at ethics reform and management in three states: Florida, Illinois, and New York.

Florida: Significant Ethics Reform in Waiting?[1]

Florida's quest for significant ethical reform remains a work in progress, although the state has had an ethics statute since 1967 and a nine-member commission on ethics since 1974. Florida's ethics statute covers all officers and employees of the state, including those in cities, counties, and special districts. In 1976, Florida voters overwhelmingly supported an amendment to the state's constitution that added an open meetings law—called the "Sunshine" amendment—with enforcement jurisdiction given to the Florida Commission on Ethics. The Sunshine amendment applies to all local governments and state agencies with the exception of the legislature. Floridians are justifiably proud of the open meetings law and alleged violations are often brought before the Commission.

Still, there is much distance to go to claim that Florida has a strong ethics management system in place. Menzel's (1996a) investigation of the Florida Commission on Ethics reinforces the view that the state's ethics, legal, and organizational infrastructure is not adequate. Indeed, there is a disturbing possibility that the ethics commission unwittingly contributes to a "trust deficit." Menzel gathered data on the complaint-making process in Florida in the early 1990s from more than 300 residents who filed ethics complaints with the commission and 555 officials who had complaints filed against them. The survey information focused on the experiences of each group in dealing with the Florida Commission on Ethics.

Public officials reported a much more positive experience with the way in which the commission handled complaints than did citizens. For example, 50 percent of the complainants rated staff courtesy as "good" or "excellent," whereas 75 percent of the public officials reported a similar rating. At the other end of the courtesy scale, one of every four citizen complainants rated the staff's courtesy as "poor" or "unacceptable." The pattern was even more pronounced for the promptness with which the staff dealt with complaints. More than 50 percent of the complainants said that staff promptness was "poor" or "unacceptable," in contrast to a majority of public officials who said that staff promptness was "excellent" or "good."

Other findings were equally disparate, with public officials generally much more positive about the work of the ethics commission than citizens were. Consider the following assessment written by a citizen:

> The public city managers and high-ranking employees of local government in Florida strongly believe that the Florida Commission on Ethics is ineffective and usually does nothing or very little about unethical conduct of local officials. I believe this directly contributes to elected local officials' and public managers' attitudes that they can misuse their power—they are above ethical laws, so to speak.

Still another citizen remarked in a lengthy three-page letter:

> As one moves thru the labyrinth of government offices one cannot escape
> the contempt [with] which the public is held by the officeholders. A great
> fear rests within each and every citizen as to whether or not they should
> speak out . . . what will happen to them? Is it worth the risk?

Some public officials view the complaint-making process as a gauntlet of
discontented citizens armed with abusive and baseless accusations. Consider
the fact that once a complaint is filed, the complainant can go public with
it; that is, an elected official has no media protection from an allegation of
wrongdoing if the complainant wishes to make the complaint public information, which can be done by simply calling a local newspaper reporter. Could
citizen complainants become "civic terrorists"? Or, might they be ethical
zealots or whistleblowers who hold worldviews vastly different from others
and are therefore more likely to have a "bad" experience following the filing
of a complaint, no matter what the final outcome is?

Comments by both citizens and officials suggest that Florida's presumably
well-intentioned ethics laws and infrastructure, the Florida Ethics Commission,
may be widening rather than closing the trust deficit. Ethics and trustworthy
government go hand in hand. They are essential components of democracy
whose very survival rests on public trust and confidence. "Democracy requires
a degree of trust that we often take for granted . . . [but] it is much harder to
build trust than to lose it" (Bellah et al. 1991, 3) And, in the United States,
"we have begun to lose trust in our institutions; the heritage of trust that has
been the basis of our stable democracy is eroding" (4). Although there may
be many conditions and circumstances that destroy trust in public authorities
and government, none is likely to do it more quickly or effectively than the
unethical conduct of public officeholders.

Florida gained the unwanted distinction of leading all states for the decade
1998–2007 in the number (824) of convicted public officials in federal public
corruption cases, surpassing New York with 704, Texas with 565, Pennsylvania
with 555, California with 547, Ohio with 547, and Illinois with 502 (Smith
2008). And, after a series of scandals and corruption arrests in Palm Beach
County in 2008–2009, Governor Charlie Crist petitioned the Florida Supreme
Court to impanel a grand jury to investigate "public officials who have abused
their powers via their public office . . . and identify any deficiencies in current
laws, punishments or enforcement efforts and make detailed recommendations to improve our anti-corruption initiatives" (State of Florida 2010). The
grand jury report paints an ugly picture of unethical behavior and corruption
in the Sunshine State and calls for significant reform. Present-day corruption
in Florida, the report states, "is pervasive at all levels of government. . . . We
believe the citizens of Florida deserve public servants who will take action

for the good of the whole even if it does not benefit them individually. While there are many good officials in Florida, our government buildings and elected bodies should be overflowing with leaders who are not afraid to set a higher standard for their conduct and serve as role models for the public" (State of Florida 2010).

The grand jury's recommendations are extensive and include specific steps that could strengthen ethical governance in Florida. These steps include (1) requiring elected and appointed officials subject to the code of ethics to undergo ethics training prior to or within 60 days of holding office, (2) encouraging local and state agencies to designate a chief ethics officer to ensure that officers and employees are trained and educated, (3) urging management to lead by example and foster a strong ethical culture, (4) encouraging metropolitan counties to establish a code of ethics and a commission on ethics and public trust similar to the Miami-Dade Commission on Ethics and Public Trust, (5) giving the commission on ethics limited authority to self-initiate investigations based on a super-majority vote of the commissioners, and (6) rewriting the code of ethics so that it clearly applies to any persons, entities, or nonprofit organizations receiving public funds to perform a government function or service. "Our State," the Florida grand jury asserted, "should be a leader when it comes to ethical accountability for our public servants and officials" (State of Florida 2010, 110).

Following on the heels of the grand jury's report, Florida elected a new Republican governor Rick Scott in November 2010 who declared that ethics and integrity are "essential to maintaining the public trust." He ordered his staff to take a close look at the grand jury's recommendations. A year later, November 2011, no recommendations have been implemented. Scott's office, a spokesman declared, determined that all the suggestions would require legislation, although no explanation has been put forward why Scott has not pushed for lawmakers to pass an ethics bill (Bender 2011).

The grand jury recommendations are meritorious and, if adopted, would move Florida further along the path of statewide ethics reform. But even more reform is needed. Indeed, the Florida Commission on Ethics put forward legislative recommendations in 2011 that would make the agency more effective. The commission seeks "limited authority to investigate situations without having to receive a complaint"; an increase in the range of penalties that could be assessed, including increasing the maximum civil penalty from $10,00 to $100,000; a prohibition to prevent a public official who has a conflict of interest from using staff members to influence the outcome of a situation; and enactment of an ethical standard that addresses action that gives the appearance of impropriety (State of Florida Commission on Ethics 2011).

The Florida Commission on Ethics is the state's ethical watchdog, but it is all too often regarded as "toothless" because of its limited ability to investigate alleged violations of ethics laws and its complete inability to sanction violators. The commission can only recommend penalties to the presiding authority who has the final say in the action taken or not taken.

Is significant ethics reform in Florida still in waiting? So it would seem.

Illinois: Race to the Top or Bottom?

Illinois, reeling from the double whammy of the past two governors—George Ryan and Rod Blagojevich, both driven from office—has been battered by ethical scandals and official misdeeds for many years. The result: a steady decline of public trust and confidence in state government. Nonetheless, efforts to strengthen the ethics infrastructure were launched more than a decade ago when the legislature passed and Governor Jim Edgar signed into law the State Gift Ban Act of 1998. The act banned the giving and receiving of gifts to and by officials and employees of all government entities in Illinois. It also (1) contained significant political campaign disclosure requirements for identifying who gives how much to whom; (2) required all local government entities to pass "gift ban" ordinances consistent with state law; and (3) called for the establishment of seven separate statewide ethics commissions. Two years after its passage, following much maneuvering and considerable legal challenge, Will County circuit judge Thomas Ewert threw out the law, ruling it was so vague and filled with so many exemptions that it was unenforceable. Thus, Illinois became lawless to prevent abuses in gifts given to and received by public officials.

Gift bans attempt to limit the influence of interested parties, including lobbyists, on decisions of public officials. Some "bans" set specific limits and circumstances, while others are "zero tolerance" bans; that is, no gifts are allowed under any circumstances.

This condition was finally brought to an end with the 2002 election of the reform-minded Democratic governor of Illinois, Rod Blagojevich. (Yes, you read that correctly.) Blagojevich issued Executive Order 3 in January 2003 to create the Office of Inspector General (OIG). The OIG's power and duties were expanded to include jurisdiction over all state agencies, with the exception of the attorney general, the secretary of state, the comptroller, and the treasurer. As an independent agency reporting directly to the governor, the OIG has subpoena power and is authorized to investigate complaints of fraud, abuse, or misconduct. When OIG reports a finding of wrongdoing, disciplinary action is then recommended to the governor and the appropriate agency director. If the recommended disciplinary action is not taken, the OIG can forward the finding to the newly established Executive Ethics Commission for a ruling.

Illinois took another step in strengthening its ethics infrastructure on December 9, 2003, when the legislature enacted and the governor signed into law the State Officials and Employees Ethics Act (Public Act 93–0617). The law provides for both civil and criminal penalties with fines of up to $10,000 and/or one year in prison for some violations. Key provisions of this legislation include the following.

- The establishment of the Executive Ethics Commission, a body of nine commissioners appointed by the state constitutional officers and the governor. The commission receives complaints, conducts administrative hearings, prepares and publishes guides regarding the ethics laws, issues subpoenas, and makes rulings and recommendations in disciplinary cases. The commission has jurisdiction over the employees and officers of the executive branch of government (Illinois Attorney General 2010).
- Legislators and constitutional officers are forbidden from using public money to pay for billboards, bumper stickers, and other paraphernalia bearing their name or image. These practices have been widely used by public officeholders to gain greater name recognition.
- State employees are banned for one year after leaving the state payroll from taking jobs with companies about which they made regulatory, licensing, or contracting decisions.

Illinois Secretary of State Paul T. Powell (1902–1970) was an undefeated politician for 42 years who never earned more than $30,00 a year. Yet, upon his death, he left an estate worth more than $2 million ($11–12 million in 2011 dollars), including $800,000 ($4.6 million in 2011 dollars) of it in bills packed into shoeboxes, briefcases, and strongboxes in the closet of his hotel suite in Springfield. His philosophy of a successful politician: "There's only one thing worse than a defeated politician, and that's a broke one" (*Time*, 1971).

- State workers are prohibited from soliciting political contributions on state property and from performing political work—another widespread abuse in years past.

- Units of local government—including park districts, municipalities, special purpose districts, school districts, and community colleges—are required to adopt an ordinance or resolution that is no less restrictive than the act.
- Unpaid advisers to the governor and other state officials must file economic disclosure statements if they act on behalf of the officials.
- Perks such as golf outings and tennis matches paid for by lobbyist are not permitted, but lobbyists may spend up to $75 per day per official for drink and food, provided they are consumed on the premises from which they were purchased, prepared, or catered.
- Ethics training for all state employees and constitutional officers is required annually.
- Lobbyists are required to register with the secretary of state, and the law broadened the definition of a lobbyist.

Have these provisions and others put Illinois on the path to integrity and sound ethics management? So it might seem. Among other things, a 24-hour ethics hotline has been established by the office of the executive inspector general, and more than 3,000 calls have been received. Nearly 1,800 complaints have been received with more than 500 investigated and closed. Eighty-five instances of wrongdoing have been found with recommendations made for disciplinary action. Additionally, the commission helped trained approximately 150,000 state officers and employees on ethics rules in FY 2010.

While these steps suggest that Illinois is in the race to the top of effective ethical reform, the Blagojevich impeachment and his subsequent removal from office sent the state into a tailspin. Pat Quinn moved into the governor's chair on January 30, 2009, and wasted little time in attempting to resolve a "crisis of integrity" by issuing Executive Order No. 1, reconstituting the Illinois Reform Commission (IRC) as an independent advisory body. The IRC was charged with evaluating existing Illinois law and the operational practices of the state from the perspective of ethics in government. Two months later, the IRC put forward a series of reform proposals covering campaign finance, procurement, enforcement, and transparency. Was the race to the top on again? Yes! Has Illinois arrived? No, but . . . the Illinois Executive Ethics Commission (IEEC) was strengthened significantly.

The general assembly enacted legislation in 2010 that "expanded the transparency and oversight of the disciplinary process of State employees who behave unethically on the job" and gave the IEEC (2011b) new "authority to oversee the purchase of goods and services procured by State agencies under the control of the Governor and State universities." State employee investigation reports containing serious, confirmed ethical misbehavior are now made available to the public. And, as of January 26, 2011, 15 such employee investigation reports were on the commission's web site (http://www2.illinois.gov/eec/Pages/default.aspx). In procurement oversight, the commission "appointed Procurement Compliance Monitors for each State agency . . . to ensure that laws, rules and best practices are followed by state employees" (IEEC 2011a, 3).

Ethics management in the state of Illinois is progressing in a manner similar to that of most other states. In all likelihood, it has deterred willful and unwillful acts of wrongdoing by public officials and government employees. However, it is not possible to know how many or what kinds of unethical behavior have been prevented. Nor is it possible to assess the consequences of the online ethics training program. Many training programs in both the private and public sector are people-to-people, hands-on experiences. The approach taken by Illinois is clearly reaching a large number of government managers and workers, but the effectiveness of online training remains unknown at the time of this writing.

Is Illinois in a race to the top or the bottom? You decide.

New York: Endless Pursuit of Ethics Reform?

New York State, as noted earlier, was the first state to adopt an ethics law in 1954 after a series of scandals surfaced involving the bribery of public officials by organized crime. Yet, more than 30 years went by before the state could claim it had an effective law to prevent further abuse. Prompted once more by scandal in which lawmakers placed no-show workers on their payrolls, the state legislature passed a sweeping reform measure—the Ethics in Government Act of 1987 (Rosenson 2005, 99). The act created the New York State Ethics Commission and gave it jurisdiction over officers and employees of the executive branch. The five-member commission was authorized to initiate its own investigations and levy civil fines (not to exceed $10,000)—both powerful tools compared to those of many other states. Other duties of the commission include rendering advisory opinions that interpret and apply the laws; distributing, collecting, and auditing financial disclosure statements; issuing rules and regulations to implement and enforce the Ethics in Government Act; and conducting training.

New ethics reform legislation, the Public Employee Ethics Reform Act (PEERA), was enacted in the spring of 2007. The law was motivated by several high-profile ethical lapses, growing discontent by good governance groups, and the "Sheriff of Wall Street" (as Eliot Spitzer was nicknamed) calling for ethics reform in his 2006 gubernatorial campaign (New York City Bar Association 2010). Among the state officials caught with their hand in the cookie jar was Comptroller Alan Hevesi, who was convicted in 2006 for misuse of state resources, and Senator Efrain Gonzalez, Jr., who was indicted for the theft of over $400,000 of state money. A third high-ranking legislator, Senator Joseph Bruno was under investigation by the FBI in connection with his outside consulting work, eventually indicted and found guilty in 2009 of taking payments from a business executive and failing to disclose a secret financial partnership with the businessman. Governor Spitzer signed PEERA into law on March 27, 2007, less than three months after taking office.

Pay-to-Play

Alan Hevesi, the state comptroller, was the sole trustee for New York's $141 billion pension fund. He pleaded guilty to accepting more than $1 million in travel expenses, sham consulting fees, and campaign contributions from people wanting to invest some of those billions. He is the highest-ranking elected official in New York's history to go to prison for corruption (*New York Times,* 2011a).

For the first time in New York State history, PEERA combined lobbying and ethics laws with monitoring and enforcement responsibilities lodged in the new Commission on Public Integrity (CPI). The CPI is composed of 13 members, seven appointed by the governor (of which only four may be members of the same party). The other six commissioners are also appointed by the governor, with nominations (one each) submitted by the attorney general, the senate president, the assembly speaker, the senate minority leader, and the assembly minority leader. The governor selects the chairman of the CPI.

The CPI's jurisdiction is quite broad, encompassing all statewide elected officials, state officers and state employees, candidates for statewide elected office, lobbyists and the clients of lobbyists, and former lobbyists or clients of lobbyists. The inclusion of "state officer or employee" covers state boards, bureaus, divisions, commissions or councils, and members of public authorities. The 2007 act does not give the CPI authority to monitor and enforce ethics lapses by city or county officials.

PEERA also enlarged the former Legislative Ethics Committee (LEC) and broadened its jurisdiction and authority to monitor lawmakers. The LEC is authorized to issue advisory opinions and adjudicate complaints regarding violation of laws by members and employees of the legislature and candidates for state legislative office. Each of the four legislative leaders appoints one member of the nine-member LEC from among the legislature and one nonlegislative member (New York City Bar Association 2010, 13). The fifth member, a nonlegislator, is appointed jointly by the assembly speaker and the senate majority leader. Somewhat skeptical of the expanded LEC to reign in unethical behavior by legislators, the New York City Bar Association (2010, 13) notes that "in their two decades of existence, the LEC and its predecessor organization have never publicly found a legislator guilty of wrongdoing."

The ethical reform initiatives launched in 2007 were regarded by the then governor Eliot Spitzer and other state leaders as the most sweeping ethics and lobbying changes in state history. Still, the state continues to roil in mishaps and scandal. Responding to legislative misdeeds and Governor Spitzer's forced resignation on March 12, 2008, following the disclosure that he was involved in a sex ring, a *New York Times* editorial declared: "The state has become a national embarrassment, a swamp of intrigue and corruption . . ." (*New York Times* 2009).

Troopergate Intrigue

It was alleged that Governor Eliot Spitzer sought to discredit the Republican Senate majority leader Joseph L. Bruno by ordering state police to conduct surveillance of his travel. The governor wanted to determine if Senator Bruno was using taxpayer funds to engage in political activities. Several investigations followed regarding Governor Spitzer's "inappropriate" order, including an investigation by the Commission on Public Integrity. The CPI investigation became complicated when allegations surfaced that the then-executive director had improperly shared information about the investigation with the Spitzer administration. Governor Paterson called for the resignation of the entire CPI, which was rejected (New York City Bar Association, 2010).

Let's take a closer look at the work of the Commission on Public Integrity.

Besides the additional responsibilities identified earlier, the former reorganized ethics commission (now the CPI) has grown in staff from approximately 20 to nearly 50, with the larger subunits being the Counsel's Office, Investigations, Program Operations Filings, and Information Technology (NYS Commission on Public Integrity 2010c).

Advisory Opinions

The CPI issues two types of advisory opinions: formal and informal. A formal opinion is issued when a state official requests it in writing. The opinion is binding on both the CPI and the person making the request. Formal opinions are made public, but the name of the requestor is held in confidence. An informal opinion merely advises the person making the request about issues previously decided by the CPI; as such, it is not binding. In 2010, the CPI issued 179 informal advisory opinions and 5 formal opinions.

Investigations and Enforcement

The commission is empowered to begin investigations either upon receipt of a complaint or on its own initiative. In 2010, the commission opened 180 cases and issued 16 Notices of Reasonable Cause (NORCs), public documents issued upon a vote of the commissioners that allege a violation of the law (not a finding of guilt). If at any stage of an investigation prior to the issuance of the notice, the commission determines either that there is no violation or that any potential conflict of interest violation has been rectified, it notifies the complainant and the subject of the complaint and terminates the investigation. The investigation then remains confidential (NYS Commission on Public Integrity 2011).

Lobbying is in full swing in New York State. In 2010, there were 6,659 lobbyists registered with the commission, representing 4,091 clients, compared to 6,624 lobbyists representing 4,145 clients in 2008. During this same period, there were 63 public corporations registered. According to commission reports, $213 million was spent on lobbying in 2010. A Random Audit Program provides another independent and objective evaluation of reports and registration statements filed by lobbyists and their clients; in 2010, the commission conducted 563 audits that produced 22 formal findings regarding potential violations of the lobbying act and 407 informal findings, which are minor errors in documentation or reporting (NYS Commission on Public Integrity 2011).

Troopergate Revisited

In 2008, the Commission on Public Integrity charged three former officials of the Executive Chamber and the former acting superintendent of the State Police with violating the Public Officers Law when they utilized the State Police to create records and gather information and documents regarding Senator Joseph L. Bruno's travel to New York City in May and June 2007. Two officials reached settlements with the commission in 2008. In 2009, the commission assessed a civil penalty of $10,000 against Darren Dopp, former communications director to then-Governor Eliot Spitzer, in regard to his involvement in the matter (NYS Commission on Public Integrity, 2010b).

Education and Training

In 2010, the commission conducted 122 training sessions for 6,836 employees; offered continuing legal education (CLE) credits to 700 individuals; and ran 179 lobbyist training sessions for 629 clients and lobbyists. An interactive online "Ethics Overview" became available in January 2009 to assist agencies unable to take advantage of the other training opportunities offered (for example, a state facility that operates on 24/7 basis). A total of 214 individuals took the online course in 2010. Another online program, "Lobbying Act Training & Education" (LATE), was launched to educate participants on common mistakes made by new filers. In 2010, 119 individuals completed the online LATE course (NYS Commission on Public Integrity 2011).

Ethics reform in New York remains much debated, with calls for further measure to strengthen the laws already in place. Indeed, Governor Andrew M. Cuomo in his 2011 State of the State message asserted:

> We have to transform the ethical environment and we have to clean up Albany. We all have seen the headlines, headline after headline, month after month, year after year with no change. . . . We will propose a clean up Albany plan with real reform. This is not going to be a situation where the people of the state will have suffered for years and lost trust and now we're going to give them a watered down or half-baked ethics reform bill. They're going to have real ethics reform. We're going to end pay to play. We're going to have full disclosure of outside income. We're going to have an independent monitor. (Cuomo 2011)

A headline in the June 4, 2011, issue of the *New York Times* read: "Cuomo and Legislators Reach Deal on Ethics Overhaul." The agreement would force legislators who have law practices to disclose the names of clients who have business before the state; allow prosecutors to seek to strip pensions from future elected officials convicted of felonies; and allow officials appointed by a governor a role in overseeing legislative compliance with ethics laws (Confessore and Kaplan 2011).

A headline in the August 15, 2011, issue of the *Wall Street Journal* read: "NY Governor Signs Government Ethics Law." Governor Cuomo hails the new ethics reform law as "an aggressive new approach to returning integrity to the halls of our Capitol. It provides for much-needed disclosure of outside income by lawmakers, creates an independent monitor to investigate corruption, and issues strong new rules for lobbyists." A new 14-member Joint Commission on Public Ethics replaces the Commission on Public Integrity. Six members are to be selected by the governor, with at least three from a different political party. Legislative leaders will select eight members—four Democrats and four Republicans (Associated Press 2011).

Has the pursuit of ethics reform in New York State reached an end? Or is this a new beginning? You decide.

Summing Up

This chapter showhighlights the diverse approaches taken by states to deter wrongdoing and encourage ethical behavior. What was said twenty years ago by Elder Witt (1992, 343) about the absence of uniformity across the American states in their ethics infrastructure might well be echoed in 2012. "What has emerged," Witt said then (1992, 343), "is not a clear system of rules, but an inconsistent and confusing patchwork." The Better Government Association uses similar language in asserting that "states have taken a patchwork approach towards promoting integrity which indicates a lack of the proper amount of concern regarding integrity and corruption" (2002, 5).

Ethics management is more than laws, rules, and regulations and the processing of ethics complaints. Obeying the law and following ethics regulations may keep state officials and employees out of legal difficulty, but abiding by the law is not sufficient to ensure ethical governance. Many states have ethics statutes, commissions with investigatory powers, and training programs, but there is little evidence that states employ the full complement of ethics management tools available to them.

Ethics Management Skill Building

Practicum 7.1. Follow the Law or Your Conscience?[2]

On July 24, 2011, it became legal for gay and lesbian couples in New York State to receive marriage licenses. Assume you are an elected town clerk with responsibility to issue same sex marriage licenses but feel strongly from a religious perspective that same sex marriages are immoral. When asked by a friend how you feel about same sex marriage, you say "Based on my Christian faith and my belief in God and what the Bible teaches, I cannot and I don't support gay lifestyles." You add: "I may have to resign because protections were not provided for us to be able to practice our freedom of religion in our jobs."

Questions

1. Do you have an obligation as a public official/civil servant to issue the licenses? Or, does this violate your conscience to the point that you refuse to do it?

2. Should you plead for an exemption given your religious views?
3. Should you look for another job?
4. What should you do?

Practicum 7.2. Getting a Code Adopted

As a newly arrived senior manager in a large state agency, you are dismayed to find that the agency has never adopted a code of ethics or considered requiring employees to sign an oath stating something like: "I do solemnly swear that I will support the Constitution of the United States and the Constitution of the State of Linconland, faithfully discharge the duties of my office, and abide by and adhere to the provisions of the agency's Code of Ethics. So help me God."

Convinced that codes and oaths contribute to ethical workplaces, you appoint a committee drawn from many different departments to draft a code and an oath for your agency. Six months later, the committee chair reports that the committee is hopelessly deadlocked over whether the code should specify appropriate behavior that could be monitored and therefore sanctioned when violations occur, or whether a statement of values and principles might suffice.

Questions

1. What advice would you offer the committee chair? Would you send him back to the committee to try once more? Would you disband the committee and start anew? Would you appear before the committee and attempt to persuade them to adopt an enforceable code and a stringent oath? A values statement? Neither?
2. What arguments would you put forward for the adoption of an enforceable code and oath? A values statement?
3. What course of action would produce the best outcome?

Notes

1. This section draws in part on material in Menzel (1996a).
2. Based on Kaplan (2011).

8

Federal Ethics Management

*In framing a government which is to be administered by men over men
. . . you must first enable the government to control the governed; and
in the next place oblige it to control itself.*

—James Madison, *The Federalist #51*

The federal government's ethics management approach can be described as
a patchwork of laws, rules, regulations, and agencies that, in a Byzantine
manner, define the government's effort to discourage unethical behavior and
encourage ethical behavior. All too often, the discourage-and-deter side is emphasized, with far less attention given to the encourage-and-inspire side. The
result is a spate of laws and statutes with accompanying rules and regulations
that prescribe and proscribe acceptable behaviors and what might happen to
those who dare, wittingly or unwittingly, to cross over the "do not do" line.
The federal effort puts the accent on "gotcha" ethics.

This chapter surveys legislative, judicial, and administrative measures
taken by the U.S. government to promote ethics and integrity in governance.
And, where possible, an assessment is offered about how well or poorly these
efforts have fared. We begin with a look at ethics laws.

Federal Ethics Laws

A variety of statutes govern the conduct of federal employees, with the oldest
one—dating from the Civil War era—aimed at curbing abuses in government
procurement. A 2008 compilation (95 pages) of federal ethics laws by the
U.S. Office of Government Ethics lists laws dealing with conflicts of interest, procurement and contracting, gifts and travel, employment, government
property and information, taxes, and political activities. A variety of executive
branch agencies, including the Executive Office of the President, the U.S.
Department of Justice, the Inspectors General, the Merit Systems Protection
Board, the Office of Special Counsel, the General Services Administration,
the Office of Personnel Management, the Federal Elections Commission, and

the General Accountability Office, have ethics responsibilities. Complex? Yes. Confusing? Yes.

The two most significant federal statutes are the Ethics in Government Act of 1978 and the Ethics Reform Act of 1989. The 1978 act followed on the heels of the Watergate crisis of the early 1970s. This legislation established the U.S. Office of Government Ethics within the Office of Personnel Management and "charged it with providing overall leadership and direction for the ethics program within the executive branch" (Gilman 1995a). The 1978 act also "established a comprehensive public financial disclosure system for all three branches" of the federal government (Gilman 1995a). Additionally, this legislation authorized the president to appoint an independent special prosecutor to investigate high-profile cases. Do you recall Special Prosecutor Ken Starr and the Clinton/Lewinsky scandal?

> "The Ethics in Government Act is 32 years old and is one of the few happy results of the Watergate scandal. History teaches us of the periodic eruption of bad government and has lessons for us. I am well aware that many find the law unduly detailed and tedious, but the Government is better for it. It would be easier by far to fill vacancies, to contract, and to run departments of government as little fiefdoms as they sometimes were earlier in our history. But it would not be easier to govern ethically."
> —Robert I. Cusick (2010),
> Director, U.S. Office of Government Ethics

The Ethics Reform Act of 1989 expanded previous legislation in several areas. Post-employment restrictions were applied to members of Congress and top congressional staff. Moreover, the public financial disclosure system was strengthened by "authorizing all three branches of government to implement a system of confidential financial reporting" (Gilman 1995a). The prohibition on solicitation and acceptance of gifts was expanded to include all three branches. Other provisions dealt with limitations on outside earned income and compensation received for service as an officer or board member of an association or corporation. Further, the 1989 act placed restrictions on the compensation that a federal official might receive for teaching without prior notification and approval of the appropriate ethics office.

Other federal legislation that should be noted is the Office of Government Ethics Reauthorization Act of 1988, the Whistleblower Protection Act of 1989, and the Lobbying Disclosure Act of 1995. The Lobbying Disclosure Act (P.L. 104–65) was signed into law by President Bill Clinton on December 19, 1995, and took effect January 1, 1996. It expanded the definition of who a lobbyist is, thereby greatly "increasing the number of registered lobbyists and the amount of information they must disclose" (Tenebaum 2002). Failure to comply with the act can result in a civil fine of up to $50,000.

The Whistleblower Protection Act of 1989 established the Office of Special Counsel (OSC) as an independent agency within the executive branch to receive complaints and "safeguard the merit system by protecting federal employees and applicants from prohibited personnel practices, especially reprisal for whistleblowing" (U.S. Office of Special Counsel 2010). The OSC is a small agency with 106 employees who are primarily personnel management specialists, investigators, and attorneys. The original version of the act was amended in 1994 with the passage of Public Law 103–424, which expanded the coverage to some government corporations and employees in the U.S. Department of Veterans Affairs.

Some critics point out that while the U.S. whistleblowing regulatory system is a positive development, there is still much room for improvement. The current approach, according to Sheryl Groeneweg (2001), is based heavily on how much money is saved by blowing the whistle on misconduct, fraud, or abuse of authority. She asserts that the U.S. system is reactive, not proactive, and therefore puts the whistleblower's career in a precarious situation. Most important, "at its core, the U.S. model displays the failure to focus on the spirit of whistleblower protections" (15). Roberta Ann Johnson (2003, 21), writing in *Whistleblowing: When It Works—and Why,* adds: "Studies of whistleblower protection suggest that the protection offered is far from perfect."

The Honest Leadership and Open Government Act of 2007 is, at this writing, the most recently enacted federal legislation concerning Congress and lobbyists. It attempts to slow the revolving door that enables former members of the Congress and top staff members to use their knowledge and connections to lobby their colleagues and federal agencies. The Jack Abramoff Indian lobbying scandal, along with several other high-profile cases (including one involving the former deputy secretary of the Department of the Interior Steven Griles, who pleaded guilty in 2007 to obstruction of justice in the Senate investigation of the Abramoff scandal), triggered the legislation. The lobbying bans, while regarded by many as a step in the right direction, are viewed by some legal experts as being too lenient. University of Minnesota law professor and former White House chief ethics lawyer Richard W. Painter (2009, 150) notes: "A former member usually has a lot of influence with former colleagues for well beyond two years. A better rule might bar former members of the House or Senate from lobbying back to Congress for a period equivalent to their time in office . . . up to a maximum perhaps of five or seven years."

Honest Leadership and Open Government Act of 2007

On September 14, 2007, President George W. Bush signed S. 1, the Honest Leadership and Open Government Act of 2007 (P.L. 110–81), into law. The act amended the Lobbying Disclosure Act of 1995 to provide, among other changes to federal law and House and Senate rules, additional and more frequent disclosures of lobbying contacts and activities. Specifically, the act tightened revolving-door rules by prohibiting

- retiring senators from directly lobbying members or employees of either House for a period of two years; retiring members of the House are banned from lobbying for one year;
- senior Senate staff and Senate officers from lobbying contacts with the entire Senate for one year, instead of just their former employing office;
- senior House staff from lobbying their former office or committee for one year after they leave House employment (Straus, 2008).

Honest Services Fraud

Federal prosecutors have been aggressive over the past 15 years in their pursuit of government officials—federal, state, local—and corporate executives who have defrauded the public. When members of Congress rewrote mail and wire fraud laws in 1988, they included 28 words that made it illegal to "deprive another of the intangible right of honest services" (Wikipedia 2011a). In a *San Diego Union-Tribune* article, Assistant U.S. Attorney Shane Harrigan described the law (18 U.S.C. § 1346) as an "extremely effective tool to fight public corruption," adding, "The essence of public corruption is that public officials deprive people in the community of their honest efforts to represent them. That's theft of honest services and that's what the statute covers" (Thornton 2006). Bribery, kickbacks, and extortion are often difficult to prove. In other words, it is much easier to prove to a jury that honest services fraud has occurred. Critics contend it "is a way for prosecutors to convert almost any kind of behavior into a felony" (Thornton 2006). Moreover, it is asserted that the language is vague and interpreted inconsistently across cases.

Honest services fraud was among the charges brought against Jeffrey K. Skilling, chief executive of Enron just prior to its 2001 collapse, and Conrad M. Black, a newspaper executive accused of defrauding his media company. Both were convicted and appealed their cases to the U.S. Supreme Court (for information on Skilling, see *Skilling v. United States,* 130 S. Ct. 2896 [2010]). In June 2010, the court—in a unanimous decision—called the broad interpretation of the law unconstitutionally vague (Liptak 2010). The justices did not strike down the law entirely; rather, the majority said the law must be limited to the offenses of bribes and kickbacks. The court remanded both Skilling's and Black's convictions to the lower court for reconsideration.

Convicted of Honest Services Fraud

- Jack Abramoff—Washington, DC, lobbyist
- Joseph L. Bruno—New York state senator (R)
- Wayne R. Bryant—New Jersey state senator (D)
- Randy "Duke" Cunningham—congressman (R) from San Diego, CA
- William Jefferson—congressman (D) from New Orleans, LA
- Kevin Geddings—North Carolina lottery commissioner
- Mary McCarty—Palm Beach, Florida, county commissioner
- Bob Ney—congressman (R) from Ohio
- Don Siegelman—governor (D) of Alabama

The Supreme Court's decision is widely viewed as narrowing if not eviscerating the Honest Services Fraud law. Elizabeth R. Sheyn, law clerk in the U.S. Court of Appeals for the Sixth Circuit, writes: "The Supreme Court's recent decision in Skilling greatly narrowed the scope of the honest-services statute, which criminalizes schemes or artifices designed to deprive another of the intangible right of honest services, by limiting the statute's application to schemes to defraud involving bribes or kickbacks" (Sheyn 2011).

The initial reaction from Congress was swift. Senate Judiciary Committee chairman Patrick Leahy (D-Vermont) introduced the Honest Services Restoration Act on September 28, 2010. The aim of the bill was to restore the scope of the statute to cover improper, undisclosed self-dealing (Aguilar 2010). The Leahy bill died when the 111th Congress (2008–10) closed.

The U.S. Office of Government Ethics

The Office of Government Ethics Reauthorization Act of 1998 is significant because it removed the Office of Government Ethics (OGE) from the Office of Personnel Management and established it as a separate executive agency. OGE is responsible "for promulgating and maintaining enforceable standards of ethical conduct for nearly 4 million civilian employees and military members in over 130 Executive Branch agencies" (U.S. OGE 2010).

The director is appointed to a five-year term by the president with the consent of the Senate. The office has no investigatory powers and does not serve the legislative or judicial branches of government. OGE has three primary functions: (1) to manage the public financial disclosure reporting system for presidential appointees confirmed by the Senate and designated agency ethics officials, (2) to conduct program reviews of "headquarters and regional offices to determine whether an agency has an effective ethics program tailored to its mission," and (3) to "develop and provide ethics training courses and materials for executive branch departments and agencies" (U.S. OGE n.d.a) (see Exhibit 8.1).

Each executive agency has a designated agency ethics official (DAEO) and an alternate deputy tasked with supporting the agency's ethics program and with whom OGE primarily deals. There are 230 DAEOs who provide guidance on how to interpret and comply with conflict-of-interest regulations, standards-of-conduct regulations, and financial disclosure policies and procedures. Pamela A. Gibson (2009, 105) examined the moral reasoning of DAEOs and found that they engage in conventional reasoning which "mirrors and supports the legalistic practice of public administration expected at the national level." In other words, federal ethics officials in the executive branch have a law-and-order orientation toward resolving ethical issues.

As might be surmised, knowing how to stay out of trouble in the executive branch of the U.S. government has become a major challenge given the numerous laws, rules, and regulations regarding unacceptable practices and behaviors. Thus, a primary mission of the OGE is to help federal employees comply with those rules and regulations so that they can avoid unintentional ethical lapses.

The development of a clear set of ethical standards for officers and employees of the executive branch was initiated in January 1989, when President George H.W. Bush issued Executive Order (E.O.) 12668. This order established the Commission on Federal Ethics Law Reform, which, in turn, produced a report titled "To Serve with Honor." The report made 27 recommendations, including one that a "1965 executive order prescribing the standards of conduct be revised and that the Office of Government Ethics be directed to consolidate all executive branch standards of conduct in a single set of regulations" (Gilman 1995a). A second order on the subject, Executive Order 12674 (April 12, 1989—see Exhibit 8.2), set forth 14 principles of ethical conduct for government officers and employees and directed the Office of Government Ethics to "promulgate a single, comprehensive, and clear set of executive branch standards of conduct that shall be objective, reasonable and enforceable" (Gilman 1995a). In August 1992, the OGE issued a final rule promulgating standards of conduct for executive branch employees, effective February 3, 1993.

The ethics infrastructure in place in the executive branch of United States government is built on rules, regulations, enforcement, education, and training. This is both good news and bad news. Rule-driven ethics management, with its legal compliance overtones, is regarded by many ethicists as reactive and

---

Exhibit 8.1
Who Is Responsible for Investigating the
Alleged Misconduct of Federal Employees?

The inspector general of the department or agency involved and, when necessary, the Federal Bureau of Investigation of the Department of Justice. The sixty-four inspectors general (IG) in the executive branch of the U.S. government conduct the majority of investigations into government wrongdoing. In addition they also coordinate investigations with their regular financial and management audits of federal agencies and programs. The coordinating body for the inspectors general is the President's Council on Integrity and Efficiency (PCIE), of which the Office of Government Ethics is a member.

Source: U.S. Office of Government Ethics, n.d.b.

---

punitive—a minimalist approach. Moreover, it can cause major disruptions in an agency. Consider the National Institutes of Health initiatives offered by the Director Elias A. Zerhouni in early 2005 to force NIH staff to divest their holdings in drug and biotechnology companies. Six thousand employees among the agency's 18,000 would have been affected had the director not backed off from the rules in August 2005. Threats of high-level defections and 1,300 mostly critical comments by employees about the proposed rules motivated the director to loosen the conflict-of-interest rules (Connolly 2005). Rules are inescapable, but a more comprehensive and inclusive approach requires officials to lead with integrity and find avenues to motivate public service employees and professionals "to serve with honor," as the 1989 President's Commission on Federal Ethics Law Reform report reads.

Presidents

Do the "Principles of Ethical Conduct for Government Officers and Employees" apply to presidents? Surely, one might think. But life in the White House can be more challenging than one might suppose. Consider President Lyndon B. Johnson (LBJ; 1963–1968) and the U.S. involvement in the Vietnam War. The military buildup of troops and equipment in Vietnam proceeded steadily in the 1960s, despite repeated claims by the president that the United States did not want to escalate the conflict. As Daniel Ellsberg, a member of the

Exhibit 8.2
Principles of Ethical Conduct for
Government Officers and Employees

By virtue of the authority vested in me as President by the Constitution and the laws of the United States of America, and in order to establish fair and exacting standards of ethical conduct for all executive branch employees, it is hereby ordered as follows:

Part I. Principles of Ethical Conduct

Section 101. Principles of Ethical Conduct. To ensure that every citizen can have complete confidence in the integrity of the Federal Government, each Federal employee shall respect and adhere to the fundamental principles of ethical service as implemented in regulations promulgated under sections 201 and 301 of this order:

(a) Public service is a public trust, requiring employees to place loyalty to the Constitution, the laws, and ethical principles above private gain.

(b) Employees shall not hold financial interests that conflict with the conscientious performance of duty.

(c) Employees shall not engage in financial transactions using non-public Government information or allow the improper use of such information to further any private interest.

(d) An employee shall not, except pursuant to such reasonable exceptions as are provided by regulation, solicit or accept any gift or other item of monetary value from any person or entity seeking official action from, doing business with, or conducting activities regulated by the employee's agency, or whose interests may be substantially affected by the performance or nonperformance of the employee's duties.

(e) Employees shall put forth honest effort in the performance of their duties.

(f) Employees shall make no unauthorized commitments or promises of any kind purporting to bind the Government.

(g) Employees shall not use public office for private gain.

(continued)

Exhibit 8.2 *(continued)*

(h)   Employees shall act impartially and not give preferential treat-
      ment to any private organization or individual.
(i)   Employees shall protect and conserve Federal property and shall
      not use it for other than authorized activities.
(j)   Employees shall not engage in outside employment or activities,
      including seeking or negotiating for employment, that conflict
      with official Government duties and responsibilities.
(k)   Employees shall disclose waste, fraud, abuse, and corruption to
      appropriate authorities.
(l)   Employees shall satisfy in good faith their obligations as citizens,
      including all just financial obligations, especially those such as
      Federal, State, or local taxes that are imposed by law.
(m)   Employees shall adhere to all laws and regulations that provide
      equal opportunity for all Americans regardless of race, color,
      religion, sex, national origin, age, or handicap.
(n)   Employees shall endeavor to avoid any actions creating the ap-
      pearance that they are violating the law or the ethical standards
      promulgated pursuant to this order.

   Source: Executive Order 12674 of April 12, 1989 (as modified by
E.O. 12731).

State Department who gained notoriety when he leaked the Pentagon papers
to the *Washington Post,* recalls: "On election day 1964, I spent the day with an
interagency working group to expand the war—contrary to Lyndon Johnson's
assertion that the administration seeks no wider war" (Ellsberg 2004). Did
President Johnson lie to the American public?

President John F. Kennedy made ethics a major policy theme during his
administration. An ethics czar was appointed to work with the head of the
Civil Service Commission. Executive Order 10939, issued May 5, 1961,
established conflict-of-interest standards for presidential nominees and
appointees, including members of the White House staff.

LBJ's successor, President Richard M. Nixon, had a different set of problems that tainted his presidency. Nixon engaged in a conspiracy to cover up

a trail of misdeeds and criminal wrongdoing when political operatives broke into the Democratic headquarters at the Watergate Hotel in 1972. Two years later, in August 1974, President Nixon resigned from office rather than face impeachment by the House of Representatives.

Fast-forward to the 1980s. President Ronald Reagan found himself in a difficult position as his administration attempted to aid Contra rebels in Nicaragua who were attempting to oust the Socialist-led government. Reagan's national security adviser, John Poindexter, and Lieutenant Colonel Oliver P. North took it upon themselves to sell arms to Iran to secure money to support the Contra rebels—a clear violation of law. Did President Reagan know about this transaction? He claims he did not. The Iran-Contra controversy certainly raised the possibility that President Reagan lied.

President Bill Clinton (1992–2000) took the ethical high ground immediately upon taking office by requiring senior members of his administration to take a "five-year" pledge that they would not represent private parties in dealing with the government after leaving office. Executive Order 12834, "Ethics Commitments by Executive Branch Personnel," President Clinton hoped, would put an end to the perception that the federal government was "hostage to special interests" (Gilman 1995b). Alas, a few years later, the president found himself in a legal and political morass of his own making when it became known that he had a sexual tryst with a young White House intern, Monica Lewinsky. The scandal grew into a political firestorm when President Clinton testified under oath that he did not have sex with Ms. Lewinsky. Many members of Congress concluded that the President lied. Consequently, the Republican-controlled House proceeded to impeach President Clinton. The Senate, however, did not convict him—that is, the U.S. Senate did not vote to remove him from office. Did President Clinton lie? So it would seem. Was lying under oath sufficient grounds for removal from office? No. Not surprisingly, the 2000 presidential campaign of George W. Bush promised to restore dignity to the office of the President.

But President Bush had his share of ethical issues as well. The list includes the invasion and occupation of Iraq, stem cell research, privacy rights, government secrecy, domestic spying by the National Security Agency without court approval, and charges that his administration sought political revenge by leaking information that revealed the name of CIA undercover agent Valerie Plume. The administration's contention that Saddam Hussein possessed weapons of mass destruction, which was the rationale for the invasion of Iraq, turned out to be untrue. Nor was a credible link found to exist between Iraq and the terrorists attacks of September 11, 2001. Many citizens have asked, "Did President Bush lie to the American public?"

The investigation into who leaked information about CIA agent Plume resulted in the indictment in 2005 of I. Lewis "Scooter" Libby, Vice President Cheney's former chief of staff, and threatened to bring down Karl Rove, President Bush's chief political adviser. Later that year, President Bush ordered mandatory ethics training for all White House staff. On June 13, 2006, it was announced that special prosecutor Patrick J. Fitzgerald would not bring charges against Rove. Scooter Libby, however, was not as fortunate. He was tried and found guilty of perjury and obstruction of justice and sentenced to 30 months in prison for stifling a CIA leak investigation. In July 2007, however, before Libby was to be imprisoned, President Bush commuted his sentence, asserting that the length of the sentence was excessive.

A *pardon* is a forgiveness of an offense or crime and the punishment associated with it. A *commutation* is a waiver or lessening of a punishment without a forgiveness of the crime or punishment. Pardons and commutations are granted by heads of state (presidents and governors in the United States).

President Bush, his critics assert, turned the ethics management clock in the federal government backward, as evidenced by appointments of individuals to high-ranking positions who used their office to advance the president's political agenda over the objections of senior managers. One example can be found in a 2005 General Accountability Office report concerning a decision made by top officials in the Food and Drug Administration (FDA). The FDA officials in question rejected an application to allow over-the-counter sales of morning-after birth control pills, ignoring contrary recommendations by both an independent advisory committee and the agency's own scientific review staff (Harris 2005). Similar intervention by top Department of Justice officials is reported to have taken place in the decision to reject senior staffers' advice on possible Voting Rights Act violations. The redistricting of congressional districts in Texas in the early 2000s, spearheaded by house majority leader Tom DeLay (R), clearly diluted minority voting rights.

President Obama has also encountered strong ethical headwinds. As a candidate, he pledged to clean up the special influence of lobbyists; on his first day in office, he issued Executive Order 13490, which imposed strict rules on lobbyists entering government positions and appointees leaving government for lobbying positions. Two days later, President Obama faced a skeptical public as he sought an "exception" for William Lynn's appointment as Deputy Secretary of Defense. Mr. Lynn previously served as a lobbyist for defense industry giant Raytheon.

President Obama's Ethics Guidelines

"Transparency and the rule of law will be the touchstones of this presidency. . . . We need to close the revolving door that lets lobbyists come into government freely and lets them use their time in public service as a way to promote their own interests over the interests of the American people when they leave" (Tapper 2009).

No president is above the law, but these cases point to the fine line between telling the truth and knowing when to do so is or is not in the public interest. Americans expect the president to do both.

Congress

While federal ethics statutes have steadily expanded the coverage of the law over the past several decades, Congress has also found it necessary to ensure that their members and top staff are engaged in appropriate behavior. As noted in Chapter 2, the Founding Fathers designed a system of government that separated and divided power among institutions and officeholders. Horizontally, the separation of powers between U.S. Congress, the president, and the judiciary sought to prevent the concentration of power. Similarly, the division of power between the central government and the states created multiple power centers. The Founding Fathers understood that men and women of ambition would seek the power of public office and, unless checked in some manner, might threaten the well-being of the republic. "Ambition must be made to counteract ambition," wrote James Madison in *The Federalist* #51.

House of Representatives

Over time, it has become evident that measures other than checks and balances would be needed to prevent the misuse and/or abuse of public power. For example, Congress has found it necessary to constrain the unacceptable behavior of its own members. The Committee on Standards of Official Conduct, a 10-member bipartisan committee, is the ethics enforcer of the House of Representatives. Complaints brought to the committee are investigated if a majority finds probable cause to do so. In the event of a 5–5 Republican-Democrat deadlock, investigations automatically resume in 45 days. In January 2005, the Republican-controlled House, by a vote of 220 to 195, changed this provision so that in the event of a deadlock, ethics investigations are dismissed. The politics behind this change had to do with the behavior of the House majority leader, Representative Tom DeLay (R-Texas), who was admonished three times in 2004 for egregious behavior. By changing this deadlock rule, Republicans claimed that the House would be able to protect the members from what could be purely partisan attacks.

Democrats strongly disagreed, arguing that the change would make the Ethics Committee impotent. By the end of April, after new revelations surfaced about Mr. DeLay's international travel supported by a lobbyist and the Democrats' vocal resistance, Speaker of the House J. Dennis Hastert of Illinois relented. By a vote of 406 to 20, the House approved a resolution that restored the rules that had been in place at the beginning of the year.

The House disciplinary procedures for dealing with an alleged violation of the ethics rules are shown in Exhibit 8.3. Several highly visible members of the House, both Democrats and Republicans, have been investigated and punished over the years (see Exhibit 8.4). They include Newt Gingrich, Republican Speaker of the House (1994–1997), and Representative James C. Wright Jr., a Democrat from Texas who resigned in 1989 over improper lobbying on behalf of a constituent. An earlier case involved the flamboyant Democratic representative from New York, Adam Clayton Powell, Jr., who was fined $25,000 and excluded from his seat following his reelection to the 91st Congress in 1967. He appealed the House's action to the U.S. Supreme Court, which ruled that his exclusion was unconstitutional. Powerful Chicago Democratic congressman Dan Rostenkowski used his office for many years to secure political favors. In 1994, he was indicted for corruption and lost his bid for reelection. He later pleaded guilty to mail fraud and was sentenced to 17 months in federal prison. Rostenkowski served 15 months before President Bill Clinton pardoned him in 2000.

The House of Representatives was stunned in 2005 when a popular senior California Republican, Randy Cunningham, a decorated combat pilot in Vietnam, resigned his seat after admitting that he received more than $2 million in money and favorable considerations from a defense contractor. In November 2003, for example, the contractor MZM purchased Mr. Cunningham's Del Mar house for $1,675,000, then put it back on the market for the same price, where it sat for nearly nine months until it sold for $975,000—a nifty $700,000 loss, or gain, depending on your point of view. Representative Cunningham sat on the House Defense Appropriations Subcommittee. In December 2005, on the heels of Cunningham's resignation, Speaker of the House Hastert proposed that lawmakers receive ethics training.

Ethics Reform

Much criticism has been directed at Congress's seeming inability to ensure that its members behave ethically. Ethics lapses and issues in recent years

Exhibit 8.3
U.S. House of Representatives
Procedures for Handling an Ethics Complaint

Step 1. A complaint is filed in writing and submitted to the Committee on Standards of Official Conduct.

Step 2. The committee chairman and ranking minority member have fourteen days to determine if the complaint meets rules that define a complaint.

Step 3. If the complaint is deemed legitimate by the chair and ranking minority member, the full committee must decide to either investigate or drop the case.

Step 4. Investigations are carried out by subcommittees that can lead to a sanction hearing to determine the level of punishment, if any. The possible sanctions include:

- expulsion
- censure
- reprimand
- fine
- limitations of rights or privileges, or
- other as determined by the committee such as letters of reproval.

Source: U.S. House of Representatives, 2008.

have received considerable attention. For instance, there was the involvement of Ohio Republican Bob Ney in the Jack Abramoff scandal. Ney pleaded guilty to conspiracy to defraud the U.S. government and served 17 months in a federal penitentiary. And you might recall William Jefferson, a Democratic congressman from Louisiana, who found himself in deep trouble after the FBI discovered $90,000 in his freezer. In all honesty, however, the clock on congressional ethics violations began ticking a long time ago. As Mark Twain (1897) once put it, "It could probably be shown by facts and figures that there is no distinctly native American criminal class except Congress."

Exhibit 8.4
House Censures and Reprimands

A censure is a more serious punishment than a reprimand. Twenty-three members have been censured in House history and nine have been reprimanded. Examples include:

Censures

December 2, 2010   Charles Rangel of New York for violating House gift rules.

July 20, 1983   Gerry E. Studds of Massachusetts for sexual misconduct with a House page.

June 6, 1980   Charles H. Wilson of California for receipt of improper gifts, "ghost" employees, and personal use of campaign funds.

July 31, 1979   Thomas L. Blanton of Texas for unparliamentary language.

Reprimands

September 15, 2009   Joe Wilson of South Carolina for a breach of decorum when President Obama spoke to the Congress.

January 21, 1997   Newt Gingrich of Georgia for allowing a member-affiliated tax-exempt organization to be used for political purposes and providing inaccurate information to the ethics committee.

July 26, 1990   Barney Frank of Massachusetts for using political influence to fix parking tickets and to sway probation officers for a personal friend.

July 31, 1984   George V. Hansen of Idaho for false statements on financial disclosure documents.

Source: New York Times, 2010b.

The House of Representatives won a Democratic majority in 2006. Shortly thereafter, future House speaker Nancy Pelosi spoke out loudly and clearly about Congress's plans to bring an end "to the culture of corruption," stating, "We will drain the swamp." In March 2008, the House established the Office of Congressional Ethics (OCE), a six-person board of directors consisting of private citizens with the authority to investigate alleged wrongdoing and *advise* the House Ethics Committee. The OCE's authority is limited in that it cannot issue subpoenas; nor can it compel witnesses or lawmakers to testify or investigate cases. In April 2009, a *New York Times* editorial asked: "is the House swamp drained yet?" A year later, another editorial declared: "They [OCE] must be doing their job."

The Charlie Rangel Case

The case of Harlem Democrat Charlie Rangel could be considered the tipping point in the short life of the Office of Congressional Ethics. Would the OCE take on such a powerful member of Congress? After all, the 80-year-old Mr. Rangel wielded the gavel on the influential Ways and Means Committee, a much-coveted post that his seniority enabled him to claim. He was first elected to Congress in 1970.

Mr. Rangel's ethical lapses involved his use of rent-stabilized apartments in Manhattan and the misuse of his office to preserve a tax loophole worth half a billion dollars for an oil executive who pledged a donation for an educational center being built in Mr. Rangel's honor (Lipton and Kocieniewski 2010). He was also charged with failing to report or pay taxes on rental income from his beachfront Dominican villa. The House ethics committee concurred with the OCE investigation and set in motion a public trial before an adjudicatory subcommittee. The subcommittee found Representative Rangel guilty of 11 counts of ethical violations. The full committee, with the concurrence of the House by a vote of 333 to 79, censured him. With Mr. Rangel standing in the well of the House before Speaker Nancy Pelosi, she read House Resolution 1737: "Resolved, that, one, Representative Charles B. Rangel of New York be censured." Chastised but not repentant, Mr. Rangel said: "I am confident that when the history of this has been written, people will recognize that the vote for censure was a very, very, very political vote. . . . I did not curse out the speaker. I did not have sex with minors. I did not steal money" (Kocieniewski 2010).

The aggressive staff director and chief counsel of the independent Office of Congressional Ethics, Leo J. Wise, announced on October 16, 2010—only a few weeks before the midterm elections—that he was stepping down to join the U.S. attorney's office in Maryland. That move allowed Wise to avoid a political fight over the future of the OCE should the Republicans recapture the House, and recapture they did. Before the election, "speculation was rampant that if the Republicans took over the House, they would kill the fledgling Office of Congressional Ethics" (Nixon 2011). After all, newly installed Speaker John Boehner had vigorously opposed the creation of the office. Would he move to kill the OCE? No; in fact, he reportedly had no plans to change the office's mandate, mission, or funding. But, as Norman J. Ornstein of the American Enterprise Institute put it: "The question is, how is the Republican leadership going to react when the OCE starts going after its people?" (Nixon 2011).

U.S. Senate

The U.S. Senate has assigned responsibility for ethics investigations to a six-member bipartisan Select Committee on Ethics. A 530-page *Senate Ethics Manual* (2003) guides the deliberations of the Select Committee and provides rules for gifts, conflicts of interest, outside earned income, financial disclosure, political activity, use of the franking privilege (free mail) and Senate facilities, employment practices, and more. The review and investigative process followed by the Senate Select Committee is similar to that followed in the House.

> Senate perks include expenses for traveling to political fundraisers on corporate jets. Senate rules require that the plane's owners are reimbursed at first-class rates, which are considered to be a bargain. Newly elected Senator Barack Obama (D-Illinois) stopped traveling on corporate jets because it created an appearance of wrongdoing (Stolberg 2006).

A four-member majority must vote in support of moving an investigation forward. Letters of admonition are also issued by the Senate Select Committee on Ethics. For example, former Senator Robert G. Torricelli (D-New Jersey) was severely admonished for violating Senate rules for gifts he received. The committee of three Republicans and three Democrats wrote in a three-page letter, stating, in part: "Your actions and failure to act led to violations of Senate Rules (and related statutes) and created at least the appearance of impropriety, and you are hereby severely admonished" (U.S. Senate Select Committee on Ethics 2002). Some critics regarded this punishment as little more than a "slap on the wrist."

Sex, Politics, Ethics: Complicated and Hazardous Mix?

Unlike the House, there has been less effort made by the Senate to more closely monitor and investigate alleged ethical breaches. Does this mean that Senators and their staff are less inclined to fall from a wobbly ethical ladder? Not likely. Consider the case of Nevada Republican Senator John

Ensign and his administrative assistant Douglas Hampton—and Mr. Hampton's wife. The senator had an extra marital affair with, yes, Mr. Hampton's wife, who worked on the senator's last campaign. Mr. Hampton was let go after learning of the affair. Some $96,000 in hush money, it was alleged, was paid to Mr. Hampton by Senator Ensign's parents. Moreover, the senator is reported to have helped Mr. Hampton land a lobbying job as a government affairs consultant to a Las Vegas airline company and an energy company. The Senate Ethics Committee launched an investigation into the scandal. In the meantime, Senator Ensign announced that he would not seek reelection in 2012. And, in December 2010, the Justice Department prosecutors, following a year-long investigation, dropped the charges against Ensign. But, in March 2011, Mr. Hampton was indicted by a federal grand jury in the District of Columbia for violating criminal conflict of interest laws, charging that he violated post-employment lobbying restrictions mandated by The Honest Leadership and Open Government Act of 2007. More specifically, he was accused of repeatedly contacting Senator Ensign's office in 2008 and early 2009 seeking assistance for the Nevada companies. Mr. Hampton claims that the senator encouraged him to contact his office.

As a nearly two-year-long Senate ethics investigation entered its final phase, Senator Ensign resigned his seat effective May 3, 2011, one day before he was to have answered questions under oath about the charges against him. In his letter of resignation, he asserted: "While I stand behind my firm belief that I have not violated any law, rule, or standard of conduct of the Senate . . . I will not continue to subject my family, my constituents, or the Senate to any further rounds of investigation, depositions, drawn out proceedings, or especially public hearings. . . . This continued personal cost is simply too great" (Lipton 2011).

Congressional ethics is not an oxymoron. Those who serve in the U.S. Congress are placed in the proverbial fishbowl of high media visibility. Acts of wrongdoing—real or perceived—receive enormous public attention. With a majority of Americans saying that members of the House and Senate have low ethical standards, congressional representatives need to stay on the high road. Fifty-seven percent of respondents in a 2010 Gallup poll ranked the ethics of members of Congress as "low" or "very low," one notch below car salespeople and one notch above the very bottom dweller—lobbyists (Gallup 2010).

Federal Judiciary

Judges are widely viewed as ethical public officials. Yet, it has long been recognized that judges need ethical guidance and advice as much as other public officials do. Federal judges receive lifetime appointments when approved by the U.S. Senate in its capacity to "advise and consent." The Code of Conduct for United States Judges (U.S. Courts 2011) sets forth seven canons to which all federally appointed judges must subscribe.

Canons are a body of standards, rules, or principles accepted as universally binding.

As can be seen in Exhibit 8.5, the canons are both proscriptive and prescriptive. Judges must "uphold the integrity and independence of the judiciary" while also "avoiding the appearance of impropriety in all activities" and "refraining from political activity." Judges who find themselves in ethically questionable situations can seek advisory opinions from the Committee on Codes of Conduct of the Judicial Conference. The Judicial Conference serves as the principal policymaking body concerned with the administration of the United States courts.

With lifetime appointments, federal judges cannot be easily removed from the bench for ethical lapses. In *The Federalist #78* (1788), Alexander Hamilton argued that judges should be appointed to serve "during good behavior" and insulated from the political process so that they could be a check on the legislative and executive branches. However, when a judge's behavior is egregious, he or she can be removed by a House vote of impeachment and a Senate trial to determine guilt—an action taken only eight times in Senate history. The most recent removal occurred on December 8, 2010. All 96 senators present voted to oust New Orleans native G. Thomas Porteous, Jr., of the Federal District Court in Louisiana for a "pattern of conduct incompatible with the trust and confidence placed in him" (Steinhauer 2010). One impeachment article states Porteous was "so utterly lacking in honesty and integrity that he is guilty of high crimes and misdemeanors and is unfit to hold the office of federal judge and should be removed from office" (Alpert 2010).

What did Judge Porteous do? He sought and accepted kickbacks and other gifts, including money, trips and free meals at expensive restaurants from lawyers and a bail bond company with business before him. He also knowingly and intentionally made false statements, under penalty of perjury, related to his personal bankruptcy filing and violating a bankruptcy court order (Wikipedia 2011c). Mr. Porteous's behavior cost him dearly. Not only did he lose his lifetime job, he lost his $174,000 annual federal pension and was forever disqualified from holding any office of honor or profit under the United States.

Exhibit 8.5
Code of Conduct for United States Judges

Canon 1.   A Judge Should Uphold the Integrity and Independence of the Judiciary

Canon 2.   A Judge Should Avoid Impropriety and the Appearance of Impropriety in All Activities

Canon 3.   A Judge Should Perform the Duties of the Office Impartially and Diligently

Canon 4.   A Judge May Engage in Extra-Judicial Activities to Improve the Law, the Legal System, and the Administration of Justice

Canon 5.   A Judge Should Refrain from Political Activity

Source: U.S. Courts, 2011.

Summing Up

Ethics management in the U.S. federal government is a work in progress with no end in sight. While much has been accomplished since the ethical meltdown called Watergate, there is no clear road ahead given the size and complexity of the undertaking. Still, one must remain optimistic in spite of the mind-numbing surprises that reach the media all too often. Sexting (sending sexually explicit texts), a creation of the high-tech age, surprised the American public in June 2011 when Anthony Weiner, a Democratic congressman from New York, admitted to placing revealing pictures of himself on Facebook and tweeting young women.

All the rules and regulations on the books and those yet to be invented are unlikely to prevent errant public officials from straying from the ethical path. In the end, the responsibility for ethical behavior remains with the individual, regardless of his or her official rank. The key for instilling those values that enable one to pursue the ethical course remains something of a mystery.

Ethics Management Skill Building

Practicum 8.1. FEMA and Hurricane Katrina

As director of the U.S. Federal Emergency Management Agency (FEMA), you have the responsibility of employing FEMA's resources (people, funds, technology) to assist communities and states devastated by natural disasters such as Hurricane Katrina, which struck the Gulf Coast states in late August 2005. Your agency is not a first responder; that responsibility belongs to local authorities. Moreover, significant FEMA resources cannot be deployed until the president declares that a county or region is in a state of emergency.

President George W. Bush issued such a declaration two days before Katrina, with deadly winds in excess of 150 miles per hour, made landfall on August 29, 2005. Soon after hurricane winds pummeled New Orleans, Louisiana, and flooding occurred with the breech of the levees protecting the city (New Orleans actually sits below sea level), law and order broke down. Looters sacked vacated stores and gangs roamed the streets. The New Orleans police force of 1,500 were overwhelmed by the flooding, a breakdown in communication, and internal stress caused by floodwaters that endangered their lives as well as the lives of the people they had pledged to protect. Some police officers resigned, others deserted, and some simply couldn't report in because of the chaos.

Under these circumstances, the National Guard is typically deployed. Unless federalized, however, a state's decision to deploy the National Guard resides with the governor. In Louisiana, Governor Kathleen Babineaux Blanco (D) activated the guard, although nearly half were serving in Iraq and therefore were unavailable. More would be needed to restore law and order.

Questions

1. As director of FEMA, you urge the president to federalize the National Guard for deployment to New Orleans, but you are unsure about the authority the president has to do this without an invitation from Governor Blanco. Due to emergency conditions, should you advise the president to act immediately and federalize (even without the governor's permission).
2. If Governor Blanco challenges the president's authority to take control of the Louisiana National Guard, what would you recommend that he do, especially in light of the fact that disorder and life-endangering conditions are worsening each day?
3. Would you advise the president to federalize national guard troops from other states for deployment to Louisiana?
4. What is the morally and/or ethically correct course of action?
5. What is likely to be the impact on FEMA if:
   a. the president acts quickly?
   b. the president acts slowly?
   c. the president doesn't act at all?

Practicum 8.2. Polish This Draft!

Annual performance appraisals typically result in anxious moments for all, especially the person receiving the appraisal. Others can be drawn into the anxiety circle, as well, with ethical or not-so-ethical overtones. Let's say you are an employee who works in a large federal agency as a staff member for a senior manager. You are routinely expected to provide "input" for the manager's annual evaluation. Suppose your input goes directly to his secretary and thus to him: Is anyone going to say anything but glowing things about what happened under his watch? Probably not.

Now consider an even more uncomfortable situation. Suppose you, as the best writer on the staff, are given the task of polishing the draft of the senior manager's performance evaluation—an evaluation put together using the "input" that everyone had provided. Trying not to violate your own ethical standards, you simply edit it, correcting grammar and rewording so it will read more smoothly. You return it to his secretary, who shares it with her boss. Then, the boss sends it back to you and pronounces, "It's not good enough. Make me look like a god."

Questions

1. Would you voice your ethical concerns to the boss?
2. Would you report your boss to his boss?
3. Would you request a transfer to another agency?
4. Would you simply turn your head and make your boss "look like a god?"

9

Ethics Management Internationally

All men are good at birth. Same are their natures.
Different are their habits.

—Wang Yinglin (1223–1296), renowned
Confucian scholar in the Song Dynasty

International ethics management is evolving rapidly, with many countries launching anticorruption initiatives and, to a lesser extent, embracing high ethical standards in government. A recent study of the 26 member countries of the European Union notes that "the focus in national public administrations and the media is on corruption, fraud and conflicts of interest, but much less on unethical behaviour in general" (Bossaert and Demmke 2005, 3). This chapter provides a broad overview of efforts worldwide to adopt public management strategies that encourage ethical behavior and combat corruption.

> *Corruption* is the (mis)use of public office for private gain. Common forms of corruption are extortion, bribery and graft, influence peddling, insider deals, and kickbacks.

Ethics and Corruption: Two Sides of a Common Coin?

Internationally, corruption has received much more attention than ethics. This is largely so because the costs and consequences associated with corruption are more visible than they are with unethical behavior, although both can be difficult to measure in a way that yields confident results. A recent report by Global Financial Integrity finds that "illicit trade in 'goods, guns, people, and natural resources' is a $650 billion enterprise, which most negatively impacts the developing world" (Global Financial Integrity 2011). Ethics and corruption are sometimes viewed as two sides of a common coin—wrongdoing. Corruption might be viewed as unethical behavior at its worst, but this might be an oversimplification. And, when placed in an international context, one might ask, are both culture bound? Does the prevailing culture define what is acceptable or unacceptable behavior? Maybe, considering the story in Exhibit 9.1.

Exhibit 9.1
A Different View of Corruption

Gathered in the guest room of a Berber friend's house in the Atlas Mountains of Morocco after Friday prayers, Hussein turned from the assembled village to me and asked me: "Is there corruption in America?"

"Yes," I answered.

"Give us an example," he gently inquired.

So, as the room quieted, I gave an example of a kickback arrangement. "Ah, no," said Hussein, as the others' heads shook in unison, "that is just buying and selling." So I mentioned the Watergate scandal. "No, no," Hussein replied to common assent, "that is just politics." So I gave an example of nepotism. "No, no, *no,*" all voices cried out, "that is just family solidarity." So, as I struggled to think of an example that would maintain the honor of my country for being every bit as corrupt as anyone else's, Hussein turned to the others and said, with genuine admiration: "You see why America is so strong—the Americans have no corruption!"

Source: Rosen, 2010.

This story, although humorous, presents a view of corruption that differs from that espoused in the Euro-American context. "Corruption is the failure to share any largess you have received with those with whom you have formed ties of dependence," muses Lawrence Rosen (2010). Is corruption culture bound? Is ethics culture bound? You will have to decide for yourself, as there is no universal agreement. However, as one well-known corruption scholar, Susan Rose-Ackerman (1999, 2), suggests:

> Obviously, subtle differences in culture and basic values exist across the world. But there is one human motivator that is both universal and central to explaining the divergent experiences of different countries. That motivator is self-interest, including an interest in the well-being of one's family and peer group. Critics call it greed. . . . Endemic corruption suggests a pervasive failure to tap self-interest for productive purposes.

International Organizations

International bodies, including the United Nations (UN), Transparency International, Global Integrity, the Utstein Group (United Kingdom, the

Netherlands, Norway, Sweden, Canada, and Germany), and the Organisation for Economic Co-operation and Development (OECD), have launched a number of anticorruption initiatives. The UN, for example, promulgated an International Code of Conduct for Public Officials in 1996 (see Exhibit 9.2). Additionally, the United Nations International Centre for Crime Prevention has developed "Anti-Corruption Tool Kits" to "help UN Member States and the public to understand the insidious nature of corruption, the potential damaging effect it can have on the welfare of entire nations and suggest measures used successfully by other countries in their efforts to uncover and deter corruption and build integrity" (U4 Anti-Corruption Resource Centre 2006).

These meritorious efforts by international bodies are sometimes challenged from within when an international agency's ethical compass is adrift. Consider the case of the International Monetary Fund (IMF), with 187 member countries. In May 2011, the agency's managing director, Dominique Strauss-Kahn, was arrested and charged with sexually assaulting a hotel housekeeper in New York City. Given this allegation of egregious behavior, the media began to take a close look at the ethical culture of the IMF; what turned up was surprising. Several years ago, the IMF tightened up its internal systems for catching misconduct among its 2,400 staff members. This included establishing a telephone hotline for complaints like harassment and appointing and empowering an ethics adviser to pursue allegations of unethical behavior. But—and it is a big "but"—the IMF's ethics policy applied only to staff, not to the managing director! The director and the IMF's 24 executive board members are above the policy and beyond the reach of the ethics adviser. Rather, the board is responsible for policing its own directors via a five-person ethics committee whose work is confidential. Moreover, the only way the board can discipline its executive members is to write a warning letter to them or to their home countries. "There are a lot of controls in place when it comes to the staff, but not for the leadership," said Katrina Campbell, a compliance and ethics expert at Global Compliance (Campbell 2011).

Transparency International, Global Integrity, and the Utstein Group

Transparency International (TI) is a nongovernmental organization devoted to combating corruption and fostering integrity through information and education. TI publishes a Bribes Payers Index, a Global Corruption Report, and a Corruption Perceptions Index (CPI) that track corruption in 178 countries. According to the 2010 CPI, Sweden, Finland, New Zealand, Denmark, and Singapore are the five most corruption-free countries in the world. The most corrupt countries, according to the CPI, are Somali, Myanmar, Afghanistan,

---

Exhibit 9.2
UN General Principles of the
International Code for Public Officials

1. A public office, as defined by national law, is a position of trust, implying a duty to act in the public interest. Therefore, the ultimate loyalty of public officials shall be to the public interests of their country as expressed through the democratic institutions of government.
2. Public officials shall ensure that they perform their duties and functions efficiently, effectively, and with integrity, in accordance with laws or administrative policies. They shall at all times seek to ensure that public resources for which they are responsible are administered in the most effective and efficient manner.
3. Public officials shall be attentive, fair, and impartial in the performance of their functions and, in particular, in their relations with the public. They shall at no time afford any undue preferential treatment to any group or individual or improperly discriminate against any group or individual, or otherwise abuse the power and authority vested in them.

Source: United Nations Economic and Social Council, 1996.

Iraq, Uzbekistan, Turkmenistan, and Sudan. The United States is tied with Belgium at number 22, one spot ahead of Chili and one spot behind Uruguay.

Transparency International also publishes guides and books that promote integrity in governance. A National Integrity System source book, available in over 20 languages, offers "a holistic approach to transparency and accountability and embrac[es] a range of accountability 'pillars'—democratic, judicial, media and civil society" (Pope 2000).

Global Integrity (GI) is a newcomer to the international arena. The organization views "corruption as a universal challenge, not a problem specific to low-income countries. It is not just about national governments, but about local government and communities as well as key sectors within economies. Corruption is not a 'development' issue; it is a political and economic one" (Global Integrity n.d.). GI evolved from a team working at the Center for Public Integrity in Washington, DC, and it became an independent nonprofit organization in 2005. A year later, GI released the first full-length *Global Integrity Report* (2006), which provided in-depth anticorruption assessments for 43 countries on five continents. GI uses online collaboration tools via a network of more than 1,200 in-country journalists, academics, and social scientists to assemble and report data that allows stakeholders to "implement evidence-based reforms" (Global Integrity n.d.). Global Integrity's comprehensive web site (www.globalintegrity.org/) contains a blog, a set of country corruption notebooks written by journalists, and easy downloads of past *Global Integrity Reports.*

The Utstein Group, with headquarters in London, was established by the ministers of international development from Germany, the Netherlands, Norway, and the United Kingdom when they gathered at the Utstein Abbey in Norway in 1999. The group has created an online resource center (www.u4.no/index.cfm) that lists studies, reports, and anticorruption projects currently under way throughout the world.

OECD

The Organisation of Economic Co-operation and Development (OECD), with 30 member countries and a history dating to the early 1960s, has long been at the forefront of promoting good governance. The OECD was instrumental in putting forward the 1997 Anti-Bribery Convention that is "the first global instrument to fight corruption in cross-border business deals" (OECD 2004). Thirty-six countries, including six non-OECD members, have enacted antibribery laws based on the OECD Convention. Estonia is the most recent party to the convention.

In 1998, the OECD also adopted a 12-principle recommendation to improve ethical conduct in the public service (see Exhibit 9.3). These principles, according to the preamble to the OECD recommendation, are intended to be a point of reference for member countries "when combining the elements of an effective ethics management system in line with their own political, administrative and cultural circumstances." The extent to which these principles have been drawn on by member countries and other countries to develop an effective ethics management system is difficult to say. Nonetheless, the 12 principles are noteworthy, and the intention is certainly meritorious.

The principles are consistent with the OECD's recommendation that countries build their ethics infrastructure "to regulate against undesirable behaviour and to provide incentives to good conduct" (OECD 1997). A well-built ethics infrastructure would include politicians who are advocates and exemplars of ethical governance; an effective legal framework; accountability mechanisms; workable codes of conduct, education, and training, and an active civic society. Admirable? Without question. Doable? Not easily.

As a working model, OECD classified nine countries along two dimensions—an integrity-compliance dimension and a public administration–

Exhibit 9.3
OECD Published Principles for
Managing Ethics in the Public Service

1. Ethical standards for public service should be clear. Public servants need to know the basic principles and standards they are expected to apply to their work and where the boundaries of acceptable behaviour lie.
2. Ethical standards should be reflected in the legal framework. The legal framework is the basis for communicating the minimum obligatory standards and principles of behaviour for every public servant.
3. Ethical guidance should be available to public servants. Guidance and internal consultation mechanisms should be made available to help public servants apply basic ethical standards in the workplace.
4. Public servants should know their rights and obligations when exposing wrongdoing. Public servants also need to know what protection will be available to them in cases of exposing wrongdoing.
5. Political commitment to ethics should reinforce the ethical conduct of public servants. Political leaders are responsible for maintaining a high standard of propriety in the discharge of their official duties.
6. The decision-making process should be transparent and open to scrutiny. The public has a right to know how public institutions apply the power and resources entrusted to them.
7. There should be clear guidelines for interaction between the public and private sectors. Clear rules defining ethical standards should guide the behaviour of public servants in dealing with the private sector, for example regarding public procurement, outsourcing, or public employment conditions.
8. Managers should demonstrate and promote ethical conduct. An organizational environment where high standards of conduct are encouraged by providing appropriate incentives for ethical behaviour . . . has a direct impact on the daily practice of public service values and ethical standards.
9. Management policies, procedures, and practices should promote ethical conduct. Government policy should not only delineate the

(continued)

Exhibit 9.3 *(continued)*

minimal standards below which a government official's actions will not be tolerated but also clearly articulate a set of public service values that employees should aspire to.

10. Public service conditions and management of human resources should promote ethical conduct. Public service employment conditions, such as career prospects, personal development, adequate remuneration, and human resource management policies should create an environment conducive to ethical behaviour.

11. Adequate accountability mechanisms should be in place within the public service. Accountability should focus both on compliance with rules and ethical principles and on achievement of results.

12. Appropriate procedures and sanctions should exist to deal with misconduct. Mechanisms for the detection and independent investigation of wrongdoing such as corruption are a necessary part of an ethics infrastructure.

Source: OECD, 1998.

managerialism dimension (see Exhibit 9.4). The United States is characterized as having an ethics infrastructure that is a mix of compliance-based ethics and managerialism; that is, the emphasis is on "getting the job done" while at the same time complying with ethics rules and regulations.

Ethics Laws and Codes Internationally

Ethics laws and codes of conduct are widely used tools in the international ethics manager's toolbox. For example, Australia's Northern Territory placed a code of conduct in the 1993 Public Sector Employment and Management Act. Neighboring New Zealand passed a nationwide code of conduct in 1998 that emphasizes obligations generally expected of civil servants in their professional lives. Each agency has been encouraged to develop specific codes of conduct consistent with the standards set out in the national code. The United Kingdom Committee on Standards in Public Life, known as the Nolan Committee, promulgated the "Seven Principles of Public Life" that have been incorporated into codes of conduct by various agencies (see Exhibit 9.5).

Exhibit 9.4   **The Integrity-Compliance and Public Administration–
Managerialism Dimensions**

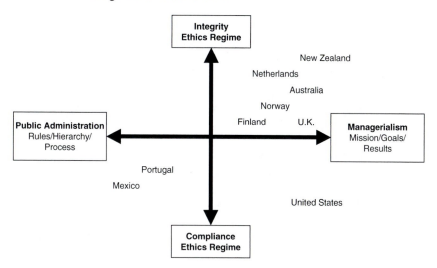

In Brazil, the Public Ethics Commission (in Portuguese, the Comissão de Ética Pública [CEP]) was established in 1999 to promote ethical behavior in the federal executive branch. The commission is also responsible for the implementation of the Federal Code of Conduct of High Administration, and it oversees and coordinates decentralized ethics initiatives in order to ensure the adequacy of the Brazilian administration's ethical standards. Another aspect of the agency's duties is to ensure that the relevant rules and procedures are known and understood, which includes publicity and training for officials and guidelines and help in dealing with ethical dilemmas (CEP n.d.).

South Korea adopted a code of conduct for maintaining the integrity of public officials in 2003. This code specifies the standards of conduct to be observed by both state and local public officials and covers conflicts of interest, the use of one's office for private purposes, and the obligation of officials to exercise neutrality and impartiality in their agencies.

The Philippines, with a workforce of 1.4 million men and women in the civil service, enacted a Code of Conduct and Ethical Standards for Public Officials and Employees in 1989. The standards include upholding the public interest over and above personal interest; discharging duties with the highest degree of excellence, professionalism, intelligence, and skill; acting with justness and sincerity; not discriminating against anyone, especially the poor and the underprivileged; and leading modest lives appropriate

Exhibit 9.5
UK Committee on Standards in Public Life:
Seven Principles of Public Life

Selflessness: Holders of public office should take decisions solely in terms of the public interest. They should not do so in order to gain financial or other material benefits for themselves, their family, or their friends.

Integrity: Holders of public office should not place themselves under any financial or other obligation to outside individuals or organizations that might influence them in the performance of their official duties.

Objectivity: In carrying out public business, including making public appointments, awarding contracts, or recommending individuals for rewards and benefits, holders of public office should make choices on merit.

Accountability: Holders of public office are accountable for their decisions and actions to the public and must submit themselves to whatever scrutiny is appropriate to their office.

Openness: Holders of public office should be as open as possible about all the decisions and actions that they take. They should give reasons for their decisions and restrict information only when the wider public interest clearly demands.

Honesty: Holders of public office have a duty to declare any private interests relating to their public duties and to take steps to resolve any conflicts arising in a way that protects the public interest.

Leadership: Holders of public office should promote and support these principles by leadership and example.

These principles apply to all aspects of public life.

Source: UK Committee on Standards in Public Life, 2001.

to their positions and income. Officials are expected to avoid extravagant or ostentatious displays of wealth in any form. The code also emphasizes positive incentives for exemplary behavior, stating that incentives and rewards to government officials and employees may take the form of bonuses, citations, directorships in government-owned or controlled corporations, local and foreign scholarship grants, and paid vacations. Public officials so honored are automatically promoted to the next higher position, with the commensurate salary suitable to their qualifications (Republic of the Philippines 1989).

One ethics management tool under development by the Philippines Civil Service Commission is an Ethics-Based Personality Test (EOPT). The commission believes that prescreening candidates for employment with this test will result in the "recruitment of the right people in all aspects and dimension" (Valmores 2005). The test will "determine the behavioral tendencies and personality profile of a job applicant [to] address the longstanding problem of hiring otherwise qualified people who are deficient on the moral and ethical requirements of public service." Ariel Ronquillo (2007) notes that the EOPT "aims to objectively evaluate the behavioral competencies and ethical values of persons wanting to enter the government service as well as existing government personnel as a critical approach to further promote ethics, transparency, and accountability."

Ethics Codes in Central and Eastern Europe

Perhaps the most active regions of the world today in the development and implementation of codes of ethics are Central and Eastern Europe, where many countries are in transition from authoritarian regimes to democratic regimes. A recent study by J. Palidauskaite (2006), a scholar from Lithuania, tracked the approaches taken in 10 countries—Albania, Bulgaria, the Czech Republic, Estonia, Latvia, Lithuania, Poland, Macedonia, Romania, and the Slovak Republic. She reports that two trends are discernable—some countries focus on the behavior of public servants through laws and codes, while other countries rely on statutory regulation only. The implementation of ethics codes and/or laws follows one of two paths. The first path is the use of an impartial council or board much like that found in the United States and the United Kingdom. The second path is left up to the individuals themselves "to interpret and apply the code of ethics" (45). The latter approach is consistent with the professional norm of self-enforcement, which is central to the codes adopted by many professional societies in the United States.

Ethics codes and statutes are not, of course, sufficient tools to ensure ethical governance. Mike Nelson (1999) notes,

> The problem with Codes of Conduct is that it is easy to stick them on the wall, but hard to make them stick in practice. . . . Without an effective development and implementation strategy which is integrated and engages with the heart and bowels issues of concern to the organization, the net result seems consistently the same: that the Code of Conduct remains a mere piece of paper, displayed or appealed to when convenient, but ignored the rest of the time.

In assessing the role of codes in European Union countries, Bossaert and Demmke (2005, 7) conclude:

> Despite their popularity, codes of ethics make little sense unless they are accepted by the personnel, and maintained, cultivated and implemented with vigor. . . . Codes are useless if staff are not reminded of them on a regular basis and given continuous training on ethics. Codes are only effective if they are impressed upon the hearts and minds of employees.

Alas, even with a vigorous implementation strategy, a code may still not deter unethical behavior.

Whistleblowing Laws

Whistleblowing laws and practices vary enormously throughout the world. The United States has numerous laws that encourage and protect individuals who blow the whistle on those who engage in corruption, waste, fraud, and abuse of power. And, there is a high incident of whistleblowing. Like those of the United States, Israel's laws provide extensive protection for whistle-blowers, although there is a low incident of whistleblowing there. India, the largest democracy in the world, has no statutes that encourage or protect whistleblowers. "In fact, whistleblowing is technically illegal, according to civil service rules, and might even be personally dangerous" (Johnson 2005, 1057). Still, there is a growing grassroots movement in India to expose government wrongdoing.

Until the collapse of the Soviet Union in 1991, whistleblowing in Russia was encouraged as a form of spying that enabled the government to sustain itself and control its citizens. This historic and unique Russian history, Roberta Johnson contends, is changing; there is evidence that a new breed of whistleblowers is emerging who are motivated to serve the public interest (2005, 1056). Johnson's case study of the United States, Israel, Russia and India has led her to conclude that there is no direct correlation between the law and the incidence of whistleblowing. Rather, she contends that the "cultural context, more than any other factor, helps explain why in some countries whistleblowers play an important role in opposing corruption and in other countries they do not" (1051).

To further assess ethics management internationally, we turn next to an in-depth look at developments in Europe, Asia, and Africa.

Europe

The founder of Transparency International and an activist European lawyer, Jeremy Pope, notes that when TI was launched in the early 1990s, the guiding philosophy was to fight corruption by building a country's "national integrity system." More than a decade later, he concluded that no matter how hard people work trying to strengthen public institutions and implement international standards, little seems to change. The bottom line is that "it does not really matter how strong one's institutions are if the wrong people are inside them" (Pope 2005). An individual's ethics, however acquired and influenced, cannot be ignored. Thus, education and training programs are essential to building an ethical infrastructure.

Moreover, he points out that the differences between ethics "best practices" in Western Europe and the United States are apparent. He suggests that the American approach can be seen in a famous cartoon in which a company's ethics adviser is shown addressing his board of directors: "My role," the adviser says, "is to draw a line between what is acceptable, and what is not. And then get the company as close to that line as possible." Drawing the line and then getting as close to it as possible is a risky, low road proposition. The Western European approach to ethics management is not, as Pope puts it, "simply a case of 'lawful conduct.'"

Still, lawful conduct has a place in Europe. Seventeen of the 27 EU countries prohibit accepting gifts and invitations, with eight of those countries prohibiting gifts above a certain amount—United Kingdom, Austria, Cyprus, Latvia, Lithuania, Italy, Slovenia, and Sweden. All but five EU countries— Luxembourg, the Czech Republic, Germany, Denmark, Belgium—require public officials to disclose financial interests (Bossaert and Demmke 2005, 105). Seventeen EU countries provide for punitive measures for those who violate ethics rules.

The European Union has stepped up its efforts to promote public service ethics. A 2004 survey (Bossaert and Demmke 2005) of member states resulted in a voluntary, non-legally binding European Code of Ethics, also known as the Ethics Framework. Six general core values were identified, and in a follow-up study (Moilanen 2007) those six were divided into eight values for analytical purposes:

1. Rule of law
2. Impartiality/objectivity
3. Transparency
4. Accountability
5. Professionalism
6. Duty of care
7. Reliability (confidence, trust)
8. Courtesy

The survey of EU states found that these "values were well reflected in the official documents with only minor exceptions" (Moilanen 2007, 4). The Ethics Framework, the study concludes, has had a positive impact on the EU, especially in helping member states draft their own code of conduct.

Ethics management among Western European countries, asserts Aive Pevkur (2007), spans a continuum of value-based, rule-based, and law-based approaches. According to Pevkur, Finland and Denmark take a value-based approach, Portugal and Great Britain pursue a rule-based approach, and Germany and France follow a law-based approach to ethics management (see Exhibit 9.6). She notes that while there is a movement away from the law or rule-based system and toward a value-based system, it remains uncertain whether it is "possible to go directly to an integrity-based system or whether a rule-based system is a necessary transitory phase" (Pevkur 2007, 20).

Russia, a non-EU country, is struggling with rampant corruption (estimated at $318 billion, one-third of GDP) in many sectors. "Surveys show that the vast majority of Russians encounter corruption at almost every turn in their daily lives, from dealing with traffic policemen to securing a place in a good school or getting a vital personal document renewed" (Weir 2009). Bribes paid by businesses are mostly directed at low-level local officials to secure licenses and fix the bidding for contracts. Higher-level officials, however, are not immune, as some business-people claim that they pay monthly bribes to federal ministries. Russian native and scholar Jasmine Martirossian (2004, 105) describes the situation in this way:

> Russia, today, has been likened to America's "wild west." Criminal elements seem to be unchecked, and it appears that people believe that efforts to expose wrongdoing are fruitless because corrupt public institutions and agencies will fail to act upon complaints, or, if they are acted upon, that the apparatus of corrupt practices will spring into action, bribes will change hands, favors will be exchanged, and no punishments will be meted out.

We turn next to an examination of ethics management in the United Kingdom and the Netherlands.

Exhibit 9.6   **Basis of Ethics Management in Countries**

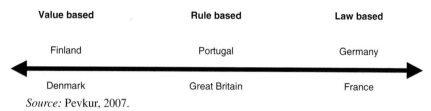

Source: Pevkur, 2007.

United Kingdom

The United Kingdom is a unitary government, although local governments exercise a great deal of autonomy. Nonetheless, the Seven Principles of Public Life put forth by the Nolan Committee in 1995 (see Exhibit 9.5) provided a starting point for more aggressive efforts to deal with ethical challenges in government. This landmark event found expression in the 2000 Local Government Act that set forth three principal components for ethics management in the United Kingdom:

1. a requirement that every local authority adopt a Code of Conduct that all councilors must sign up to;
2. a requirement that authorities set up a standards committee to oversee ethical issues and provide advice and guidance on the Code of Conduct and its implementation; and,
3. the establishment of an independent body (the Standards Board) with responsibility for investigating alleged breaches of a Council's Code of Conduct and promoting and maintaining high standards of conduct (Committee on Standards in Public Life 2004).

The Standards Board became operational in March 2001 and has regulatory responsibility for 386 local authorities, 8,000 parish councils, 31 fire and civil defense authorities, and 44 police authorities. It also covers the Greater London Authority and other regional assemblies. More than 4,000 complaints have been received by the Standards Board, with less than half investigated. Lecturer Michael Hunt describes this number of complaints as very high (Hunt 2005). A significant number of complaints deal with a failure to register a personal or financial interest. Other complaints allege councilors bring disrepute on their community and do not treat others with respect. Eighty-two councilors have been disqualified from holding office, and 15 members were suspended following a hearing by the adjudication panel, an independent judicial tribunal that hears and adjudicates serious matters concerning the conduct of elected officials (Committee on Standards in Public Life 2004, 13–14).

Another agency, the Audit Commission, is involved in ethics management. The commission describes itself as an "independent body responsible for ensuring that public money is spent economically, efficiently and effectively, to achieve high-quality local and national service for the public" (Audit Commission 2003, ii). Its approach is not to define ethical governance but to include it as part of an overall definition of governance in the public sector—that is, the commission is expected to audit the ethical standards and practices of local governments. The audits can result in a Public Interest Report that focuses on any governance issue, including failure to maintain high ethical standards.

Of central importance to the Audit Commission is determining whether poor ethical governance adversely affects performance—a very difficult task. Indeed, the commission's more traditional focus has been on performance compliance and risk assessment. However, it has developed a toolkit, *Changing Organisational Cultures,* that tests "the operation of ethical standards." This includes an assessment of officers' understanding of the local authority's code of conduct.

In 2004, the Audit Commission conducted ethical audit reviews of 38 local authorities and concluded that "it is questionable as to whether or not the problems identified by these audits will lead to service failure or poor quality services" (Fawcett and Wardman 2005, 10). At the same time, more than 1,700 middle and senior managers completed the *Changing Organisational Cultures* exercise and were quite positive about their local government's commitment to combating fraud and corruption.

These meritorious efforts were strengthened even more in 2006, when the head of the civil service, Sir Gus O'Donnell, published the new Civil Service Code. Among other things, the code calls for greater transparency, responsiveness, and professionalism in government. "Creating a culture of excellence," Sir O'Donnell asserts (2006), is an achievable goal. "My vision is for a civil service that exudes pride, pace, passion and professionalism" undergirded by the core values of honesty, objectivity, integrity and impartiality.

Altogether, the approach taken to ethics management in the United Kingdom is not as heavily compliance-driven as that in the United States, but it may be moving in that direction, despite Sir O'Donnell's vision for a revitalized civil service. Pope points out that should a litigation culture take hold in the United Kingdom and Western Europe like that in the United States, "the ethics scene here may well shift to that of the United States"—adversarial and "gotcha" oriented (Pope 2005, 6).

The Netherlands

The Netherlands, a decentralized unitary state with a population of 16.5 million, has begun to shift its ethics and integrity policy from a strong focus on complying with rules and regulations to one that emphasizes personal integrity and moral judgment (Hoekstra et al. 2005). This has been described by senior policy advisers in the Ministry of the Interior and Kingdom Relations as going "beyond compliance": The government recognizes the need for rules and regulations but also recognizes that these are not sufficient to ensure ethical governance. Thus, the emerging strategy is one that combines "structure and rules on the one hand and . . . culture and awareness on the other" (7). This shift in emphasis began slowly in the 1990s but has moved rapidly since 2003. That year, an investigation into the building industry found that many attempts had been made to bribe civil servants. Responding to this situation, lawmakers in the Netherlands amended the Civil Servants Act in 2005. The act obligates government bodies to adopt a code of conduct for civil servants and requires all new civil servants to take an oath of office.

The central government's commitment is reflected as well in the establishment in 2005 of a Bureau for Ethics and Integrity Stimulation in the Dutch Ministry of Interior and Kingdom Relations. The bureau provides guidance to managers on the development and implementation of ethics management programs, supports various studies, and analyzes trends and international developments in the ethics management field.

Another significant development occurred in March 2006, when the Netherlands required all government organizations to develop an integrity policy, which includes a mandatory code of conduct. To facilitate the adoption of this policy, the government published a Model Integrity Code as a guide and reference. Most important among its stipulations is that the "Model Code can be adopted only if the changes reflect stricter regulations than required" (Moilanen and Salminen 2006). In other words, an agency cannot simply copy the Model Code as its own and go about its business as usual.

The Netherlands Tax and Customs Administration is suggestive of a Dutch agency's attempt to go beyond the establishment of a code of ethics. In 2000, the Tax Administration embarked on an ambitious project to infuse its 30,000 employees with values inherent in the nature of the agency's work. As the director general states, "Due to the nature of their work, employees of the Tax Administration can easily find themselves in uncertain or even precarious situations . . . where guidelines and rules alone are not sufficient" (Van Blijswijk et al. 2004, 725). Tax employees must deal with the public fairly and apply the rules in a consistent manner, which is not always easy to do on a case-by-case basis. Thus, rules are not enough. Other necessary steps include (1) training new and current employees on how to handle dilemmas, (2) appointing integrity counselors who will "serve as the first line of inquiry to employees' questions with regard to integrity," (3) creating reflection groups from among integrity counselors to "discuss real-life cases and what actions have been taken," and (4) offering intranet group discussion opportunities for employees (723). The integrity project points to the value of striking a balance between codifying ethics and meeting the day-to-day challenges of acting with integrity.

Asia

Asian values—with an emphasis on personalism, paternalism, and particularlism—are sometimes asserted to be different than Western values, which focus on impersonalism, merit, and rationalism. Thus, the giving of gifts in return for favors, for example, is commonplace in much of Asia. Indeed, bribing public officials for favorable considerations is not uncommon. Consider the small South Pacific island country of Vanuatu, located about three-quarters of the way from Hawaii to Australia. With a tiny population of 205,754, one might expect high ethical standards to prevail. Apparently, this is not so, according to Marie-Noelle Ferrieux-Patterson (2003), the president of Transparency International, Vanuatu. She asserts that there is no recognizable moral or ethical code to define right and wrong in the public sphere. Conflicts of interest are especially rampant in Vanuatu because people are linked by strong tribal allegiances and "take actions or decisions to pay back past favors or to store up future favors or rewards, such as jobs or contracts."

The biggest democracy in the world, India, has been wracked by corruption and governmental inaction for decades. A 2005 study involving more than 14,000 Indians across 20 states found that "corruption in public services affecting the day to day needs of citizens is far more serious than is commonly realized" (Transparency International). The worse cases involved the police, judiciary, and land administration. Indeed, the history of corruption in India has been so persistent and severe that in April 2011, a longtime anticorruption activist, Anna Hazare, 74, began a hunger strike to persuade the government to draft new legislation for a Lokpal (ombudsman). In August, the police in New Delhi arrested Hazare and detained more than 1,200 protesters who had joined with him in an upsurge of popular outrage. Hazare's arrest fueled even more unrest and brought about peaceful demonstrations throughout India (*New York Times* 2011b). The protest movement has prompted the Indian Parliament to agree to "create an independent ombudsman with the staff and powers to investigate and prosecute corruption at every level of Indian governance," asserts Tom Friedman (2011) on a recent visit to India. And, he adds, "A furious debate is now raging here over how to ensure that such an ombudsman doesn't turn into an Indian 'Big Brother,' but some new ombudsman position appears likely to be created" (2011).

The situation in all Asian countries is certainly not as dire as suggested by the Indian or Vanuatu experience. There is a strong movement to embrace the rule of law throughout the Pacific, Asia, and Southeast Asia. Many countries are putting into place legal and institutional barriers to combat corruption and promote ethical governance. Let's look at what's happening in China and Japan.

China

Public service ethics in China in the twenty-first century is embedded in a Confucian legacy, one that emphasizes "a system of ethics that focuses on virtues that officials and governments should possess" (Dong et al. 2010). The former Chinese president Jiang Zemin put it this way in 2001: "We should combine the rule of law with the rule of virtue in order to build a lofty . . . ethical foundation for maintaining a good public order and practice" (Jiang 2001). Law and virtue in combination would indeed be a powerful antidote to corruption and unethical behavior. China, with a population of 1.3 billion and more than 6 million persons in the civil service, has long strived to break the grip of corruption. Since 1981, five major anticorruption campaigns have taken place, but the struggle continues. The 2010 Corruption Perceptions Index published by Transparency International places China seventy-eighth among 178 countries—ranked just above Colombia and Greece and below Panama and Bulgaria. In 1995, the first year that TI published the index, China placed next to last among the forty-one countries surveyed.

Building organizations of integrity among China's 29 ministries of the central government, 32 provincial governments, 1,735 counties, and 48,000 townships is a substantial challenge. Nonetheless, it is one that officials are committed to meeting. China is a single-party-dominated government. Both the Communist Party as represented by the Central Disciplinary Committee and government Ministry of Supervision share responsibility for disciplining civil servants who engage in illegal and unethical acts. The approach taken by China, according to Robert W. Smith (2004), is strikingly similar to that of the United States, although more formalistic; there are fewer opportunities for informal, negotiated settlements of cases in China than in the United States.

Smith (2004) also asserts that China has many anticorruption and ethics entities, perhaps more than any other country (311). Audit bureaus, centers for reporting corruption, offices of general inspection of financial and fiscal discipline, nonofficial corruption monitors, and nonofficial bureaus of anti-graft and bribery have been established at various levels of government. These bodies possess strong investigatory and sanctioning powers and invoke harsh penalties, even death penalties, on offenders. In 1999, 4,322 public servants were found guilty of ethics violations, 58 senior officials among them. In corruption cases, the death penalty "has been exercised with great frequency during the past few decades" (Smith 2004, 314).

In 2005, six years and 13 drafts later, the Chinese national legislature approved a code of conduct law that outlines the rights and obligations of civil servants. China's civil servant law stipulates that civil servants must (Dong, Yang, and Wang 2010, 106):

- abide by the constitution and laws;
- work responsibly and effectively;
- serve the public interest wholeheartedly with oversight from people;
- be devoted to their duties;
- obey their superiors;
- scrupulously follow work ethics; and
- work with senses of courtesy, integrity, and honesty.

The law, however, stopped short of requiring top civil servants to disclose their personal financial obligations, which critics assert is a significant omission. "There should be no doubt that the public's right to know should weigh more heavily than officials' right to privacy," noted the author of an article that appeared in the *China Daily* (2005). As this criticism suggests, mainland China's approach to ethics management is limited in scope.

Whistleblowing is encouraged in some Chinese provinces. For example, the Guangdong provincial government began rewarding whistleblowers in 1995 to root out corruption in its ranks. Financial rewards were paid out to 55 whistleblowers totaling 140,000 yuan—at that point in time approximately $18,000 U.S. dollars (Gong 2000). Whistleblowing in China can be done by telephone, letter, or personal visits. Whistleblowing "centers" also exist in many localities; they provide toll-free hotlines for reporting wrongdoing. The effectiveness of whistleblowing in China is difficult to estimate. Ting Gong, who has studied whistleblowing in the Chinese culture, claims that many potential whistleblowers remain silent because corrupt officials "are often protected by an organizational network involving lower and higher ranking officials and sometimes even people in anti-corruption agencies. They collaborate with each other to cover up their corrupt activities" (2000, 1915).

Public Service in China

Efforts to instill a public service ethos in the Chinese civil service face significant obstacles. Among other things, there is little evidence that universities are undertaking this Herculean task. Ninety-two Chinese universities offer graduate study in public administration (compared to 250 U.S. universities).[1] The course subject matter for the MPA (master's of public administration) degree in China includes two courses with heavy ideological content—the construction of socialism and Marxist theory. Others subjects include those commonplace in the West—public policy analysis, management, information technology, administrative law, and economics. Courses on ethics are noticeably absent. However, this deficiency has been recognized, and Chinese scholars have called for curriculum reform. Lan Xue and Zongchao Peng (2004, 26) assert that Chinese educators "should improve students' ethical self-cultivation and their ethical analysis ability in the public administration process."

Calls have also been made to strengthen the competency training of Chinese public servants. Currently, the training emphasis is more knowledge oriented than competency oriented (Wang 2004). Moreover, Zukun He (2004, 148) claims that "the government should care about public servants' moral and ethical education, strengthen their sense of responsibility and sense of service; only in this way can the efficiency of the government's responsiveness be better." As the civil servant law indicates, although the Chinese government stresses administrative ethics, there are no codes of ethics directed specifically at public administrators (Dong et al. 2010, 106). Ethics management in China remains a reach—with the possible exception of Hong Kong.

Hong Kong

Hong Kong, a crown colony of Great Britain until 1997, is a Special Administrative Region (SAR) in China with a population of 7 million. Scholars describe the prevailing brand of administrative ethics in Hong Kong as "a curious mix of modern Weberian notions on the one hand and traditional Confucian values on the other" (Lui and Scott 2001, 650). Hong Kong civil servants are expected to be competent administrators who subscribe to the values of neutrality and loyalty to the hierarchy—Weberian notions. Confucian values enter in as well, stressing virtue and rule by scholar-officials; that is, good government depends on the kindness and wisdom of those who rule. This is a form of "rule by man," whereas the Weberian notions emphasize the "rule of law." The result, according to Lui and Scott, is that the Hong Kong bureaucracy "operates as a corporate moral entity" (657). As the authors note,

> The individual official remains a faceless, anonymous bureaucrat, a cog in a machine who has no moral identity outside his place in the collectivity. An "ethical" civil servant is one who abides by the norms of the organization and the orders of his superiors. (657)

Hong Kong civil servants do not espouse values "beyond what the bureau-cracy has inculcated in them" (653). Although rules and regulations abound, "they are largely designed to facilitate efficient organizational operations rather than to prescribe norms of moral behavior" (653). While Hong Kong has an ombudsman and an anticorruption body, the Independent Commission Against Corruption, they have not been capable of drawing much attention to the significance of administrative ethics (653). Professionally oriented codes of conduct also exist but are not well publicized and remain nearly unenforceable (Lui 1988).

Ethics management in China, as well as in Hong Kong, is at a nascent stage in its development, with much distance to go before a claim to ethical governance can be asserted. At the same time, there is promise of a more professional civil service; the management of civil servants is increasingly merit oriented, with an emphasis on performance, character, ability, self-discipline, and achievement as the basis for promotion and reward (Zhu 2000). Nonetheless, administrative behavior is dependent on self-control, because there are few significant controls outside the institution of govern-ment (2000, 1961).

Japan

Japan has 4.4 million public employees, of which one-quarter work for the national government and the remaining three-quarters work for local governments in prefectures, cities, towns, and villages. Schoolteachers are considered public employees and constitute one-fifth of the public-employee workforce.

Ethics management in Japan is a work in progress. In 1999, the Japanese Diet (the National Assembly) enacted the National Public Service Ethics Law. This law set in motion a limited but nonetheless important approach to advancing ethics and integrity in the governance of Japan. Among other things, the law set forth three general ethical principles, established an ethics board in the national administration, created ethics supervisors, called for the promulgation of a National Public Service Officials Ethics Code (see Exhibit 9.7), and provided for the introduction of ethics management in lo-cal government.

The ethics board was placed in the National Personnel Authority, an inde-pendent agency whose mission is to ensure fairness in personnel management and develop personnel management policies. The board comprises a president and four members. All members of the board are appointed by the Cabinet. A 15-person staff supports the work of the board (Kudo and Maesschalck 2005). The board's central ethics management responsibilities include:

Exhibit 9.7
General Ethical Principles in Japan's
National Public Service Ethics Law

1. Employees shall not give unfair, discriminative treatment to the public . . . and shall always engage in their duties with fairness, recognizing that they are servants of the whole nation and not of any group thereof.
2. Employees shall always distinguish between public and private affairs and shall not use their duties or positions for private gain for themselves or the organization they belong to.
3. Employees shall not take any actions that create public suspicion or distrust against the fairness of public service while performing their duties, such as receiving a gift from entities influenced by their duties.

Source: National Personnel Authority, 2000.

- preparing and revising standards for disciplinary action against employees who violate ethics principles or rules;
- planning and coordinating ethics training programs within and across ministries and agencies; and
- investigating alleged violations of the ethics law and taking disciplinary actions against violations or requesting ministers to do so for violations in their ministry.

The law also called for the appointment of an ethics supervisory officer in each ministry or agency. The ethics supervisory officers are expected to provide guidance and advice to co-workers on ethics issues and to establish management systems that foster ethical behavior consistent with directions provided by the National Public Service Ethics Board.

The ethics code incorporated the three earlier mentioned ethical principles and added two more standards for ethical behavior:

- Employees shall, in performance of their duties, aim at increasing public interests and exert their utmost efforts.
- Employees shall always behave recognizing that their actions may influence the trust in the public service, even outside of their official hours.

Following the inclusion of these two principles, the code then becomes "very specific and in fact focuses on only one issue of ethics management: whether or not public servants can accept favours (presents, hospitality, benefits, etc.) from individuals or entities" that could be affected by the actions of government officials during the course of their work (Kudo and Maesschalck 2005, 13–14).

The National Personnel Authority (NPA) is responsible for the development of two types of training programs: general training for improvement of administrative duties and professional training that focuses on specific skills and techniques (NPA n.d.b). Ethics sensitivity training is available to junior and mid-level managers, although senior-level administrators are exempted (NPA n.d.a). Training for ethics managers is organized by the ethics board and is typically a "detailed explanation of the Ethics Law and Ethics Code and the discussion of specific cases, including actual case of violations against the Law or the Code" (Kudo and Maesschalck 2005, 15). The board has also published and distributed an ethics handbook that explains ethics regulations.

In summary, ethics management in Japan is narrowly focused on compliance with the ethics law and code, as evidenced by the fact that, among other things, it is directed at curbing expensive wining and dining of senior bureaucrats by those who seek favors from them. The approach taken in Japan parallels closely the legalistic approach taken by many American states, with an emphasis on prescribing and proscribing acceptable behavior.

Africa

With a total population of more than 1 billion and 53 countries within its borders, Africa is a large, ethnic and culturally diverse continent. Many of the world's poorest countries can be found in sub-Saharan Africa and are often plagued by endemic diseases and protracted conflicts (Armstrong 2005, 5). These conditions challenge the most committed leaders who want to manage with integrity. Moreover, the dark shadow of corruption looms large over the entire continent.

Despite the challenges, there is steady, although uneven, movement toward raising ethical standards in public service. A UN study involving 10 African nations found that there is both a heightened awareness and movement toward the enhancement of public service ethics and the fight against corruption (United Nations 2001). Nine of the ten countries conducted public opinion polls or surveyed users' perception of service delivery to promote good governance or democratization. Five countries (Cameroon, Namibia, Nigeria, South Africa, and Uganda) conducted campaigns to promote codes of conduct, raise public awareness, and advocate public service charters. South Africa focused on society-wide initiatives to bring together "the country's religious and other leaders to sign a Code of Conduct and adopt a humanitarian ethics pledge" (United Nations 2001).

Specific measures to "manage" the conduct of public servants, however, are reported as lacking effective enforcement procedures. These include inadequate steps for receiving and handling complaints, "thus making corrupt and unethical acts difficult to report" (United Nations 2001). Moreover, reporting wrongdoing is often a risky matter. While whistleblowing protection may exist in writing, practical measures are not in place to ensure anonymity and prevent retaliation. Finally, few countries are found to take the final step in enforcement—actual prosecution of violations.

Another initiative whose promise is yet to be realized is the "Charter for the Public Service in Africa" (African Public Service Ministers 2001), which was adopted by the Third Biennial Pan-African Conference of Ministers of Civil Service in Windhoek, Namibia. The charter puts forth a highly meritorious set of principles to strengthen public service throughout Africa. Included in the charter is a code of conduct for public service employees that emphasizes professionalism and ethics. Public service employees are expected to carry out their duties with "integrity and moral rectitude," avoid conflicts of interest, declare assets upon taking and leaving office, and be politically neutral and respect the confidentiality of official information to which they are privy. There has been much discussion about these charter provisions. In September 2010, African Union experts met in Maputo, Mozambique, to discuss the charter's provisions, including its implementation. Mozambique's Minister for the Public Service, Vitoria Diogo, speaking at the opening of the three-day meeting, noted that the charter supports "the public interest ahead of individual interest; the maintenance of public confidence in the integrity and objectivity of our governance; openness to public inspection; transparency and accountability; and the ceaseless concern to fight against poverty" (allAfrica.com 2010). The Charter has yet to be ratified by African Union states or by the AU itself.

Moving Forward

Are nations around the globe embracing ethics management strategies? Yes, but primarily from the perspective of combating corruption through laws, rules, and regulations. The limitations of this approach are straightforward: It reduces ethical behavior to a minimalist conception (don't break the law or regulations) and encourages a narrow, legalistic approach to defining acceptable behavior.

> Ultimately, ethics in the public service must be understood as an integral element of the role of public administrations in the achievement of good governance.
>
> —United Nations Report, 2001

However, there is reason to be optimistic about a change in direction. Kenneth Kernaghan (2003), a Canadian ethics scholar, points to changes in Australia, New Zealand, the United Kingdom, and Canada. He suggests that these countries are moving toward a value-driven approach to strengthening the ethical culture of their governments. He points to the 1999 Vision and Values Statement intended to complement the U.K. Civil Service Code as evidence. In Canada, he notes that the Office of Values and Ethics, which was established in 1999, published a Values and Ethics Code for the Public Service in 2003. In New Zealand, the State Services Commission put the accent on core values in public service with the publication of *Walking the Talk: Making Values Real* (2001). This guide encourages public servants to uphold core values such as trust and integrity in their decisions and actions. Australia, Kernaghan asserts, "is the most notable for its recognition of the central importance of leadership to effective integration of the right values into public service" (2003, 718).

Summing Up

Ethics management worldwide is important. Indeed, the United Nations has been at the forefront of the global push to embrace ethics and integrity in governance. At a 1997 conference on Public Service in Transition held in Greece, more than 20 countries from Eastern and Central Europe and representatives from international organizations such as the European Commission gathered to discuss what could be done to facilitate "capacity building in the broad areas of governance, public administration and finance" (United Nations 1999, 15). Ranked near the top of the list was the critical importance of probity and integrity. The raising of ethical standards and performance in government requires more than a plan to combat corruption. "Public service ethics encompass a broad and widening range of principles and values . . . objectivity, impartiality, fairness, sensitivity, compassion, responsiveness, accountability, and selfless devotion to duty" (2). More than anything else, the conference participants concluded, "the transition to a free and open society calls for rededication to democratic values, the respect of human rights, and belief in the service of citizens and of the common good" (2).

There is little question that corruption impedes the possibility of a universal public service ethic and, therefore, international agreement on the adoption of effective ethics management strategies. There is another important reason why a universal public service ethic has yet to emerge. It is the belief that cultural and religious norms and traditions strongly influence the ethics of a society. Consequently, what is an acceptable ethical practice or behavior in one society may not be acceptable in another. This culturally deterministic definition of ethics suggests that right and wrong behavior is relative, not universal. Put differently, ethical norms and behaviors are embedded in and defined by a country's culture. But does this mean that there are no values that transcend the cultural diversity of societies? Not necessarily, Gilman and Lewis contend. "There are fundamental values—treated at a high level of abstraction—that are closely associated with democracy, market economy, and professional bureaucracy" (Gilman and Lewis 1996, 518). These fundamental values include respect for human dignity, freedom from oppression, fairness, and truth and honesty in civic life.

Ethics Management Skill Building

Practicum 9.1. The Greater Good

As a contract manager for the U.S. Department of Defense with an office located in Saudi Arabia, your job is to ensure that contracts are managed properly so that the procurement of goods and equipment reaches American military forces in a cost-effective and timely manner. Several months ago, the U.S. Air Force ordered more than $250,000 worth of equipment that is now sitting at the customs agency on the other side of the country. The Saudi customs agency has held up delivery for some unknown reason, perhaps a technicality. The politics of the situation is such that the United States does not want to rock the boat by challenging Saudi officials.

As the contracting officer, you feel obligated to get the equipment released as quickly as possible. To accomplish this you know it is necessary to secure a release document notarized by a high-ranking U.S. official. The document is time sensitive. To your dismay, you discover that the finance officer dropped the ball and will delay securing the signature by one day. To make matters worse, the release document will become null and void if not secured immediately.

Frantic, you make every effort to reach the official whose signature is needed but discover that he is not available. What should you do under these circumstances?

Although you have no authority to do so, you decide to call the legal officer on the western end of the country and request that he redo the whole document. Furthermore, you encourage him to do whatever needs to done, including changing the date. He asks a lot of questions, so you instruct him on how to cut, paste, and copy and reapply the official seal—in essence, you explain how to falsify the document.

You rationalize that you had no choice. The process of getting the equipment out of customs would take several months. Lining up and coordinating all of these agencies would be very time consuming, and you are not going to let legal requirements blow the deal, "I am not about to blow it on a stupid piece of legally required document."

Furthermore, you muse, there are only two of us who will ever know the document is falsified—myself and the attorney. Your success in securing the release of the equipment motivates the Department of Defense to give you an award. Further reflecting on what you did, you say to yourself—"I did not pay for those goods, U.S. taxpayers did. And if it were my money, I'd have done the same. If I had not been able to secure the release of the equipment, it was going to go into the country's local market. They were not going to return it to the vendor."

Musing further, "Every situation violates some person's ethics, so, whose do we choose? And at what point do we as administrators determine that our ethics are above that of another employee's? There are some things we say we'll never do—knowingly falsifying documents for one. But, I'm thinking . . . you know, there may be a situation in which doing that particular thing would be more ethical than not doing it."

Questions

1. Do you think it is ever ethical to falsify a document?
2. Did falsifying the document to secure the release of U.S. Air Force equipment justify the act?
3. Are there career risks for falsifying a document?

Practicum 9.2. Religious Expression in the Workplace

You are the chief of the State Division of Vehicular Licensing with 1,250 employees located at six district offices. The director of District 2 approaches you about a thorny problem—what to do about providing employees who are Muslims a suitable time of the day to worship. The problem began on October 30, when the state shifted from Central Daylight Savings Time to Central Standard Time. As it turns out, the "fall back" of the clock pulled the Muslim sunset prayer back into the work hours.

A group of Muslim workers requested that the district office allow them to conduct their sunset prayer at 5 P.M. The district office closes at 6 P M. The group said that they would be willing to work from 6 P M. to 7 P M. to make up for the time lost.

The director is unsure what other districts have done and does not know if state law requires public agencies to accommodate employees' religious beliefs. It is, of course, clear to all that public agencies cannot promote religious beliefs and practices, but this is not quite the same thing.

As the division chief, you inform the director that other district offices have not faced this issue before. Moreover, state law is reasonably clear—employers (public and private) must accommodate employees' religious beliefs as long as the requests are reasonable and do not create a hardship for the agency.

Questions

1. Is the request by the workers reasonable?
2. Would shifting the sunset prayer hour to 5 P.M. create a hardship for the District Office of Vehicular Licensing? (Remember that the primary work of the District Office is to issue licenses to the public on a first-come, first-served basis.)
3. Would agreeing to the request be viewed as favoritism toward one group of employees? If so, would this create morale problems?
4. What recommendation would you, as division chief, make to the district director?

Note

1. Along with the schools of administration in China, there is a system of Communist Party training schools that have a much longer history. Programs at party schools, while focusing more on political and ideological areas, are increasingly management oriented (Wang 2004, 36).

10

Ethical Governance in the Twenty-First Century

Most of the things worth doing in the world had been declared impossible before they were done.

—Justice Louis Brandeis (2011)

What emerging issues and challenges should we focus on to ensure that ethical governance moves forward, not backward, in the twenty-first century? There are many. Among them are privatization, the Information Age, the global pursuit of economic well-being and democratic governance, and ethics education. The future, it so often seems, is here with the historic boundary between public and private sectors a vast blur. Equally blurred is the timeline between the past, present, and future. The time warp of cyberspace and instantaneous worldwide communication has all but collapsed our calendars. In this concluding chapter, we take a close look at the challenges that must be overcome to foster ethical governance.

Ethical governance is an awareness and commitment to high ethical standards by those who govern and all who enter the governance arena, including institutions and processes that are fair and just.

The Privatization Challenge

The privatization of public services and facilities is in full force worldwide. Governments of all sizes and descriptions are redefining their roles and responsibilities in providing and delivering public services. Cities, counties, states, and the U.S. government are entering into new relationships with private-sector organizations—profit and nonprofit—to "create a government that works better and costs less," to borrow the title of the *Report of the National Performance Review* (1993). In some instances, the result has been load shedding—disengaging entirely as a governmental service provider. In other instances, government contracting with a private profit-making firm or a nonprofit organization to deliver public services has been the preferred modus operandi.[1]

When David Osborne and Ted Gaebler issued their clarion call in *Reinventing Government: How the Entrepreneurial Spirit Is Transforming the Public Sector* (1992), the response was nearly instantaneous and widespread. The reinventors endorsed privatization and called for public managers to be entrepreneurial in leading their agencies. Precious little was uttered about what privatization or entrepreneurialism might mean for ethical management. Indeed, there is no mention of ethics in their book. Perhaps Osborne and Gaebler believed there is little to be concerned about, since they are not calling for managers to engage in illegal activities—merely to manage differently within the law.

Laura Abbott (2006) who worked for 26 years as a uniformed officer of the U.S. Public Health Service in the Department of Health and Human Services, describes her experience with contractors in this way:

> It has been frustrating because even if the legal means are available to force contractors to meet their deliverables, at least in my department, the will to enforce them is seriously impaired or perhaps intentionally ignored. As government has turned to greater and greater use of contractors, supposedly for support functions, the chain of accountability and sense of common purpose has been much diminished.

H. George Frederickson (1997, 194) pulls no punches in asserting that the privatization movement will eventually collapse or, at a minimum, retreat on the heels of greed and corruption amid renewed "calls for administrative competence in government." Contracting in particular, Frederickson (193) reminds us, has "always made a tempting environment for kickbacks and fraud. Doesn't anyone remember why Spiro Agnew resigned as vice president?" Frederickson's indictment is unflinching. "As more privately inclined people are appointed to governmental positions and as more governmental services are based on the enterprise model," the more likely it is that we will experience corruption and unethical behavior (180).

Meeting the Privatization Challenge

Cuyahoga County (Cleveland, Ohio) Executive Ed FitzGerald challenged 175 construction industry contractors that to win county business they would need to "engage in the highest ethical standards; nothing less will be tolerated." He also told contractors that to work for Cuyahoga County, they must join the Northeast Ohio Business Ethics Coalition, sign a membership pledge to abide by the new county ethics ordinance, and promote a high ethical standard throughout their businesses (Miller 2011a).

Linda deLeon takes a more optimistic view of ethics, privatization, and public management entrepreneurship. She argues that "public entrepreneurship can be, and at its best is, ethical" (1996, 496). She acknowledges, however, that the values commonly associated with successful private-sector entrepreneurs—egotism, selfishness, waywardness, domination, and opportunism—if not adequately constrained or checked may result in norms antithetical to the public interest. Self-serving, profit-seeking, calculating public entrepreneurial managers may be able, if successful, to spot opportunities and marshal resources to produce innovation, but the trade-off may be a diminished ethical environment. Nonetheless, deLeon believes that ethical entrepreneurship is possible and should be encouraged in public organizations.

But what evidence do we have that privatization or reinvention or entrepreneurialism threatens ethical management in government or, at worst, evokes corrupt and unethical behavior? Some evidence is supplied by Cohen and Eimicke (1999), who have investigated three cases of public entrepreneurship—the Orange County, California, financial bankruptcy case resulting from a $1.6-billion loss; a risky hotel partnership project in Visalia, California; and the successful privatization of Indianapolis's wastewater-treatment plants.

The Orange County, California, case is an example of entrepreneurship gone amok ethically, crossing over into the realm of the illegal. Robert Citron, the county treasurer, invested locally pooled funds in fiscal instruments known as derivatives that produced spectacular financial gains until interest rates began to rise. When this happened, the financial bottom fell out and eventually forced the treasurer out of office and Orange County into bankruptcy in 1994. Two years later, Mr. Citron was sentenced to one year in jail and fined $100,000.

The Visalia case is more problematic as an ethics failure or success story. What is clear is that the city took risks with taxpayer dollars. Its partnership with the Radisson hotel chain to build and operate a hotel on city-owned property floundered, which ultimately forced the city into buying the hotel and assuming its debts.

In Indianapolis, the city often cited as the epicenter of municipal privatization, the former mayor Stephen Goldsmith set about privatizing more than 40 city services in the early 1990s. Among those services were the wastewater-treatment plants. Although the city's plants were considered efficient, the city administration decided to contract out the services. The result was that a firm based in France with 51 percent ownership by the local Indianapolis Water Company won the contract and was able to achieve significant financial savings. Based upon their examination of the experiences of these three cases, authors Cohen and Eimicke conclude that public entrepreneurship can be ethical, but that a large measure of care, caution, and competence should be exercised.

As a case in point, Richard K. Ghere (1996) describes the arguable if not unethical results of a partnership forged between a metropolitan county in a midwestern state and a local chamber of commerce. The county sought to promote tourism, attract convention business, and develop a regional economic development strategy that would lure international business. A 3 percent hotel/motel bed tax was earmarked for this purpose, and the local chamber of commerce was contracted to provide these services. Suffice it to say that chamber officials were delighted with this arrangement and were energetic partners—perhaps too energetic. As time passed, a number of "irregularities" began to accrue. These included noncompetitive awards made to vendors who had family connections with chamber officials, falsification of expense reports and convention business activities, golf and dinner outings for county commissioners paid for by the chamber, and questionable international travel provided by the chamber for county officials. Ghere's analysis does not detail the extent to which the chamber's practices may have permeated county government as a whole, but it is clear that the relationship or partnership at the top did little to foster an ethical climate. Indeed, this case points out how the privatization of a public function amounted to the diminishment, if not privatization, of ethical behavior ordinarily expected of public officials. The contract, of course, was the vehicle for this transformation.

Other stories of privatization challenges to ethical governance can be found in Florida. The next sections illustrate three of these stories.

Use and Abuse of Insider Information

Another contractual ethical issue is the use and abuse of insider information. Consider the state of Florida, which, under the Republican governor Jeb Bush (1998–2006), moved full force into the privatization of Florida government. Insider information was apparently used by a private firm in securing a $126-million state technology contract. An investigation by the Florida Department of Law Enforcement concluded that the company had access to insider information that helped it easily win the contract over 19 competitors. Here's what happened: A company employee who was hired as a consultant also served as the de facto chief of staff for the State Technology Office, the granting agency. An editorial in the *St. Petersburg Times* (2005) described the situation as "a curious work environment, one in which government employees and those hired under contract were virtually indistinguishable." The Florida Department of Law Enforcement and the state attorney, despite having misgivings about this "curious work environment," decided they lacked sufficient evidence to criminally prosecute the company.

One unexpected outcome, however, was the finding that Florida's ethics laws do not apply to private-sector employees when they have acted in a state agency executive capacity. This "finding" prompted a 2010 statewide grand jury to call for an expansion of the definition of "public servant" to include individuals who work for any entity "authorized by law or contract to perform a governmental function or provide a governmental service" (State of Florida 2010, 17). The 2011 Florida legislature did not act on this recommendation.

Private Contracting for Prison Management

In 2008, 37 American states, Florida among them, awarded contracts to private profit-making firms to operate prisons. The state had contracted with private firms back in 1993 to manage its prison system. Florida law created the eight-member Correctional Privatization Commission (CPC) to oversee the contractors who managed five prisons at a cost of $106.4 million a year. A decade later, however, dissatisfaction with the lack of management oversight by the commission had reached the point where the Florida legislature said "enough." In 2005, the Florida legislature terminated the CPC and transferred all of its powers and duties to the Florida Department of Management Services (DMS). What happened?

A review by the Florida Office of the Inspector General (2005) of the financial transactions of the CPC uncovered sordid details about this particular form of private-public cooperation. It seems as if the two for-profit prison companies overbilled the state by $12.7 million during this period (2001–2004). The commission paid the two contractors—Corrections Corporations of America and the GEO Group—for guards that did not exist at the prisons. The overbilled funds were then remitted back to the CPC's Grants and Donations Trust Fund to enable the CPC to pay staff salaries. As it turns out, the legislature eliminated the commission's budget in 2001, but not the commission itself. Thus, the commission found a creative, entrepreneurial way to keep its 10-member staff employed. Is it any wonder that the CPC failed at overseeing the contractors?

Privatizing Home Building Reviews and Inspections

The privatization of home building plan reviews and inspections to ensure that codes are met illustrates another side to public-private cooperation in Florida. Between 2000 and 2002, many communities were experiencing a significant building boom. Consequently, the building departments of local governments were not able to process permits and conduct inspections in a manner deemed timely by the building industry. Some building departments took up to six weeks or more to turn around a building permit. Thus, the Florida legislature came to the rescue. In 2002, the legislature enacted the Private Provider Law (FS 553.791), enabling a building owner to use a private provider to satisfy building code compliance plans and carry out inspections for the structural, mechanical, electrical, and plumbing components of a building. The law required the builder to notify the local government of the owner's intent to use a private provider. The local building official then issued the requested permit or provided written notice to the permit applicant identifying the specific plan features that did not comply with the code within 30 business days. If the local building official did not provide a written notice of the plan's deficiencies within the 30-day period, the permit application would be deemed a matter of law and the permit would be issued by the local building official on the next business day.

The Private Provider Law has resulted in a new industry with several engineering firms hiring plan reviewers and inspectors who, by law, must be state certified and licensed. The president of Capri Engineering, Gary H. Elzweig whose firm has 10 offices throughout Florida, asserts that "The private provider law came along at the right time. It's an amazing win-win situation. The private sector takes on the responsibility of processing compliance paperwork in a timely manner while freeing up municipal resources that can be better used for more important services such as hurricane rehabilitation" (CAPRI Engineering 2005; Schweers 2005). Others are not so sure, describing the situation as the classic "fox in the hen house." One county building official put it this way: "They are a for-profit business. Our duty is to serve the public—they're not doing this as a public service. We are here to protect the public in that sense" (Schweers 2005). The verdict is still out regarding how successful the cooperation will be between the corps of private providers and local government building departments. Time will tell.

These Florida experiences illustrate the challenging nature that the privatization movement poses for public officials who want to embrace sound ethical management practices. Frederickson (1997, 171) notes, "It is no small irony that government is moving in the direction of privatization at the same time that there is a rising concern for governmental ethics."

Information (R)Age Challenges

The privatization "rage" is occurring at a time that coincides with another "rage"—the information "rage." Americans and citizens worldwide are acquiring PCs, tablets such as the iPad, e-readers like the Nook and Kindle, and MP3 players. The language of the Internet, the World Wide Web, browsers, video sharing, search engines, e-mail, listservs, blogs, chat rooms, and more has become commonplace vocabulary. Today's workplace, whether in the central office, field office, or home office, is an increasingly high-tech, information-driven workplace.[2]

Governments throughout the United States have climbed onto the Information Highway en mass. The technical aspects of accessing the Internet pale alongside the attempt to understand and abate the undesirable, and sometimes unethical, consequences that this technology can have on group life in public agencies. A study of the negative effects of e-mail on social life in the corporate workplace found that some effects, such as making the workplace less personal, were a product of two factors—the technology itself (for example, the depersonalization of social relations due to the absence of face-to-face interaction) and intentional choices by users or employees "to avoid unwanted social interactions" (Markus 1994, 119). In other words, technology is not singularly responsible for "negative" social effects in the workplace. Employees can and do make intentional choices in deciding with whom they wish to communicate. Managers committed to promoting a strong ethical climate are likely to find this situation especially difficult, particularly in light of our rudimentary knowledge of such behavior.

Another ethical challenge facing managers is implementing and monitoring Internet usage practices. These include surfing the web on agency time for personal pleasure, downloading or viewing obscene material, advertising or soliciting for personal gain, making political statements, posting or downloading inflammatory racial or sexual material, waging or selling chances, and using pseudo names when transmitting electronic messages. What can be done to discourage these practices? One approach is to adopt Internet Acceptable Use policies. But what if these policies do not work and abuse still occurs? Ethics management leaders may then have to take further steps. This has happened in the City of Tampa, Florida, where four city parking division employees were fired after sending e-mails with discriminatory references to sex, race, and ethnicity. Human Resources director Sarah Lang said that "their e-mails were specifically directed at specific employees in a pattern of e-mails that lent themselves to sexual harassment" (Varian 2005). A followup investigation of employees' work habits found that other city workers, 44 in fact, had sent e-mails that violated the city's business-only e-mail policy. Disciplinary letters were sent to these individuals with a copy placed in their personnel file. To promote the city's zero-tolerance Internet-abuse policy, the HR director sent letters to all personnel reminding them that it is against the rules to send personal e-mails from city-owned computers. Additionally, when employees now sign on to their computers, they are greeted with an on-screen message requiring them to acknowledge the city rule banning the personal use of e-mail.

There is awareness that the Internet can be a vital gateway to innovative, responsive government. Thus, there is an incentive to provide employees access to and encourage experimentation with the vast storehouse of data and information on the World Wide Web. Consider the approach taken in 2006–2007 by the city manager of Sarasota, Florida, Michael McNees, who created a blog to communicate with residents. His blog (McNees 2007) had more than 10,000 visitors in the first six months after it went live. Although opinions are mixed regarding the value of the blog as a vehicle for communicating with city residents, his willingness to use this medium to reach out to citizens earned him the 2006 Courage in Communication award from the Florida City/County Management Association.

Cities and counties are increasingly setting up community blogs to share information and engage the citizenry. City Manager Rick Cole, of Ventura, California, says "the goal of this blog is to provide a civic forum for real time news and dialogue regarding the City of Ventura" (Cole 2011). Citrus County, Florida (2011), has a blog primarily to disseminate news and information. Blogs promote transparency and, if managed responsibly, can aid in building trust in government (see Hillsborough disclaimer 2011).

Blog Disclaimer

While Hillsborough County welcomes and values comments from citizens about any issue or concern in this forum, the comments made to this blog are moderated. To ensure your comments are posted, they should be made in a spirit of cooperation and mutual respect and in a manner to help resolve the issue presented, no matter which side of the issue you are on (Hillsborough County, Florida, 2011).

Other ethical, perhaps legal, issues go beyond citizen and employee access and use of the Internet and have to do with the posture of government itself. Online governments and their leaders must position themselves to promote democratic practices such as citizen access to public information while at the same time ensuring that sensitive information is protected. It is one thing to post data about crime rates or AIDS statistics and another to allow access to names or addresses of victims. Likewise, the question might be asked: Is a public service being provided when the county property appraiser's office creates a searchable database containing property values and locations? Or is this merely making it easier for criminals to employ the same technology to target would-be victims?

Many local governments facing lean budget years might be encouraged to adopt entrepreneurial practices such as selling advertising space on their home page or endorsing a commercial product as the official product of their government. Are these practices ethical? Legal? The commercialization of the Internet is well under way. But how far should we go in commercializing government?

Finally, there is the matter of electronic communication between and among public officials and citizens. Few (small *d*) democrats would object to e-mail replacing fax messages between citizens and officials, but it may be an entirely different matter when the communication path is between officeholders. Will the Information Age, especially in its electronic form, effectively dismantle government in the sunshine? Or, will officials exercise due care, diligence, and caution before jumping on the keyboard and sending an important message to colleagues or top managers?

The Winds of Globalization[3]

A popular saying in the 1970s was that "small is beautiful," a reaction to big government, big corporations, and big policy failures in America. Four decades later, it can truly be said that small is beautiful globally. With the advent of high-powered technology, instant communication transmissions, endless choice through direct satellite TV programming, and shrinking travel distances and time, the world has never been so small. Elected and appointed officials in places as far-flung as Beijing, Lima, Moscow, Cairo, Johannesburg, London, and Brisbane are instantly aware of the latest political and economic developments in Washington, DC, New York, Chicago, Sacramento, and Tallahassee.

The winds of globalization blew with powerful market-driven force during much of the 1990s. First thought to be only an *economic* force, as countries such as China, Russia, and Vietnam embraced market-based reforms, globalization began to expand its reach as a *social* and *political* agent of change with increasing democratization and engagement in increasingly transparent policy making. The rule of law became more than a mantra; it became a means through which political leaders envisioned the possibility of seismic shifts in improving their countries' well-being and, in some instances, lifting their people out of poverty.

Globalization writ large began to touch Americans as well. Appointed and elected officials found themselves scrambling to connect their communities with the opening and exciting opportunities abroad. Sister-city programs sprung up, along with international trade delegations from cities, counties, and states traveling far and wide to explore the new world order, as it was sometimes labeled. In the second decade of the twenty-first century, there is scarcely a large city or county that does not have an international affairs office.

Public managers soon learned that it was important for them and their organizations to "think globally." This perspective is reinforced by professional associations such as the International City/County Management Association and the American Society for Public Administration. Both associations have launched initiatives that emphasis international affairs. Thus, managers are increasingly confronted by the norms and ways of different cultures. This has been especially challenging in situations where the cultures vary regarding what is and is not ethical. Giving and receiving gifts among public officeholders in Asian cultures, for example, is both commonplace and perfectly acceptable. Similar practices in the United States are viewed with suspicion, and many cities and counties have zero-gift policies.

These differences continue to be debated, with one argument calling for a global ethic—a framework for defining right and wrong that knows no social, economic, or political borders. Easier said than done? No question about it. Still, the search for a global ethic is meritorious.

Ethics Education Challenges

Education for professional public administrators in the United States is carried out primarily through 268 member-institutions of higher education that provide graduate or undergraduate study in public affairs and administration. As of June 2011, 169 graduate programs at 161 schools were accredited by the National Association of Schools of Public Affairs and Administration (NASPAA). The master's of public affairs/policy/administration (MPA) degree is increasingly viewed by the practitioner community as the degree of preference. The inclusion of professional ethics in the course of study adds considerable value to the MPA.

The teaching of ethics is a multifaceted and often controversial enterprise. It is multifaceted because the field of public administration ranges broadly within and across organizations, nations, and cultures. It is controversial because there is disagreement in the field of ethics on what to teach and how to teach it. Indeed, some persons believe that ethics cannot be taught in a traditional class or course context. Rather, the best that can be hoped for is to teach *about* ethics. Still, there is a widespread view among practicing administrators and educators that an ethical public service is essential to a well-functioning democracy. Accordingly, teaching ethics to men and women who occupy positions of public trust should and must be pursued regardless of the uncertain outcomes.

There are three approaches to teaching ethics: sensitivity and awareness, moral reasoning, and leadership and exemplar modeling.

Sensitivity and Awareness Teaching

A sensitivity and awareness approach to the teaching of ethics has moved along two primary paths. The first path is legalistic and is often reflected in the advice and instruction provided by state ethics commissions to state and local public employees and elected officials. This approach puts the accent on the "do's and don'ts" of state ethics laws. These laws, as noted in Chapter 3, emphasize conflicts of interest, financial disclosure, whistleblowing protection, and confidentiality of information. Using a "how to stay out of trouble" approach brings both good news and bad news. The bad news is that this approach often reduces acceptable behavior to the lowest level of "if it's not illegal, it's okay!"—which, as John Rohr reminds us in *Ethics for Bureaucrats: An Essay on Law and Values* (1978), is the "low road" to public service ethics. The good news is it sets down benchmark behaviors that all members of an organization can understand, even if they do not always follow suit.

The second path is semi-legalistic, with a focus on professional codes of ethics or agency rules of acceptable behavior. At the professional association level, for example, nearly every public service group has a code of ethics that its members are expected to support. Two associations are illustrative in this regard—the American Society for Public Administration (ASPA) and the International City/County Management Association (ICMA).

ASPA is an 8,500-member organization consisting primarily of educators, students, and public employees drawn from local, state, and federal agencies and members of nonprofit associations. The ASPA code, first adopted in 1984, identifies five key principles: (1) serve the public interest, (2) respect the Constitution and the law, (3) demonstrate personal integrity, (4) promote ethical organizations, and (5) strive for professional excellence (ASPA 2006). Members who violate the code can be expelled from ASPA.

The ICMA is a 7,500-member organization consisting primarily of practicing public managers in cities and counties in the United States and abroad (for example, Ireland and Australia). The ICMA code dates to 1924 and provides specific guidance on acceptable and unacceptable behaviors for local government managers. For example, it is deemed unethical for a city manager to leave her management post with less than two years of service, unless there are extenuating circumstances such as severe personal (medical/mental/financial) problems. It is also viewed as unethical for a city manager to endorse a commercial product that a vendor might sell to a local government (see ICMA 1998). The ICMA actively enforces the code with a half-dozen or more members sanctioned nearly every year for violations (see, for example, ICMA 2010).

The teaching of ethics based on codes or administrative rules of behavior stress the contents of the codes or the rules themselves, which unfortunately, can become ends in themselves. The teaching of codes and rules is often conducted by personnel within a governmental agency, management consultants, and college and university instructors, especially those in graduate-degree-granting programs that prepare men and women for public service careers.

Moral Reasoning

A second approach to teaching ethics in public administration is moral reasoning. The effort here presumes that one can learn to reason through a difficult moral or ethical dilemma. Learning how to act ethically in public service is just that—a learning process, which when a real-world ethical dilemma arises can be applied with desirable outcomes. The reasoning process puts the accent on decision making through ethical reflection based on the interplay of moral rules, ethical principles, self-appraisal, and justification. At the heart of this exercise is what Cooper (2006a) calls exercising one's moral imagination to sort through right or wrong decision outcomes.

Another proponent of teaching ethical decision making is Carol W. Lewis who, in *The Ethics Challenge in Public Service* (1991) and a later edition with Stuart C. Gilman (2005) presents the reader with a problem-solving guide. Her guide engages the learner with real and hypothetical decision-making scenarios, self-assessment tools, and questions that stimulate ethical reflection. She contends that neither the "low" road of compliance nor the "high" road of integrity is a realistic guide for navigating the often stormy political and bureaucratic environments of public service. Rather, it is necessary to develop a two-pronged, systematic strategy that incorporates the path of compliance with formal standards and the path of individual integrity. She labels this approach as the "fusion route" to meeting the ethics challenge in public service (1991).

How does one learn to engage in moral reasoning? One learns how to reason and make ethical decisions by practicing; the learner can engage himself with decision dilemmas and work through them. A teacher of ethics can use scenarios and small group processes to help the learner practice ethical decision making and acquire skill in doing so. Menzel (2010) offers many scenarios that, with hands-on practice, can help an individual become an ethically competent leader and builder of organizations of integrity.

This methodology has much in common with virtue ethics espoused by Aristotle in the age of antiquity. Aristotle believed that one could acquire a virtue only by engaging in virtuous acts. But, he was wise to add, one does not acquire a virtue by engaging in foolhardy acts. Jumping into a lion's cage to acquire the virtue of courage is not what he had in mind! Moreover, it is the pursuit of virtue—a lifelong effort—that defines the virtuous person.

Leadership and Exemplar Modeling

A third way to teach ethics centers on leadership and exemplars in public service. This approach has had a time-honored tradition in the U.S. military academies at West Point and Annapolis's Stockdale Center for Ethical Leadership and is increasingly reflected in the curricula of graduate schools that award the master's of public administration degree. A handful of schools (for example, the Lyndon B. Johnson School of Public Affairs at the University of Texas) have established a Center for Ethical Leadership that is designed to attract men and women with a strong desire for leadership responsibilities (see the Center's web site at www.utexas.edu/lbj/research/leadership).

Leading with Integrity

To paraphrase Martin Luther King, Jr., "The ultimate measure of a leader is not where they stand in moments of comfort and convenience, but where they stand at times of challenge and controversy." For me, that requires defining a vision and goals others can embrace. Achieving that vision with integrity of leadership requires optimism, strong ethical behavior, personal accountability, decisive decision making when needed, and empathetic patience.
　　　　　—Martin P. Black (2011),
　　　　　AICP, ICMA-CM, former city manager, Venice, Florida

The study of leadership, of course, is wide reaching, encompassing commercial, political, and educational sectors. Interestingly, the study and teaching of administrative leadership has been problematic, as Larry Terry notes in *Leadership of Public Bureaucracies* (1995). Several factors have contributed to this situation—the complexity of modern public organizations, including the growing interdependency of private- and public-sector organizations; the antibureaucratic ethos that permeates American politics; and the challenge of distinguishing administrative leadership from political leadership. New administrative leadership paths, however, are being forged by scholars such as Monty Van Wart, who offers "the competencies that organizational leaders at all levels need" (2005, xiii). More recently, Van Wart (2011) draws our attention to the rise of the postmodern perspective in leadership studies, citing topics such as discourse theory, complexity and relational theory, integral leadership studies, and network and collaboration theory.

Effectiveness of Ethics Education[4]

What can be said about the effectiveness of ethics education in graduate public affairs and administration programs? Are professional schools and programs preparing public administrators to be effective ethics managers? Are they making a difference? These are difficult questions to answer. There is no question that ethics educators believe they are making a difference (Menzel 1997). Survey data collected from 78 of the member schools of the National Association of Schools of Public Affairs and Administration (NASPAA) offering an ethics course showed that seven out of 10 believe students find the subject matter valuable. A smaller percentage (67 percent) said they believe that students who receive ethics instruction become more ethically sensitive. Finally, one out of every two respondents asserts that, perhaps most important, students use the ethical knowledge gained in their program of study to resolve ethical dilemmas.

These findings are encouraging for those who believe that ethics education is important and does make a difference in the lives of practitioners. But impressions, of course, can be wrong. Moreover, since many educators may bring to their task a professional advocacy (which is presumably neither a brand of moral indoctrination nor ethical zealotry), a self-fulfilling prophecy may be at work; ethics educators may want to believe that they are making a difference and are therefore inclined to report such on a survey. A more definitive measure of ethics education outcomes is necessary.

Concern about the effectiveness of public management education prompted NASPAA to revisit its accreditation standards in 2006. Three years later, in 2009, new competency-driven standards were approved. NASPAA accredited programs are now expected to assess student competencies and deliver educational experiences that ensure responsible and effective performance in public management.

The "New" Ethics[5]

The proliferation of ethics courses is an important development in what Derek Bok (1990) calls teaching the "new" ethics. The applied ethics course, he contends, "does not seek to convey a set of moral truths but tries to encourage students to think carefully about complex moral issues" (73). He adds, "The principal aim of the course is not to impart right answers but to make students more perceptive in detecting ethical problems when they arise, better acquainted with the best moral thought that has accumulated through the ages, and more equipped to reason about the ethical issues they will face in their own personal and professional lives" (73).

The "new" ethics should also include a focus on teaching future public administrators how to be effective ethics managers. There is little evidence that professional education in public administration even touches on this subject, although one is hopeful that the shift in NASPAA standards noted above will make a difference. The irony, of course, is that the leaders of public organizations are engaged in ethics management day in and day out. The present approach is learning by the "seat of your pants." Educators and NASPAA have much to do in cultivating men and women to be ethics managers and leaders who know how to build organizations of integrity. There is no "one best way" to teach or acquire ethics, nor is there one best way to educate ethics managers. NASPAA's (2008) call for programs to "enhance the student's values, knowledge, and skills to act ethically and effectively . . . in the management of public and, as appropriate, third sector organizations" cannot be contested. At the same time, there is evidence that other factors such as the ethical environment of the educational program are at work and must be taken into account in order to obtain a more complete understanding of ethics education.

Nearly two decades ago, the Hastings Center released a report calling for the higher educational community to act with greater vigor and conviction in placing ethics and values in campus curricula. Educators should not lose sight of their message. The report asserted that we cannot afford, wittingly or unwittingly, to be a partner in producing "a new generation of leaders who are ethically illiterate at best or dangerously adrift and morally misguided at worse" (Jennings, Nelson, and Parens 1994, 2).

A New Generation of Leaders

The teaching of ethics in public administration has a promising future, but much more effort is needed, especially in educating men and women to be effective in leading and building organizations of integrity. The findings reported by Paul C. Light in *The New Public Service* (1999) are revealing and disturbing. Light's study focused on the graduates of the nation's leading public policy and administration programs (including those at Syracuse, Kansas, University of Southern California, University of Michigan, and Harvard). He reports that these graduates, regardless of their current sector of employment (government, nonprofit, private), placed "maintaining ethical standards" at the top of the list of skills considered very important for success in their current job. At the same time, when asked if their school was helpful in teaching skills that would enable one to maintain ethical standards, most rated their education as insufficient. In fact, Light reports that this gap between how helpful a school is in teaching ethics and how important ethics is to one's job success was the largest of all skills listed. (The list included such important skills as "budgeting and public finance," "doing policy analysis," "managing motivation and change," and "managing conflict.")

NASPAA, through its Commission on Peer Review and Accreditation, incorporated language in its previous accreditation standards (4.21) that graduates should be able "to act ethically." Standard 4.21 encouraged schools to put into place ethics courses or otherwise demonstrate that they are teaching ethics across the curriculum. The 2009 restructured standards no longer identify "to act ethically" as a standard. Rather, NASPAA calls for programs seeking accreditation review to meet four preconditions, one of which is a commitment to public service values.

Public Service Values . . .

include pursuing the public interest with accountability and transparency; serving professionally with competence, efficiency, and objectivity; acting ethically so as to uphold the public trust; and demonstrating respect, equity, and fairness in dealings with citizens and fellow public servants.
—NASPAA, 2009

This change in approach to ethics education in public administration graduate schools has produced considerable uncertainty and concern among ethics educators about the capability of programs to prepare men and women to lead with integrity. Yet, it is too early to make a more definitive judgment as 2011 eligible programs have just entered the accreditation cycle.

Four years before it restructured its standards, however, NASPAA had taken a step toward encouraging schools to emphasize ethics with its adoption in 2005 of a Member Code of Good Practice. The code admonishes all programs holding membership in NASPAA—not just those accredited—to integrate "ethics into the curriculum and all aspects of program operation, and expects students and faculty to exhibit the highest ethical standards in their teaching, research, and service" (NASPAA 2005). Perhaps the next significant step that NASPAA should take is to require all accredited programs to either (a) offer an ethics course and/or (b) place an ethics course in the core curriculum. Dennis F. Thompson (1992, 255) remarked, "From the truth that ethics is mainly instrumental, it does not follow, as many critics seem to think, that ethics is always less important than other issues." In other words, acquiring the ability to "to act ethically" should not be relegated to the educational rear.

NASPAA might also encourage MPA programs to adopt an ethics code for students. A student code might be useful in introducing students to professional ethics. Curious about whether any NASPAA school has such a code, your author placed the following question on the NASPAA listserv—does your school have a student code of ethics? Of course, universities have conduct rules and codes but they are seldom discipline specific. Thus, the answer was a resounding and deafening silence. Should a student code of ethics such as the one in Exhibit 10.1 be adopted by MPA programs? Perhaps NASPAA should draft a model student code that academic programs could draw on to fashion their own code.

Teaching ethics is a diverse, dynamic, and challenging enterprise. There is considerable evidence that a greater emphasis will be placed on ethics in the decades ahead in the United States and abroad. A chapter in the *Handbook of Administrative Ethics* (Cooper 2001) tracks the emergence of administrative ethics as a field of study in the United States and leaves little doubt that more attention will be devoted to teaching ethics in public administration programs and schools in the years ahead. Added emphasis, as noted earlier, will be placed on defining and measuring one's ethical competency. A forthcoming volume (Cooper and Menzel 2013) explores in some depth what it means to become ethically competent for public service leadership.

Promoting ethical behavior in public service is not limited to MPA programs. Many universities have established ethics centers and institutes to carry out a myriad of programs and activities. The Markkula Center for Applied Ethics (n.d.) at Santa Clara University in California is one of the most active. The center's ethics programs are quite comprehensive, ranging from business ethics to global ethics, government ethics, technology ethics, and more. Among the innovative government ethics programs is the "Ethics and Leadership Camp for Public Officials." This two-day camp, which was launched for the first time in June 2006, attracted more than two dozen local city council members and ethics officers from California, Texas, and Arizona (Brown 2006). One novelty intended to heighten the campers' sensitivity to ethics and accountability was a "moral compass" that was slung around their necks. Exercises and group discussions were directed at enabling the campers to:

- Find ways to strengthen their city's ethics program.
- Identify the 10 most common ethical pitfalls of cities.
- Learn the best practices for city ethics program.
- Fulfill California's AB1234 ethics training requirement.

Exhibit 10.1
MPA Student Code of Ethics

1. I will abide by procedures, rules, and regulations as described in the MPA Student Handbook and the college catalog.
2. I will respect the guidelines prescribed by each professor in the preparation of academic assignments and other course requirements.
3. I will be objective, understanding, and honest in academic performance and relationships.
4. I will strive toward academic excellence, improvement of professional skills, and expansion of professional knowledge.
5. I will neither engage in, assist in, nor condone cheating, plagiarism, or other such activities.
6. I will respect and protect the rights, privileges, and beliefs of others.
7. I will become familiar with and adhere to the standards of ethical conduct established by each of the professional societies to which I am admitted as a member.
8. I will not tolerate unethical conduct on the part of others who claim membership in a professional society of which I am a member and will take appropriate action to disclose a violation of ethical standards.

Sources: This code was adapted and developed by the author from the following sources—University of Wisconsin–Madison, 1992; Florida Gulf Coast University, 2009.

In addition to university-based ethics centers, there are a number of non-profit organizations that promote ethics and integrity in the public service. The more prominent ones are the Ethics Resource Center (www.ethics.org), the Council on Governmental Ethics Laws (www.cogel.org), City Ethics (www.cityethics.org), the International Institute for Public Ethics (www.iipe.org), and the Government Accountability Project (www.whistleblower.org).

Public service professional associations such as the American Society for Public Administration (ASPA—www.aspanet.org), the International City/County Management Association (ICMA—www.icma.org), and the Government Finance Officers Association (www.gfoa.org) place a great deal of emphasis on ethical behavior. All have professional codes of ethics. ASPA and ICMA also offer resource materials and training activities for their members. ASPA's ethics section is especially focused on promoting ethics and integrity in governance. The section's web site (www.aspaonline.org/ethicscommunity) offers visitors access to decision scenarios, slide presentations, and an ethics compendium.

Internationally, there is considerable movement to promote ethical behavior, especially among emerging democracies that are struggling for economic and political independence. Nations like Russia and China are trying to loosen the grip of corruption and embrace the rule of law. The United Nations has stepped up its efforts to lend a hand as well. A report titled *Public Service in Transition* (United Nations 1999) by the Division of Public Economics and Public Administration emphasizes "the critical importance of probity and integrity" of governments worldwide to conduct the public's business. The United Nations has developed an impressive web site, the UN Public Administration Network (n.d.), that provides valuable advisory and training resources. The United Nations has also led by example with the establishment on January 1, 2006, of the Ethics Office. The new office has set up an ethics hotline and is counseling the UN's 29,000 personnel worldwide on financial disclosure and conflicts of interest. "Other tasks will eventually include awareness training on ethics issues" (United Nations 2006).

Staying the Ethical Course

Public managers are increasingly drawn into the ethical haze of privatization and the ethical time warp of the Information Age. Privatization and entrepreneurialism are here to stay (at least for a while) and cannot be ignored. Nor can we turn our heads and ignore the realities of the Information Age and the necessity to rethink what motivates the behaviors and practices of workers in local and global workplaces. We must recognize that while the individual is a moral agent and therefore responsible for his/her actions, he or she functions in a more, not less, complex and dynamic social and organizational environment.

What, then, are the implications for managers who wish to navigate these troubling waters? Most compelling is the need to think and act in terms of organizational ethics. Managers should ask themselves day in and day out: "What can and should I do to foster an ethical environment in my organization?" Leading by example is, of course, a starting point, but it is hardly sufficient. Another factor is recruiting honest employees. Easier said than done? Certainly.

How can managers foster a strong ethical environment in their organizations? Many suggestions have been provided in this book. But to truly succeed, managers must strive to instill an ethical consciousness in their organizations and in their relationships with members of other organizations, both private and public. Among other things, steps should be taken to develop and implement a code or values statement, provide ethics training, establish an ombudsman, or add an ethics element to annual performance reviews. These efforts, separately and collectively, support the view of "ethics as organization development" (Zajac and Comfort 1997).

Twenty-First-Century Challenges

There are several conclusions that can be drawn about the challenges facing ethical governance in the twenty-first century. First, ethics issues and efforts to deal with them are not limited to the American experience. These matters are ubiquitous. Moreover, it is clear that efforts to manage ethics internationally cannot be reduced to a "one size fits all" boilerplate. Creative solutions are needed that allow for cultural differences but at the same time do not treat ethics as something that depends on the situation.

Second, building organizations of integrity is not a one-shot affair. Rather, it is an ongoing process in much the spirit of the cliché that it is the journey, not the destination, that matters. Still, the destination is very important even if it's never reached. What is that destination—workplaces where individuals treat each other with respect, take pride in their work, care about one another, promote accountability, and place the public interest over individual and organizational self-interest. This is the idea and ideal of an organization of integrity.

A third conclusion is that a compliance approach to building an organization of integrity is not sufficient. Indeed, in its most pernicious form it can lead to the lowest common denominator that if it's legal, it's ethical. This low-road approach will never lead to an ethical workplace. Rather, the workplace becomes one in which rule evasion and dodging go hand in hand with a "gotcha" mentality. The high road of aspirational ethics must be taken. Members of the organization must always ask themselves, "What is the right thing to do?" Rules and regulations may help answer this question, but they will never be sufficient. Each person must strive to ensure that his or her ethical compass is working correctly. A faulty ethical compass is the surest way to get lost in the quagmire of today's complex organizations.

A final conclusion offered here is that there is no checklist for building organizations of integrity. Public managers must engage in exemplary leadership, promote ethics training, support codes, conduct ethics audits, and find ways to promote an ethical climate through the use of human resources management processes such as hiring, annual evaluations, and promotion. These tactics can be powerful when combined in a systematic, comprehensive manner—similar, perhaps, to that of an orchestra conductor who must be able to produce harmonious music from diverse musicians and instruments. No single tactic is the best one to transform the sour notes of unethical behavior into the reassuring culture of an organization of integrity.

The ethical challenges facing elected and appointed public officeholders are real and ever more complex, and they must be met. A failure to do so will erode public trust and confidence in government and faith in our more than 200-year-old experiment called the United States of America. Are you ready to meet the challenges of ethics management?

Ethics Management Skill Building

Practicum 10.1. Nonprofit Contracting

As a recent retiree from the U.S. Air Force, you decide to take a position with a nonprofit agency that manages the city's federally funded low-income housing program. On four separate occasions over the next few months, you are told by the city's program administrator to use money from one federal grant to pay for a project that wasn't covered by the grant. One month later you are asked to approve the expenditure of $87,150 on a private residence that would sell for $70,000.

Increasingly uncomfortable with the situation, you object, asserting that federal guidelines prohibit the city from spending that much money on low-income housing. The city administrator complains to your boss that you are not attentive, productive, or responsive to city staff. Your boss decides to remove you from the project. Frustrated but convinced that you did the right thing, you write to the mayor detailing your concerns about the misuse of federal funds. The mayor never responds.

A few months later the city's internal auditing staff reports that the city administrator has issued questionable loans, kept poor records, and awarded noncompetitive bids. Housing and Urban Development (HUD) officials warn the mayor that the administrator may have misused $1.4 million in federal funds. The administrator claims that the feds are applying ridiculous rules. The mayor backs him. The administrator appears before city council and asserts that "we do not intend to follow HUD's direction at this point." All but one member of city council praises the administrator.

Fast-forward two years . . . a federal indictment charges that the city housing administrator used government jobs to reap thousands of dollars in gratuities. HUD requires the city to return $1,402,650 to the U.S. Treasury.

Questions

1. Did your boss do the right thing in removing you from the project?
2. Did you do the right thing in going around your boss by writing directly to the mayor?
3. What policy would you draft to prevent a city administrator from misusing federal grants for low-income housing? Would your policy apply to the director of the nonprofit agency?

Practicum 10.2. Entrepreneurialism at the Office

Jan and Bill are ambitious, energetic urban planners employed by the U.S. Department of Transportation (DOT) in Atlanta's regional headquarters. Their work on several comprehensive plans brings them much praise, including several positive stories published in the *New York Times.* One day, Jan says to Bill, "Why don't we try to make some money as planning consultants? We can advertise ourselves on the web with our own site. The costs would be minimal, and as long as we don't contract with clients doing business with our agency, there shouldn't be any ethical or legal issues to contend with."

Bill gives Jan's suggestion a few days of thought, and a week later they have a web site in place. On the site, Jan and Bill are presented as Jones & Greene Associates, Urban Planners. Services that their firm can provide include, among other things, market analysis, community planning, business site selection, and geographic information systems.

Assume you are Jan and Bill's boss at the DOT and you happen to come upon their web site. While it does not identify the U.S. DOT as Bill and Jan's employer, the site does state that they have significant government experience as urban planners. Moreover, the page contains their firm's e-mail address and Bill's home office telephone number.

Two weeks later while at work, you happen to overhear Bill talking by telephone with an apparent client about his consulting services.

Questions

1. What would you do? Would you call Bill and Jan aside and tell them that they cannot do private business while at the office?
2. Would you consult with your agency's Designated Ethics Officer?

3. Would you report them to the U.S. Office of Government Ethics?
4. Would you ignore the situation?

Notes

1. See Henry (2011) for a critical review of contracting by the U.S. government.

2. See Bretschneider and Mergel (2011) for a comprehensive treatment of technology and public management information systems.

3. There is a growing body of literature regarding the plight of public administration in a "postglobal" world. See Schultz (2011) for an overview.

4. See Raffel, Maser, and Calarusse (2011) for an in-depth discussion of NASPAA competencies in education for leadership in public service.

5. This discussion draws on Bowman and Menzel (2004).

References

Abbott, L. 2006. Personal e-mail communication, July 8.

Abramson, A. 2010. "Palm Beach County Ethics Commission Launches Its Fight Against Corruption." *Palm Beach Post,* July 15.

Adam, A.M., and D. Rachman-Moore. 2004. "The Methods Used to Implement an Ethical Code of Conduct and Employee Attitudes." *Journal of Business Ethics* 54: 225–244.

African Public Service Ministers. 2001. "Charter for the Public Service in Africa." Meeting of the Third Biennial Pan-African Conference of Ministers of Civil Service, Windhoek, Namibia. February 5. www.ictregulationtoolkit.org/en/Document.1430. pdf (accessed December 5, 2011).

Aguilar, Melissa. 2010. "Post-Skilling, Movement Afoot on Honest Services Fraud." *Compliance Week,* October 4. www.complianceweek.com/post-skilling-movement-afoot-on-honest-services-fraud/article/187439/ (accessed April 17, 2011).

allAfrica.com. 2010. "Experts Discuss African Public Service Charter." September 6. http://allafrica.com/stories/201009061127.html (accessed February 11, 2011).

Alpert, Bruce. 2010. "Judge Thomas Porteous Not Trustworthy, Task Force Declares." Nola.com, January 22. www.nola.com/crime/index.ssf/2010/01/judge_thomas_porteous_not_trus.html (accessed March 31, 2011).

American Society for Public Administration (ASPA). 2004. "Integrity at the United Nations." *Ethics Moments* (October). www.aspaonline.org/ethicscommunity/moments/oct04.htm.

———. 2006. "ASPA's Code of Ethics." http://www.aspanet.org/scriptcontent/index_codeofethics.cfm.

Anderson, Gavin. 2004. Telephone conversation, December. Gavin Anderson is a Deputy District Attorney in Salt Lake County.

———. 2011. Personal e-mail communication, May 19.

Anechiarico, F., and J.B. Jacobs. 1994. "Visions of Corruption Control and the Evolution of American Public Administration." *Public Administration Review* 54:465–473.

———. 1996. *The Pursuit of Absolute Integrity: How Corruption Control Makes Government Ineffective.* Chicago, IL: University of Chicago Press.

Armstrong, E. 2005. "Integrity, Transparency and Accountability in Public Administration: Recent Trends, Regional and International Developments and Emerging Issues." United Nations, Economic & Social Affairs, 1–10.

Associated Press. 2011. "NY Governor Signs Government Ethics Law." *Wall Street Journal,* August 15. http://online.wsj.com/article/APc2da03d25ded42f3a28f31-adc99bb8c0.html (accessed August 16, 2011).

Audit Commission. 2003. *Corporate Governance.* Report, October. www. audit-commission.gov.uk/SiteCollectionDocuments/AuditCommissionReports/ NationalStudies/CorporateGovernance.pdf (accessed January 3, 2006).

———. 2011. *Changing Organisational Cultures.* March. http://www.intecpublicsector. com/system/files/FinalChangingorganisationalflyerMarch2011.pdf (accessed May 2, 2011).

Ayres, Walter C. 2005. Personal e-mail communication.

Bailey, S. 1964. "Ethics and the Public Service." *Public Administration Review* 24: 234–243.

Barnard, C. 1938. *The Functions of the Executive.* Cambridge, MA: Harvard University Press.

Barton, P., and L. Shames. 2003. *Not Fade Away.* New York: HarperCollins.

Bass, B.M., and P. Steidimeier. 1999. "Ethics, Character, and Authentic Transformational Leadership Behavior." *Leadership Quarterly,* 10:181–208.

Bazerman, M.H., and A.E. Tenbrunsel. 2011. *Blind Spots: Why We Fail to Do What's Right and What to Do About It.* Princeton, NJ: Princeton University Press.

Bellah, R.N., R. Madsen, S.M. Tipton, W.M. Sullivan, and A. Swidler. 1991. *The Good Society.* New York: Random House.

Bellamy, Calvin. 2010. Letter to the Editor. *Chicago Tribune,* September 17. http://articles.chicagotribune.com/2010-09-17/news/ct-vp-0917voiceletters-briefs-20100917_1_chicago-mayor-richard-daley-fresh-face-china-shop/2 (accessed May 2, 2011).

Bellomo, T. 2005. "The Making of an Ethical Executive." *New York Times,* February 14.

Bender, M.C. 2011. "Tea Party Picks Up Ethics Issue as Gov. Scott Retreats." November 11. http://www.tampabay.com/news/politics/stateroundup/tea-party-picks-up-ethics-issue-as-gov-scott-retreats/1201061 (accessed November 14, 2011).

Bennett, C.G. 1959a. "Strict City Code of Ethics Voted by Estimate Board." *New York Times,* August 21.

———. 1959b. "City Code of Ethics Signed by Wagner." *New York Times,* September 4.

———. 1960. "Mayor Inducts Board of Ethics." *New York Times,* January 8.

Bennis, W.G. 1993. *An Invented Life: Reflections on Leadership and Change.* Reading, MA: Addison-Wesley.

Berman, E.M. 1996. "Restoring the Bridges of Trust: Attitudes of Community Leaders Toward Local Government." *Public Integrity Annual,* 31–49.

Berman, E.M., M.J. Moon, and H. Choi, eds. 2010. *Public Administration in East Asia.* Boca Raton, FL: CRC Press.

Berman, E.M., and J.P. West. 1997. "Managing Ethics to Improve Performance and Build Trust." *Public Integrity Annual,* 23–31.

———. 2003. "Solutions to the Problem of Managerial Mediocrity." *Public Performance and Management Review* 27 (December): 30–52.

———. 2012. "Public Values in Special Districts: A Survey of Managerial Commitment." *Public Administration Review* 72 (Jan/Feb).

Berman, E., J. West, and A. Cava. 1994. "Ethics Management in Municipal Governments and Large Firms: Exploring Similarities and Differences." *Administration & Society* 26 (August): 185–203.

Better Government Association. 2002. "The BGA Integrity Index." www.bettergov. org/2008_bga-alper_integrity_index_/.

Black, M.P. 2011. Personal e-mail message March 21. Marty Black is the former city manager of Venice, Florida.

The Boeing Company. n.d. "Boeing Code of Conduct." In *Boeing Ethical Business Conduct Guidelines.* http://boeing.com/companyoffices/aboutus/ethics/ethics_booklet.pdf.

Bok, D. 1990. *Universities and the Future of America.* Durham, NC: Duke University Press.

Bonczek, S.J. 1998. "Creating an Ethical Work Environment: Enhancing Ethics Awareness in Local Government." In *The Ethics Edge,* ed. E.M. Berman, J.P. West, and S.J. Bonczek. Washington, DC: International City/County Management Association, 72–79.

Bossaert, D., and C. Demmke. 2005. *Main Challenges in the Field of Ethics and Integrity in the EU Member States.* Maastricht, The Netherlands: European Institute of Public Administration.

Bowley, Graham. 2011. "At I.M.F., a Strict Ethics Code Doesn't Apply to Top Officials." *New York Times,* May 30, B1.

Bowman, J.S. 1977. "Ethics in the Federal Service: A Post-Watergate View." *Midwest Review of Public Administration* 11 (March): 3–20.

———. 1981. "Ethical Issues for the Public Manager." In *A Handbook of Organization Management,* ed. William B. Eddy. New York: Marcel Dekker.

———. 1990. "Ethics in Government: A National Survey of Public Administrators." *Public Administration Review* 50 (May/June): 345–353.

Bowman, J.S., and D. Menzel. 2004. "Ethics Practices and Experiences in Graduate Public Administration Education." Paper presented at the 65th Annual Conference of the American Society for Public Administration. Portland, Oregon, March 27–30.

Bowman, J.S., and J.P. West. 2011. "The Profession of Public Administration: Promise, Problems, and Prospects." In *The State of Public Administration: Issues, Challenges, and Opportunities,* ed. D. Menzel and H. White. Armonk, NY: M.E. Sharpe, 25–35.

Bowman, J.S., and R.L. Williams. 1997. "Ethics in Government: From a Winter of Despair to a Spring of Hope." *Public Administration Review* 57: 517–526.

Brady, W.D. 2011. *Procurement Management Review.* Sarasota County, Procurement Department, Final Report, June 7. National Institute of Governmental Purchasing. www.scgov.net/CFPO/ProcurementPurchasing/documents/NIGPFinalReport.pdf.

Brandeis, L. 2011. http://www.goodreads.com/author/quotes/1287729.Louis_Dembitz_Brandeis (accessed November 16, 2011).

Bretschneider, S.I., and I. Mergel. 2011. "Technology and Public Management Information Systems: Where We Have Been and Where We Are Going." In *The State of Public Administration: Issues, Challenges, and Opportunities,* ed. D. Menzel and H. White. Armonk, NY: M.E. Sharpe, 187–203.

Brewer, G.A., and S. Coleman Selden. 1998. "Whistleblowers in the Federal Civil Service: New Evidence of the Public Service Ethic." *Journal of Public Administration Research and Theory* 8 (July): 413–439.

Brown, P.L. 2006. "At Ethics Camp, Not-So-Tall Tales from the Dark Side." *New York Times,* June 23.

Brown, S. 2005. "Managing Municipal Ethics." www.gmanet.com/event_detail/default.asp?eventid=6445&menuid=GeorgiaCitiesNewspaperID (accessed December 29, 2005).

Bruce, W. 1994. "Ethical People Are Productive People." *Public Productivity and Management Review* 17 (Spring): 23–30.

Brumback, G.B. 1998. "Institutionalizing Ethics in Government." In *The Ethics Edge,* ed. E.M. Berman, J.P. West, and S.J. Bonczek. Washington, DC: International City/County Management Association, 61–71.

Burke, F., and A. Black. 1990. "Improving Organizational Productivity: Add Ethics." *Public Productivity and Management Review* 14 (Winter): 121–133.

Burke, J.P. 1986. *Bureaucratic Responsibility.* Baltimore, MD: Johns Hopkins University Press.

California Fair Political Practices Commission. 2011. "AB 1234 Ethics Training for Local Officials." www.fppc.ca.gov/index.php?id=477 (accessed November 10, 2011).

California State Controller's Office. 2010. "Controller's Bell Audit Finds Mismanaged Bonds, Unlawful Payments and Illegal Taxes." Press release, September 22. www.sco.ca.gov/eo_pressrel_controller_chiang_2010_bell_audit.html (accessed March 6, 2011).

Campbell, K. 2011. "At I.M.F., a Strict Ethics Code Doesn't Apply to Top Officials." *New York Times,* May 30: B1.

CAPRI Engineering. 2005. "CAPRI Engineering Applauds the Private Provider Law." *Business Wire,* April 12. www.businesswire.com/news/homes/2005041200557/en/CAPRI-Engineering-Applauds-Private-Provider-Law (accessed November 16, 2011).

Carnevale, D.G. 1995. *Trustworthy Government: Leadership and Management Strategies for Building Trust and High Performance.* San Francisco, CA: Jossey-Bass.

Carter, S.L. 1997. *Integrity.* New York: HarperPerennial.

Chan, S. 2005. "Transit Leader to Pay Fine in Ethics Case." *New York Times,* August 27.

Chiang, John. 2010. *City of Bell Audit Report: Administrative and Internal Accounting Controls, July 1, 2008, Through June 30, 2010.* California State Controller, September 22. www.sco.ca.gov/Press-Releases/2010/sco_bell_audit_2010.pdf (accessed March 6, 2011).

China Daily. 2005. "Top Civil Servants Must Disclose Finances." April 29. www2.chinadaily.com.cn/english/doc/2005–04/29/content_438416.htm (accessed January 3, 2006).

Citrus County, Florida. 2011. Board of County Commissioners—Blog. http://bocc.citrus.fl.us/blog/.

City of Chicago, Illinois. 2010. "Department: Ethics." www.cityofchicago.org/city/en/depts/ethics.html.

———. 2011. "Government Ethics Ordinance." Chapter 2–156, Municipal Code of Chicago, June 8. www.cityofchicago.org/city/en/depts/ethics/supp_info/governmental_ethicsordinance.htm (accessed November 16, 2011).

City of Chicago Board of Ethics. 2004. *Annual Report 2003–04.* http://www.cityofchicago.org/dam/city/depts/ethics/general/AnnualReports/ann-rpt-03-04.pdf (accessed January 3, 2006).

———. 2009. *Annual Report 2008–2009.* www.cityofchicago.org/content/dam/city/depts/ethics/general/AnnualReports/Ann-Rpt-08-09.pdf (accessed March 6, 2011).

City of Jacksonville, Florida. 1999. "Introduction." Jacksonville Ethics Code, Office of the General Counsel, August 24. http://generalcounsel.coj.com/documents/2007JacksonvilleEthicsCode.pdf (accessed January 3, 2006).

———. 2004. *Compliance Report 2004.* Jacksonville Ethics Commission.

———. 2007. Report No. 08-01. Office of the Inspector General, November 29.

www3.coj.net/Departments/Ethics-Office/Docs/inspector-general-report-no-08-01. aspx (accessed May 12, 2011).

———. 2009. "Ethics Education Program." Jacksonville Ordinance Code, Sec. 602.1001, February 11. Available at www.coj.net/Departments/Ethics-Office/ Ethics-Code-%28Current%29.aspx (accessed March 6, 2011).

———. n.d.a. "Duties of the Ethics Officer." www.coj.net/Departments/Ethics-Office/ Duties-of-the-Ethics-Officer.aspx.

———. n.d.b. "Ethics Office." www.coj.net/Departments/Ethics-Office.aspx.

———. n.d.c. "Inspector-General: Background." www3.coj.net/Departments/ Inspector-General/Background.aspx (accessed May 12, 2011).

City of New York Conflicts of Interest Board (COIB). 2010. *Annual Report 2010: Ethics Lights the Way to Good Government.* http://www.nyc.gov/html/conflicts/ downloads/pdf2/annual_reports/final_report_2010.pdf (accessed May 25, 2011).

City of San Diego, California. 2002. "Chapter 2, Article 7, Division 35: City of San Diego Ethics Ordinance." Municipal Code, April 29. http://docs.sandiego.gov/municode/ MuniCodeChapter02/Ch02Art07Division35.pdf (accessed August 8, 2011).

———. 2007. "Office of Ethics & Integrity," *Annual Fiscal Year 2008 Budget,* 241–247. www.sandiego.gov/fm/annual/pdf/fy08/30v20fficeofethics.pdf (accessed August 8, 2011).

City of Sweet Home, Oregon. 2011. www.sweet-home.or.us (accessed March 6, 2011).

City of Tampa, Florida. 2003a. "Mission and Duties of the City Ethics Officer." Article VII: City of Tampa Ethics Code, Division 2, Sec. 2–621, October 2. www.tampagov. net/dept_human_resources/files/City_of_Tampa_Ethics_Code.pdf.

———. 2003b. "Powers, Duties and Jurisdiction of Ethics Commission." Article VII: City of Tampa Ethics Code, Division 2, Sec. 2–657, October 2. www.tampagov. net/dept_human_resources/files/City_of_Tampa_Ethics_Code.pdf.

———. 2003c. "Procedure on Complaints of Violations." Article VII: City of Tampa Ethics Code, Division 2, Sec. 2–658, October 2. www.tampagov.net/dept_human_ resources/files/City_of_Tampa_Ethics_Code.pdf.

———. 2003d. "Prohibited Activities Relating to Fraternization." Article VII: City of Tampa Ethics Code, Division 2, Sec. 2–548, October 2. www.tampagov.net/ dept_human_resources/files/City_of_Tampa_Ethics_Code.pdf.

———. 2003e. "Purpose and Legislative Intent." Article VII: City of Tampa Ethics Code, Division 2, Sec. 2–501, October 2. www.tampagov.net/dept_human_ resources/files/City_of_Tampa_Ethics_Code.pdf.

———. 2003f. "Recommended." Article VII: City of Tampa Ethics Code, Division 2, Sec. 2–659, October 2. www.tampagov.net/dept_human_resources/files/ City_of_Tampa_Ethics_Code.pdf.

———. 2010. *Ethics Commission 2010 Annual Report.* www.tampagov.net/dept_ human_resources/files/2009%20Ethics%20Commission%20Report.pdf (accessed June 30, 2011).

CityEthics.org. 2006. "Jacksonville, FL." May 14. www.cityethics.org/city/ jacksonville.

Cohen, S., and W. Eimicke. 1999. "Is Public Entrepreneurship Ethical?" *Public Integrity* 1 (Winter): 54–74.

Cole, Rick. 2011. Ventura City Manager Blog. http://cmblog.cityofventura.net.

Comissão de Ética Pública (CEP). n.d. "Sobre a Comissão: O que é." (Public Ethics Commission. n.d. "About the Commission: What It Is"). http://etica.planalto.gov. br/sobre/o_que_e.

Committee on Standards in Public Life. 2004. *Getting the Balance Right—Implementing Standards of Conduct in Public Life.* Tenth Report. Presented to Parliament by the Prime Minister by Command of Her Majesty. http://www.official-documents. gov.uk/document/cm64/6407/6407.pdf.

Confessore, N., and T. Kaplan. 2011. "Cuomo and Legislators Reach Deal on Ethics Overhaul." *New York Times,* June 4.

Connolly, C. 2005. "Director of NIH Agrees to Loosen Ethics Rules." *Washington Post,* August 26.

Conquergood, M. 2005. Personal e-mail communication.

Constitution of the United States. 1787. America's Historical Documents. College Park, MD: U.S. National Archives and Records Administration. http://www. archives.gov/historical-docs/document.html?doc=3&title.raw=Constitution%20 0f%20the%20United%20States.

Cook County, Illinois. 2011a. "Board of Ethics." Cook County Web site. http://www. co.cook.il.us/portal/server.pt/community/board_of_ethics/293/ethics%2C_board_ of/401.

———. 2011b. "Board of Ethics Meetings & Members." Cook County Web site. http://www.co.cook.il.us/portal/server.pt/community/board_of_ethics/293/board_ meetings_members/402.

Cooper, T.L. 1982. *The Responsible Administrator: An Approach to Ethics for the Administrative Role.* Port Washington, NY: Kennikat Press.

———. 1984. "Citizenship and Professionalism in Public Administration." *Public Administration Review* 44 (March): 143–149.

———. 1986. *The Responsible Administrator: An Approach to Ethics for the Administrator Role.* 2d ed. Millwood, NY: Associated Faculty Press.

———. 1987. "Hierarchy, Virtue, and the Practice of Public Administration: A Perspective for Normative Ethics." *Public Administration Review* 47 (July/August): 320–328.

———. 1998. *The Responsible Administrator.* 4th ed. San Francisco, CA: Jossey-Bass.

———, ed. 2001. *Handbook of Administrative Ethics.* 2d ed. New York: Marcel Dekker.

———. 2006a. *The Responsible Administrator.* 5th ed. San Francisco, CA: Jossey-Bass.

———. 2006b. Personal e-mail communication, February 27.

Cooper, T.L., and D.C. Menzel, eds. 2013. *Achieving Ethical Competency for Public Service Leadership.* Armonk, NY: M.E. Sharpe.

Cooper, T.L., and N.D. Wright, eds. 1992. *Exemplary Public Administrators.* San Francisco, CA: Jossey-Bass.

Cooper, T.L., and D.E. Yoder. 2002. "Public Management Ethics Standards in a Transnational World." *Public Integrity* 4 (Fall): 333–352.

Corporate Leadership Council. 2003. "Fact Brief: Administering Ethics Hotlines." Catalog No. CLC1YFAG9, March. https://cfo.executiveboard.com/public/ documents/ADR_Administering_Ethics_Hotlines.pdf.

Council for Excellence in Government. 1992–1993. "Ethical Principles for Public Servants." *Public Manager* 21: 37–39.

Council of Governmental Ethics Laws (COGEL). 2004. *COGEL Blue Book: 2004 Ethics Update.* Jacksonville, FL.

———. 2010. *COGEL Blue Book: 2010 Ethics Update.* Jacksonville, FL.

Covey, S. R. 2004. *Seven Habits of Highly Effective People.* New York: Free Press.
Cuomo, Andrew M. 2011. State of the State Address. Albany, NY, January 5. www.governor.ny.gov/s12/stateofthestate2011transcript (accessed April 9, 2011).
Cusick, Robert I. 2010. Director's Welcome Remarks. The 17th National Government Ethics Conference, May 10–14, Chicago, IL. www.usoge.gov/conference/pdf/17th_cusick_welcome.pdf (accessed June 2, 2011).
Dao, J. 2005. "Governor of Ohio Is Charged with Breaking Ethics Law." *New York Times,* August 18.
Davey, M. 2008. "Illinois Governor Arrested in Inquiry into Filling Obama's Senate Seat." *New York Times,* December 9. www.nytimes.com/2008/12/09/world/americas/09iht-10illinois.18524701.html.
Davey, M., and E.G. Fitzsimmons. 2011. "Jury Finds Blagojevich Guilty of Corruption." *New York Times,* June 28, A1.
Davey, M., and G. Ruethling. 2006. "Former Illinois Governor Is Convicted in Graft Case." *New York Times,* April 18.
Davies, M. 2005. Personal e-mail communication, February 7.
Davis, M. 1999. Cited in R.W. Smith, "Local Government Ethics Boards: A Panel Discussion on the New York Experience." *Public Integrity* 1 (Fall): 397–416.
Daytona Beach Morning Journal. 1954. Editorial. November 1.
deLeon, L. 1996. "Ethics and Entrepreneurship." *Policy Studies Journal* 24 (Autumn): 496–514.
Denhardt, K.G. 1988. *The Ethics of Public Administration: Resolving Moral Dilemmas in Public Organizations.* New York: Greenwood.
———. 1989. "The Management of Ideals: A Political Perspective on Ethics." *Public Administration Review* 49 (March/April): 187–192.
Denhardt, R.B. 1981. *In the Shadow of Organization.* Lawrence, KS: Regents Press of Kansas.
Dobel, J.P. 1993. "The Realpolitik of Ethics Codes: An Implementation Approach to Public Ethics." In *Ethics and Public Administration,* ed. H.G. Frederickson. Armonk, NY: M.E. Sharpe.
———. 1999. *Public Integrity.* Baltimore, MD: Johns Hopkins University Press.
———. 2009. "Value Driven Leading: A Management Approach." Case Teaching Resources from The Electronic Hallway at The Evans School of Public Affairs, University of Washington.
Dobuzinskis, A. 2011. "City Manager Pleads Not Guilty in Bell, California, Pay Scandal." Reuters, March 24. www.reuters.com/article/2011/03/24/us-pay-scandal-idUSTRE72N8HJ20110324 (accessed April 9, 2011).
Dong, K.Y., H.S. Yang, and X. Wang. 2010. "Public Service Ethics and Anticorruption Efforts in Mainland China." In *Public Administration in East Asia,* ed. E.M. Berman, M.J. Moon, and H. Choi. Boca Raton, FL: CRC Press.
Drucker, P.F. 2004. Cited in S.R. Covey, *Seven Habits of Highly Effective People,* p. 101.
Dugan, K., and K. Woodhouse. 2011. "A Code of Ethics that Packs a Punch." *Public Management.* 93 (November), 6–10.
Dunlap, A. 1997. *Mean Business: How I Save Bad Companies and Make Good Companies Great.* New York: Fireside.
Eckhart, R. 2011. "Indicted Project Manager Received Gifts from Another Firm." *Herald-Tribune.com* (Sarasota, FL), May 10. www.heraldtribune.com/article/20110510/ARTICLE/110519964 (accessed May 12, 2011).

Edmunds, F. 2011. Personal e-mail to the author. March 3. Frank Edmunds is the city manager of Seminole, Florida.

Ellsberg, D. 2004. "Truths Worth Telling." *New York Times,* September 28.

Executive Order 10939. 1961, To Provide a Guide on Ethical Standards to Government Officials. May 5. http://www.thecre.com/fedlaw/lega115/eo10939.htm (accessed November 18, 2011).

Executive Order 11222. 1965. "Prescribing Standards of Ethical Conduct for Government Officers and Employees." May 8. www.usoge.gov/laws_regs/exec_orders/eo11222.html (accessed February 28, 2006).

Executive Order 12668. 1989. "President's Commission on Federal Ethics Law Reform," George H.W. Bush, *Federal Register:* 54 FR 3979, January 27.

Executive Order 12674. 1989. "Principles of Ethical Conduct for Government Officers and Employees," *Federal Register* 54 FR 15159, April 14, as modified by E.O. 12731. April 12. http://www.usoge.gov/laws_regs/exec_orders/eo12674.html.

Executive Order 12834. 1993. "Ethics Commitments by Executive Branch Personnel." January 20. http://search.archives.gov/cs.html?url=http%3A//www.archives.gov/federal-register/executive-orders/pdf/12834.pdf&charset=iso-8859-1&qt=12834&col=1arch+social&n=1&la=en (accessed November 18, 2011).

Executive Order 13490. 2009. "Section 1: Ethics Pledge." January 21. www.whitehouse.gov/the-press-office/ethics-commitments-executive-branch-personnel (accessed June 5, 2011).

Fawcett, G., and M. Wardman. 2005. "Ethical Governance in Local Government in England: A Regulator's View." Paper presented at the Ethics and Integrity of Governance: The First Transatlantic Dialogue, Leuven, Belgium, 2–5 June.

Federal Bureau of Investigation (FBI). 2004. "Investigations of Public Corruption: Rooting Crookedness Out of Government." March 15. www.fbi.gov/news/stories/2004/march/greylord_031504 (accessed June 23, 2006).

Ferrieux-Patterson, M.N. 2003. "Conflict of Interest-Vanuatu's Experience." Paper presented at the 4th Regional Anti-Corruption Conference of the ADB/OECD Anti-Corruption Initiative for Asia and the Pacific, Kuala Lumpur, Malaysia, 3–5 December.

Finn, R. 2005. "Albany's Ethics Policeman Would Like More Muscle." *New York Times,* March 25.

Florida Commission on Ethics. 2004. *Annual Report to the Florida Legislature for Calendar Year 2004.*

Florida Gulf Coast University. 2009. "Code of Ethics." In *2009–2010 MPA Student Handbook,* pp. 13–15. http://cps.fgcu.edu/PA/MPA/Files/handbook.pdf.

Florida Office of Inspector General. 2005. *Contract Management of Private Correctional Facilities.* Internal Audit Report Number 2005–61, June 30.

Folks, S.R. 2000. "A Potential Whistleblower." *Public Integrity* 2 (Winter): 61–74.

Follet, M.P. 1924. *Creative Experience.* New York: Longmans, Green.

Frederickson, H.G. 1992. "Elmer B. Staats: Government Ethics in Practice." In *Exemplary Public Administrators,* ed. T.L. Cooper and N.D. Wright. San Francisco, CA: Jossey-Bass.

———, ed. 1993. *Ethics and Public Administration.* Armonk, NY: M.E. Sharpe.

———. 1997. *The Spirit of Public Administration.* San Francisco, CA: Jossey-Bass.

————. 2011. Personal e-mail communication, May 18.

Frederickson, H.G., and D.K. Hart. 1985. "The Public Service and the Patriotism of Benevolence." *Public Administration Review* 45 (5): 547–553.

Frederickson, H.G., and M.A. Newman. 2001. "The Patriotism of Exit and Voice: The Case of Gloria Flora." *Public Integrity* 3 (Fall): 347–362.

Friedman, T. 2011. "Two Peas in a Pod." *New York Times.* November 8.

Fry, B.R. 1989. *Mastering Public Administration: From Max Weber to Dwight Waldo.* Chatham, NJ: Chatham House.

Gallup. 2010. "Honesty/Ethics in Professions." Poll, November 19–21. www.gallup.com/poll/1654/honesty-ethics-professions.aspx (accessed April 23, 2011).

Garvey, G. 1993. *Facing the Bureaucracy: Living and Dying in a Public Agency.* San Francisco, CA: Jossey-Bass.

Gawthrop, L.C. 1984. *Public Sector Management, Systems, and Ethics.* Bloomington, IN: Indiana University Press.

————. 1998. *Public Service and Democracy: Ethical Imperatives for the 21st Century.* Chappaqua, NY: Chatham House.

————. 1999. "Public Entrepreneurship in the Lands of Oz and Uz." *Public Integrity* 1 (Winter): 75–86.

George C. Marshall Foundation. 2003. "George C. Marshall Foundation Award: A Gala Occasion Honoring Secretary of State Colin L. Powell." *Topics,* December (insert). www.marshallfoundation.org/pdfs/Topics-Gala-Insert.pdf (accessed June 28, 2011).

Georgia Municipal Association (GMA). 2009a. "Becoming a City of Ethics." January 30. www.gmanet.com/CitiesOfEthics.aspx?CNID=19980 (accessed August 5, 2011).

————. 2009b. "Sample Ethics Ordinance." January 30. www.gmanet.com/Assets/PDF/gma_sampleethicsordinance.pdf.

————. 2010. *Ethics in Government: Charting the Right Course.* GMA Legal Report, July (revised). www.gmanet.com/Publications.aspx?CNID=19954.

Gerth, H.H., and C.W. Mills, eds. and trans. 1946. *From Max Weber: Essays in Sociology.* New York: Oxford University Press.

Ghere, R.K. 1996. "Aligning the Ethics of Public-Private Partnership: The Issue of Local Economic Development." *Journal of Public Administration Research and Theory* 6 (October): 599–621.

Gibson, P. 2009. "Examining the Moral Reason of the Ethics Adviser and Counselor: The Case of the Federal Designated Agency Ethics Official." *Public Integrity* 11: 105–120.

Gilman, S.C. 1995a. *The Management of Ethics and Conduct in the Public Service: The United States Federal Government.* Report, December. www.oecd.org/dataoecd/30/22/2731902.htm (accessed January 2, 2006).

————. 1995b. "Presidential Ethics and the Ethics of the Presidency." *Ethics in American Public Service: The Annals of the American Academy of Political and Social Science* 537: 58–75.

————. 2005. "Ethics Codes and Codes of Conduct as Tools for Promoting an Ethical and Professional Public Service: Comparative Successes and Lessons." Paper prepared for the Poverty Reduction and Economic Management (PREM) Network, the World Bank, Washington, DC. http://www.oecd.org/dataoecd/17/33/35521418.pdf.

————. 2006. Personal e-mail communication, July 6.

Gilman, S.C., and C.W. Lewis. 1996. "Public Service Ethics: A Global Dialogue." *Public Administration Review* 56 (November/December): 517–524.

Glazer, M.P., and P.M. Glazer. 1989. *The Whistleblowers: Exposing Corruption in Government and Industry.* New York: Basic Books.

Global Financial Integrity. 2011. *Transnational Crime in the Developing World.* Report, February. http://transcrime.gfip.org (accessed February 13, 2011).

Global Integrity. n.d. "About Us." www.globalintegrity.org/about (accessed July 15, 2011).

————. 2006. *Global Integrity Report.* http://www.globalintegrity.org/information/downloads.

Goldsmith, S., and W.D. Eggers. 2004. *Governing by Network: The New Shape of the Public Sector.* Washington, DC: Brookings Institution Press.

Gong, T. 2000. "Whistleblowing: What Does It Mean in China?" *International Journal of Public Administration* 23 (11): 1899–1923.

Gore, A. 1993. *Creating a Government That Works Better and Costs Less: The Report of the National Performance Review.* New York: Plume.

Gorman, S. 2011. "Voters in California's Corruption-Hit Bell Make Clean Sweep." Reuters, March 9. http://www.reuters.com/article/2011/03/09/us-corruption-bell-election-idUSTRE7286GZ20110309.

Gottlieb, J., R. Vives, and J. Leonard. 2010. "Bell Leaders Hauled Off in Cuffs." *Los Angeles Times,* September 22. http://articles.latimes.com/2010/sep/22/local/la-me-bell-arrest-20100922.

Graham, K. 2005. "Parks Worker Accused of Taking Bribe." *St. Petersburg Times,* February 24.

Groeneweg, S. 2001. "Three Whistleblower Protection Models: A Comparative Analysis of Whistleblower Legislation in Australia, the United States and the United Kingdom. Public Service Commission of Canada." www.psc-cfp.gc.ca/research/merit/whistleblowing_e.htm (accessed January 3, 2006).

Grosenick, L. 1995. "Federal Training Programs: Help or Hindrance?" *Public Manager* 24 (4): 43.

Gustafson, C. 2006. "City Ethics groups Get Looked At by Council." *San Diego Union-Tribune,* May 6.

Hamilton, A. 1787. *The Federalist #6.* http://thomas.loc.gov/home/histdox/fed_06.html.

————. 1788. *The Federalist #78.* http://thomas.loc.gov/home/histdox/fed_78.html.

Harris, G. 2005. "Report Details F.D.A. Rejection of Next-Day Pill." *New York Times,* November 15.

Harlow, L.F. 1977. *Without Fear or Favor: Odyssey of a City Manager.* Provo, UT: Brigham Young University Press.

————, ed. 1981. *Servants of All: Professional Management of City Government.* Provo, UT: Brigham Young University Press.

Hart, D.K. 1984. "The Virtuous Citizen, the Honorable Bureaucrat, and 'Public' Administration." *Public Administration Review* 44: 111–120.

Haynes, W., and B. Gazley. 2011. "Professional Associations and Public Administration: Making a Difference?" In *The State of Public Administration: Issues, Challenges, and Opportunities,* ed. D. Menzel and H. White. Armonk, NY: M.E. Sharpe.

He, Z. 2004. "Improving Responsiveness in Government." In *Windows on China,* ed. M.T. Gordon, M.C. Meininger, and W. Chen. Amsterdam: IOS Press, 143–150.

Hejka-Ekins, A. 1992. "Marie Ragghianti: Moral Courage in Exposing Corruption." In *Exemplary Public Administrators,* ed. T.L. Cooper and N.D. Wright. San Francisco, CA: Jossey-Bass.

———. 2001. "Ethics in In-Service Training." In *Handbook of Administrative Ethics,* 2d ed., ed. T.L. Cooper. New York: Marcel Dekker, 79–103.

Henry, N. 1995. *Public Administration and Public Affairs.* 6th ed. Englewood Cliffs, NJ: Prentice Hall.

———. 2011. "Federal Contracting: Government's Dependency on Private Contractors." In *The State of Public Administration: Issues, Challenges, and Opportunities,* ed. D. Menzel and H. White. Armonk, NY: M.E. Sharpe, 221–237.

Herrmann, F.M. 1997. "Bricks Without Straw: The Plight of Government Ethics Agencies in the United States." *Public Integrity Annual,* 13–22.

Hess, A. 2003. "Assessing the Ethical Judgment of a Potential Employee—II." *Public Administration Times,* September.

Hill, L.A. 2006. "Exercising Moral Courage: A Developmental Agenda." In *Moral Leadership: The Theory and Practice of Power, Judgment, and Policy,* ed. D.L. Rhode. San Francisco, CA: Jossey-Bass.

Hillsborough County, Florida. 2005. "Hillsborough County: Statement of Ethics." June 13. www.hillsboroughcounty.org/administrator/resources/publications/statementOfEthics.pdf (accessed June 29, 2011).

———. 2011. "Disclaimer!" Official Citizen Participation Blog. http://hillsboroughfl.blogspot.com (accessed June 7, 2011).

Hirt, M.J. 2003. "Assessing the Ethical Judgment of a Potential Employee." *Public Administration Times,* July.

Hoekstra, A., A. Belling, and E. Van Der Heide. 2005. "Beyond Compliance—A Practitioners' View." Paper presented at the Ethics and Integrity of Governance: The First Transatlantic Dialogue, Leuven, Belgium, 2–5 June.

Hoge, W. 2005. "Citing Abuse of Authority, U.N. Dismisses Elections Chief." *New York Times,* December 7.

Hunt, M. 2005. "Ethics and British Local Government: The Relevance of Compliance Strategies." Paper presented at the Ethics and Integrity of Governance: The First Transatlantic Dialogue, Leuven, Belgium, 2–5 June.

Illinois Attorney General. 2010. "Ethics and Public Integrity." www.ag.state.il.us/government/ethics.html (accessed July 1, 2011).

Illinois Executive Ethics Commission (IEEC). 2011a. *Fiscal Year 2010 Annual Report.* March. www2.illinois.gov/eec/Documents/FY%202010%20%20AnnualRep.pdf.

———. 2011b. "Letter from James J. Faught, Chair, to Employees and Citizens of the State of Illinois." In *Fiscal Year 2010 Annual Report.* March. www2.illinois.gov/eec/Documents/FY%202010%20%20AnnualRep.pdf.

———. 2011c. http://www2.illinois.gov/eec/Pages/default.aspx. (accessed December 21, 2011).

International City/County Management Association (ICMA). 1998. "Code of Ethics." http://icma.org/en/icma/ethics/code_of_ethics.

———. 2005. "ICMA Rules of Procedure for Enforcement of the Code of Ethics." September. http://icma.org/en/icma/knowledge_network/documents/kn/Document/100266/ICMA_Rules_of_Procedure_for_Enforcement_of_the_Code_of_Ethics (accessed April 20, 2011).

———. 2010. "ICMA Censures Former City Manager for Ethics Violation." December 20. http://icma.org/en/icma/newsroom/highlights/Article/100857/ICMA_Censures_Former_City_Manager_for_Ethics_Violation (accessed April 20, 2011).

———. n.d. "Practices for Effective Local Government Management." http://icma.org/en/university/about/management_practices/overview (accessed December 27, 2008).

Iorio, P. 2011. *Straightforward: Ways to Live & Lead.* Tampa, Florida: Pam Iorio.

Jacksonville Ethics Commission. *Annual Compliance Report 2004.*

Jefferson, T. 1807/1824. *A Winter in Washington.* Memoir in two volumes by Margaret Bayard Smith. New York: E. Bliss and E. White.

Jenkins, C. 2005. "Penalty for Judge Is Seen Two Ways." *St. Petersburg Times,* November 19.

Jennings, B., J.L. Nelson, and E. Parens. 1994. *Values on Campus: A Report.* Briarcliff, NY: Hastings Center.

Jensen, D.P. 2004. "County Ethics Reform Stalled." *Salt Lake Tribune,* December 6.

Jiang Zemin. 2001. Keynote speech at the Communist Party of China's 80th Anniversary. China Internet Information Center, July 2. http://china.org.cn/english/features/35725.htm (accessed August 2, 2005).

Johnson, A. 2011a. Personal e-mail communication, April 28. Alan Johnson is the executive director of Palm Beach County's Commission on Ethics (Florida).

———. 2011b. Personal e-mail communication, May 27.

Johnson, E. 2011. Personal e-mail communication, April 11. Eric Johnson is Director. Strategic Planning and ERP Implementation, Hillsborough County, Florida.

Johnson, R. 2003. *Whistleblowing: When It Works—and Why.* Boulder, CO: Lynne Rienner.

———. 2005. "Comparative Whistleblowing: Administrative, Cultural, and Ethical Issues." Proceedings of 2005 International Conference on Public Administration, October 21–22, Chengdu, P.R. China.

Jos, P.H. 1989. "In Praise of Difficult People: A Portrait of the Committed Whistleblower." *Public Administration Review* 49: 552–561.

Kant, Immanuel. 1785/1989. *Foundations of the Metaphysics of Morals.* Translated from the German by Lewis White Beck. 2d ed. Upper Saddle River, NJ: Prentice Hall.

Kaplan, Thomas. 2011. "Settled in Albany, Gay Marriage Is Still Drawing Opposition," *New York Times,* July 13, A20.

Kaptein, M. 2011. "Toward Effective Codes: Testing the Relationship with Unethical Behavior." *Journal of Business Ethics* 99: 233–251.

Keller, E.K., ed. 1988. *Ethical Insight, Ethical Action: Perspectives for the Local Government Manager.* Washington, DC: International City/County Management Association.

Kennedy, John F. 1961. "Special Message to the Congress on Conflict-of-Interest Legislation and on Problems of Ethics in Government." April 27. http://www.presidency.ucsb.edu/ws/index.php?pid=8092#axzz1bkR1C11c.

Kernaghan, K. 2003. "Integrating Values into Public Service: The Values Statement as Centerpiece." *Public Administration Review* 63 (November/December): 711–719.

King, Martin Luther, Jr. 1963. "Letter from Birmingham Jail." April 16. http://abacus.bates.edu/admin/offices/dos/mlk/letter.html (accessed March 5, 2011).

King County, Washington. 2010. *Ombudsman 2009 Annual Report.* Office of Citizen Complaints. www.kingcounty.gov/operations/Ombudsman/publications.aspx.

King County Board of Ethics (Washington). 2005. *2004 Annual Report.* March. http://your.kingcounty.gov/ethics/annualreport2004.pdf.

———. 2006. *2005 Annual Report.* March. http://your.kingcounty.gov/ethics/annualreport2005.pdf.

———. 2009. "History of the Ethics Program." January 26. http://www.kingcounty.gov/employees/ethics/aboutus/history.aspx (accessed June 23, 2006).

———. 2010a. "2010 Ethics Quiz and Survey Executive Summary." December. http://your.kingcounty.gov/ethics/2010QuizSurveyExecutiveSummary.pdf (accessed June 30, 2011).

———. 2010b, *2010 Annual Report.* 1–20.

Koch, Ed. 2010. "The Mayor and Public Integrity: Remarks Delivered at the National Watchdog Conference Gracie Mansion, New York City, October 24, 2008 by the Hon. Edward I. Koch, 105th Mayor of New York City." Ed. and comp. Eric Kuhn. *Public Integrity* 12 (4): 359–362.

Kocieniewski, D. 2010. "Rangel Censured over Violations of Ethics Rules." *New York Times,* December 3, A1.

Kormanik, B. 2007. "Do You Know When and Where Your City Council Is Meeting?" *Florida Times Union,* June 14.

Kudo, H., and J. Maesschalck. 2005. "The Ethics Law and Ethics Code in Japanese Public Administration: Background, Contents, and Impact." Paper presented at the Ethics and Integrity of Governance: The First Transatlantic Dialogue, Leuven, Belgium, 2–5 June.

Lambert, B. 2005. "Audit Describes 8 Years of Looting by School Officials." *New York Times,* March 3.

Lasthuizen, K. 2008. Leading to Integrity. Dissertation. Amsterdam: VU University.

Lawton, A., and F. Six. 2011. "New Public Management: Lessons from Abroad." In *The State of Public Administration: Issues, Challenges, and Opportunities,* ed. D. Menzel and H. White. Armonk, NY: M.E. Sharpe, 409–423.

Lee, T., and A.G. Bense. 2006. Memorandum. The Florida Legislature. January 20.

Leinbach, K. 2011. Personal e-mail communication, March 4.

Lewis, C.W. 1991. *The Ethics Challenge in Public Service: A Problem-Solving Guide.* San Francisco, CA: Jossey-Bass.

Lewis, C.W., and S.C. Gilman. 2005. *The Ethics Challenge in Public Service: A Problem-Solving Guide.* 2d ed. San Francisco, CA: Jossey-Bass.

Lewis, N.A. 2000. "Obituary: Elliot Richardson Dies at 79; Stood Up to Nixon and Resigned in 'Saturday Night Massacre.'" NYTimes.com—On This Day, January 1. www.nytimes.com/learning/general/onthisday/bday/0720.html (accessed March 7, 2011).

Light, P.C. 1999. *The New Public Service.* Washington, DC: Brookings Institution Press.

Liptak, A. 2010. "Justices Limit Use of 'Honest Services' Law Against Fraud." *New York Times,* June 24.

Lipton, E., and D. Kocieniewski. 2010. "Panel in House Will Try Rangel in Ethics Cases." *New York Times,* July 23, A1.

Lipton, R. 2011. "G.O.P. Senator Resigning Post amid Scandal." *New York Times,* April 22, A1.

Los Angeles County Metropolitan Transportation Authority. 2011. "Codes of Conduct." www.metro.net/about/ethics/code-conduct/ (accessed August 5, 2011).

Lovell, Alan. 2003. "The Enduring Phenomenon of Moral Muteness: Suppressed Whistleblowing." *Public Integrity* 1.5 (Summer): 187–204.

Lui, T.T. 1988. "Changing Civil Servants' Values." In *The Hong Kong Civil Service and Its Future,* ed. I. Scott and J.P. Burns. Hong Kong: Oxford University Press.

Lui, T.T., and I. Scott. 2001. "Administrative Ethics in a Chinese Society: The Case of Hong Kong." In *Handbook of Administrative Ethics,* ed. T.L. Cooper. New York: Marcel Dekker, 649–670.

Mackenzie, G.C. 2002. *Scandal Proof: Do Ethics Laws Make Government Ethical?* Washington, DC: Brookings Institution Press.

Madison, J. 1788. *The Federalist #51.* http://thomas.loc.gov/home/histdox/fed_51.html#.

Manske, M.W., and H.G. Frederickson. 2004. "Building a Strong Local Government Ethics Program." *Public Management* 86 (June): 18–22.

Markkula Center for Applied Ethics. n.d. Santa Clara, CA: Santa Clara University. www.scu.edu/ethics/.

Markus, M.L. 1994. "Finding a Happy Medium: Explaining the Negative Effects of Electronic Communication on Social Life at Work." *ACM Transactions on Information Systems* 12 (April): 119–149.

Martirossian, J. 2004. "Russia and Her Ghosts of the Past." In *The Struggle Against Corruption: A Comparative Study,* ed. Roberta Ann Johnson. New York: Palgrave Macmillan.

Mayer, J.P., ed. 1969. *Democracy in America.* New York: Harper & Row.

McAllister, K. 2005. Personal e-mail communication, May 5.

McAuliffe, D. 2002. "Social Work Ethics Audits: A New Tool for Ethical Practice." Paper presented at the IIPE/AAPAE Conference, Brisbane, Australia.

McAuliffe, M.F., P. Zacks, and A. Johnson. 2009. "Final Presentment of the Palm Beach County Grand Jury: Investigation of Palm Beach County Governance and Public Corruption Issues." May 21. http://www.palmswest.com/clientuploads/pdfs/Government%20Affairs/Final%20Presentment%200f%20the%20Palm%20Beach%20County%20Grand%20Jury.pdf.

McFadden, R.D. 2005. "Obituary: Stanley Kreutzer, 98, Author of New York City Ethics Code." *New York Times,* February 22.

McNees, M. 2007. "(Former) Sarasota City Manager." Blog, May 25. http://srqcm.blogspot.com.

Menzel, D.C. 1992. "Ethics Attitudes and Behaviors in Local Governments: An Empirical Analysis." *State and Local Government Review* 24 (Fall): 94–102.

———. 1993. "The Ethics Factor in Local Government: An Empirical Analysis." In *Ethics and Public Administration,* ed. H. George Frederickson. Armonk, NY: M.E. Sharpe, 191–204.

———. 1995. "The Ethical Environment of Local Government Managers." *American Review of Public Administration* 25 (September): 247–262.

———. 1996a. "Ethics Complaint Making and Trustworthy Government." *Public Integrity Annual,* 73–82.

———. 1996b. "Ethics Stress in Public Organizations." *Public Productivity and Management Review* 20: 70–83.

———. 1997. "Teaching Ethics and Values in Public Administration: Are We Making a Difference?" *Public Administration Review* 57 (May/June): 224–230.

————. 2001a. "Ethics and Public Management." In *Handbook of Public Management Practice and Reform,* ed. K.T. Liou, 349–362. New York: Marcel Dekker.

————. 2001b. "Ethics Management in Public Organizations." In *Handbook of Administrative Ethics,* 2d ed., ed. Terry L. Cooper, 355–366. New York: Marcel Dekker.

————. 2005a. "Research on Ethics and Integrity in Governance: A Review and Assessment." *Public Integrity* 7 (Spring): 147–168.

————. 2005b. "Building Public Organizations of Integrity." Proceedings of 2005 International Conference on Public Administration, Chengdu, P.R. China, October 21–22.

————. 2006. "Ethics Management in Cities and Counties." *Public Management* 88 (January/February): 20–25.

————. 2010. *Ethics Moments in Government: Cases and Controversies.* Boca Raton, FL: CRC Press.

————. 2011. "Ethics and Integrity in Public Service: Issues and Challenges." In *The State of Public Administration: Issues, Challenges, and Opportunities,* ed. D. Menzel and H. White. Armonk, NY: M.E. Sharpe, 108–124.

Menzel, D.C., and K. Carson. 1999. "A Review and Assessment of Empirical Research on Public Administration Ethics: Implications for Scholars and Managers." *Public Integrity* 1 (Summer): 239–264.

Menzel, D., and H. White, eds. 2011. *The State of Public Administration: Issues, Challenges, and Opportunities.* Armonk, NY: M.E. Sharpe.

Merle, R. 2004. "Long Fall for Pentagon Star: Druyun Doled Our Favors by the Millions." *Washington Post,* November 14, A01. www.washingtonpost.com/wp-dyn/articles/A48241-2004N013.html (accessed November 10, 2011).

Metropolitan Transportation Authority (MTA). 2009. "Vendor Code of Ethics." December. www.mta.info/mta/compliance/pdf/vendorethics.pdf (accessed August 5, 2011).

Miami-Dade County Ethics Commission. 2005a. "Miami/Dade Best Practices: Community Outreach—Public Schools." CityEthics.org, May 2. http://www.cityethics.org/best-practice (accessed June 21, 2006). Also see www.miamidadeethics.com.

————. 2005b. "Miami/Dade Best Practices: Training and Education," CityEthics.org, May 2. www.cityethics.org/best-practice (accessed June 21, 2006). Also see www.miamidadeethics.com.

Miceli, M., and J.P. Near. 1985. "Characteristics of Organizational Climate and Perceived Wrongdoing Associated with Whistle-Blowing Decisions." *Personnel Psychology* 38: 525–544.

Miller, C. 2005. Personal e-mail communication, April 25. Carla Miller is the ethics officer in the Ethics Office, City of Jacksonville, Florida.

————. 2011a. "Hotline Analysis Dated August 2007–May 2011." Presented to the Council of the City of Jacksonville, Florida, June 14.

————. 2011b. Personal e-mail communication, November 14.

Miller, J. 2011. "Contractors Gather to Learn of New Cuyahoga County Ethical Standards." *Crain's Cleveland Business,* July 1.

Moilanen, T. 2007. "The Adoption of the Ethics Framework in EU Member States." Paper presented at the Conference on Public Integrity and Anticorruption in the Public Service, Bucharest, Romania. May 29–30.

Moilanen, T., and A. Salminen. 2006. "Comparative Study on the Public-Service Ethics of the EU Member States." A Report from the Human Resources Working Group, EUPAN.

Morin, R., and D. Balz. 2005. "Bush's Popularity Reaches New Low." *Washington Post,* November 4. www.washingtonpost.com/wp-dyn/content/article/2005/11/03/AR2005110301685.html.

Mosley, L. 1982. *Marshall: Hero for Our Times.* New York: Hearst Books.

Nagourney, A., and R. Cathcart. 2010. "City Officials Arrested in Los Angeles Suburb." *New York Times,* September 22: A14.

National Association of Schools of Public Affairs and Administration (NASPAA). 2005. *NASPAA Member Code of Good Practice.* October. www.naspaa.org/codeofgoodpractice/CodeOfGoodPractice.pdf.

———. 2008. *Standards: 2008.* January. www.naspaa.org/accreditation/seeking/reference/standards.asp.

———. 2009. *NASPAA Standards 2009: Accreditation Standards for Master's Degree Programs.* Commission on Peer Review and Accreditation, October 16. www.naspaa.org/accreditation/doc/NS2009FinalVote10.16.2009.pdf (accessed June 7, 2011).

National Conference of State Legislatures. 2010. "Ethics: Links to States' Online Ethics Training Programs, Training Manuals, and Slide Presentations." July. http://www.ncsl.org/?TabId=15349 (accessed April 4, 2011).

National League of Cities. 2010. "The Athenian Oath." http://nlc.org/build-skills-networks/resources/cities-101/the-athenian-oath (accessed June 11, 2011).

National Personnel Authority (NPA). 2000. "Outline of the National Public Service Ethics Law (Law No. 129 of 1999)." www.jinji.go.jp/rinri/eng/detai11/main.htm.

———. n.d.a. "Main Training Courses Conducted by the NPA." www.jinji.go.jp/english/fig/fig_15.htm (accessed January 3, 2006).

———. n.d.b. "Training." www.jinji.go.jp/english/int_05.htm.

Nelson, M. 1999. "The Challenge of Implementing Codes of Conduct in Local Government Authorities." Paper presented at the Ninth International Anti-Corruption Conference, Durban, South Africa, October 10–15. http://9iacc.org/papers/day4/ws3/d4ws3_mnelson.html.

New York City Bar Association. 2010. "Reforming New York State's Ethics Laws the Right Way." Report of the Committee on State Affairs and Committee on Government Ethics. February.

New York State (NYS) Commission on Public Integrity. 2007. The Public Employee Ethics Reform Act of 2007 (PEERA). March 26. http://www.nyintegrity.org/pubs/annual_report_2007/ann_rept_07.html (accessed October 27, 2011).

———. 2010a. "Governor Paterson Fined for Soliciting Yankees Tickets." News release, December 20. http://www.nyintegrity.org/pubs/2010/122010_press.html (accessed April 8, 2011).

———. 2010b. "Investigations." In *2009 Annual Report.* April. www.nyintegrity.org/pubs/annual_report_2009/investigations.html (accessed April 9, 2011).

———. 2010c. "Staff." In *2009 Annual Report.* April. http://www.nyintegrity.org/pubs/annual_report_2009/staff.html (accessed April 9, 2011).

———. 2011. *Annual Report: 2010.* May. www.nyintegrity.org/pubs/annual_report_2010/2010%20Annual%20Report.pdf (accessed May 10, 2011).

New York State Ethics Commission. 2004. *The Ethics Report.* September.

New York Times. 2009. "Editorial: Fed Up with Albany." October 19, A26.

———. 2010a. "Editorial: Untenable Judicial Ethics." November 28, 7.

———. 2010b. "Punishment in the House." November 19, A3. http://www.nytimes.com/2010/11/19/nyregion/19rangelside.html.

————. 2011a. "Editorial: From Pay-to-Play to Jail." April 16, A20. www.nytimes. com/2011/04/16/opinion/16sat3.html.

————. 2011b. "Anna Hazare." http://topics.nytimes.com/top/reference/timestop-ics/people/h/anna_hazare/index.html?scp=10&sq=india%20corruption&st=cse (accessed November 16, 2011).

New Zealand State Services Commission (SSC). 2001. *Walking the Talk: Making Values Real.* Wellington, NZ: SSC. September. http://www.ssc.govt.nz/sites/all/ files/Walking_the_Talk-_full_text.pdf.

Nixon, R. 2011. "G.O.P. Grants Reprieve to House Ethics Office." *New York Times,* January 21.

Obama, B. 2009. President Barack Obama's Inaugural Address. January 20. http:// www.whitehouse.gov/blog/inaugural-address/.

O'Donnell, G. 2006. "Our 21st Century Civil Service—Creating a Culture of Excellence." Speech, June 6. www.egovmonitor.com/node/6303 (accessed July 6, 2006).

O'Leary, R. 2006. *The Ethics of Dissent: Managing Guerrilla Government.* Washington, DC: CQ Press.

Organisation for Economic Co-operation and Development (OECD). 1997. "Managing Policy Ethics." PUMA Policy Brief. February. www.oecd.org/ dataoecd/59/60/1899269.pdf (accessed January 3, 2006).

————. 1998. "Principles for Managing Ethics in the Public Service." PUMA Policy Brief No. 4. May. www.oecd.org/dataoecd/60/13/1899138.pdf.

————. 2004. "OECD Reviews Progress in the Worldwide Fight Against Corruption." News release, January 12. http://www.oecd.org/document/30/0,2340,en_2649_20 1185_33989854_1_1_1_1,00.html (accessed January 3, 2006).

Osborne, D., and T. Gaebler. 1992. *Reinventing Government: How the Entrepreneurial Spirit Is Transforming the Public Sector.* Reading, MA: Addison-Wesley.

Ouchi, W.G. 1981. *Theory Z: How American Business Can Meet the Japanese Challenge.* Reading, MA: Addison-Wesley.

Paine, L.S. 1994. "Managing for Organizational Integrity." *Harvard Business Review* 72 (March/April): 106–117.

Painter, R.W. 2009. *Getting the Government America Deserves: How Ethics Reform Can Make a Difference.* Oxford: Oxford University Press.

Palidauskaite, J. 2006. "Codes of Ethics in Transitional Democracies: A Comparative Perspective." *Public Integrity* 8: 35–48.

Palka, M.K. 2007. "City's Hiring of Tech Firm Faces Review." *Florida Times Union,* Ausust 7.

Palm Beach County, Florida. 2009. Commission on Ethics Ordinance, Revised 10/21/2009. http://southflorida912.0rg/wp-content/uploads/2009/10/Commission-on-Ethics-Ordinance-10-21-09.pdf.

————. 2011. "Louis Dembitz Brandeis: Quotes." Goodreads. www.goodreads.com/ author/quotes/1287729.Louis_Dembitz_Brandeis.

Patterson, S. 2011. "Jacksonville Ethics Commission gains more autonomy." http:// jacksonville.com/news/metro/2011-06-15/story/jacksonville-ethics-commission-gains-more-autonomy (accessed November 13, 2011).

Perry, J.L. 1993. "Whistleblowing, Organizational Performance, and Organizational Control." In *Ethics and Public Administration,* ed. H. George Frederickson. Armonk, NY: M.E. Sharpe, 79–99.

Peters, T.J., and R.H. Waterman. 1982. *In Search of Excellence.* New York: Harper & Row.

Pevkur, A. 2007. "Compatibility of Public Administration Systems and Ethics Management." State Chancellery of the Republic of Estonia, Department of Public Service, Tallinn, Estonia, 16–24.

Pinellas County, Florida. n.d. "Pinellas County Statement of Ethics." http://www.co.pinellas.fl.us/persnl/PCethics.pdf.

Plunkitt, G.W. 1903. "The Curse of Civil Service Reform." In *Plunkitt of Tammany Hall*, ed. W.L. Riordan. New York. http://www.yale.edu/glc/archive/993.htm.

Pope, Jeremy. 2000. *Source Book 2000—Confronting Corruption: The Elements of a National Integrity System.* Transparency International. www.transparency.org/publications/publications/sourcebook2000 (accessed January 3, 2006).

———. 2005. "Observations Concerning Comparative Administrative Ethics in Europe and the U.S." Paper presented at the Ethics and Integrity of Governance: The First Transatlantic Dialogue, Leuven, Belgium, June 2–5.

Pops, G. 2006. "The Ethical Leadership of George C. Marshall." *Public Integrity* 8:165–186.

Public Broadcasting Service. 2005. "Selecting State Judges." *NOW,* June 17. www.pbs.org/now/politics/choosingjudges.html (accessed July 1, 2011).

Rabin, J., ed. 2003. *Encyclopedia of Public Administration and Public Policy.* 2 vols. New York: Marcel Dekker.

Raffel, J.A., S.M. Maser, and C. Calarusse. 2011. "Accreditation and Competencies in Education for Leadership in Public Service" In *The State of Public Administration: Issues, Challenges, and Opportunities,* ed. D. Menzel and H. White. Armonk, NY: M.E. Sharpe, 70–88.

Ragghianti, M. 1992. Cited in A. Hejka-Ekins. "Marie Ragghianti: Moral Courage." In *Exemplary Public Administrators: Character and Leadership in Government,* ed. T.L. Cooper and N.D. Wright. San Francisco: Jossey-Bass.

Reamer, F.G. 2000. "The Social Work Ethics Audit: A Risk-Management Strategy." *Social Work* 45 (July): 355–366.

Reid, A. 2009. "Palm Beach County Approves New Ethics Rules After Corruption Scandals." *South Florida Sun-Sentinel,* December 15.

Report of the National Performance Review. 1993. *Creating a Government That Works Better and Costs Less.* Washington, DC: U.S. Government Printing Office.

Republic of the Philippines. 1989. Republic Act No. 6713. Congress of the Philippines, Metro Manila, Eighth Congress, February 20. www.lawphil.net/statutes/repacts/ra1989/ra_6713_1989.html (accessed June 25, 2006).

Rhode, D.L., ed. 2006. *Moral Leadership: The Theory and Practice of Power, Judgment, and Policy.* San Francisco, CA: Jossey-Bass.

Richardson, E. 1996. *Reflections of a Radical Moderate.* New York: Pantheon Books.

Roberts, R.N. 1988. *White House Ethics: The History of the Politics of Conflict of Interest Regulation.* New York: Greenwood.

Rohr, J.A. 1978. *Ethics for Bureaucrats: An Essay on Law and Values.* New York: Marcel Dekker.

———. 1986. *To Run a Constitution: The Legitimacy of the Administrative State.* Lawrence: University Press of Kansas.

———. 1989. *Ethics for Bureaucrats: An Essay on Law and Values.* 2d ed. New York: Marcel Dekker.

———. 1998. *Public Service, Ethics, and Constitutional Practice.* Lawrence: University Press of Kansas.

Ronquillo, A. 2007. "Ethics in Government: The Philippine Scenario." Paper presented at EUROPA, Tehran, Iran. November 18–22.

Rose-Ackerman, S. 1999. *Corruption and Government: Causes, Consequences, and Reform.* New York: Cambridge University Press.

Rosen, L. 2010. "Understanding Corruption." *The American Interest,* March–April. www.the-american-interest.com/article.cfm?piece=792 (accessed February 13, 2011).

Rosenson, Beth A. 2005. *The Shadowlands of Conduct: Ethics and State Politics.* Washington, DC: Georgetown University Press.

Salt Lake County, Utah. 2011. "County Ethics Code." Salt Lake County, Utah, Code of Ordinances, Chapter 2.07, May 16. http://library.municode.com/HTML/16602/leve12/TIT2ADPE_CH2.07COETCO.html#TOPTITLE (accessed November 13, 2011).

Scheer, Robert. 1976. "The Playboy Interview: Jimmy Carter," *Playboy* 23, no. 11 (November): 63–86. http://www.arts.mcgill.ca/history/faculty/troyweb/courseweb/jimmycartertheplayboyinterview.htm (accessed February 27, 2006).

Schneider, B., ed. 1990. *Organizational Climate and Culture.* San Francisco, CA: Jossey-Bass.

Schultz, D. 2011. "The Crisis of Public Administration Theory in a Postglobal World." In *The State of Public Administration: Issues, Challenges, and Opportunities,* ed. D. Menzel and H. White. Armonk, NY: M.E. Sharpe, 453–464.

Scott, W.G., and D.K. Hart. 1979. *Organizational America.* Boston, MA: Houghton Mifflin.

———. 1989. *Organizational Values in America.* New Brunswick, NJ: Transaction Publishers.

Schweers, J. 2005. "Concern Builds as Home Inspection Goes Private." *Florida Today.* July 25.

Senge, P. 1990. *The Fifth Discipline: The Art and Practice of the Learning Organization.* New York: Currency Doubleday.

Sheyn, E.R. 2011. "Criminalizing the Denial of Honest Services After Skilling." ExpressO. Available at http://works.bepress.com/elizabeth_sheyn/2 (accessed June 21, 2011).

Shorstein, H.L., and G.E. Schulz, Jr. 2008. *Open Government: Restoring Accountability and Public Confidence in Jacksonville's Local Government.* Final Report of the Duval County Grand Jury, January 17. www3.coj.net/Departments/Ethics-Office/Docs/grandjurypresentment.aspx (accessed May 12, 2011).

Simmons, C.W., H. Roland, J. Kelly-DeWitt. 1998. *Local Government Ethics Ordinances in California.* California Research Bureau, California State Library.

Slackman, M. 2005. "Albany Ethics Case That Died Points to Loophole, Not a Crime." *New York Times,* February 25.

Smith, A.C. 2008. "Florida Wears U.S. Corruption Crown." *St. Petersburg Times,* December 21, B3.

Smith, M.K. 2001. "Peter Senge and the Learning Organization." *E-Journal of Organizational Learning and Leadership* 2 (1). www.leadingtoday.org/weleadinlearning/msapr03.htm (accessed December 6, 2005).

Smith, R.W. 2003. "Enforcement or Ethical Capacity: Considering the Role of State Ethics Commissions at the Millennium." *Public Administration Review* 63 (3): 283–295.

———. 2004. "A Comparison of the Ethics Infrastructure in China and the United States." *Public Integrity* 6 (Fall): 299–318.

Smothers, R. 2005. "11 New Jersey Officials, Including 3 Mayors, Face Charges of Corruption." *New York Times,* February 25.

Stainer, L., A. Stainer, and A. Gully. 1999. "Ethics and Performance Management." *International Journal of Technology Management* 17 (7/8): 776–785.

State of California. 2011. "Ethics Training Courses for State Offices." Department of Justice, Office of the Attorney General. http://ag.ca.gov/ethics/ (accessed November 10, 2011).

State of Connecticut General Assembly. 2004. *State Ethics Organizations.* OLR Research Report 2004-R-0881, Office of Legislative Research. www.cga.ct.gov/2004/rpt/2004-R-0881.htm (accessed July 1, 2011).

State of Florida. 2007. Office of the Governor Executive Order 07–01.

———. 2010. *Nineteenth Statewide Grand Jury, First Interim Report: A Study of Public Corruption in Florida and Recommended Solutions.* Case No. SC 09–1910, December 17. www.fappo.org/2011Tradeshow/documents/19th1stInterimReport.pdf.

State of Florida Commission on Ethics. 2011. *Annual Report to the Florida Legislature for Calendar Year 2010.* www.ethics.state.fl.us/publications/2010_annual.pdf.

State of Florida. Statutes. Section 112.313.

State of Illinois. 1993. State Officials and Employees Ethics Act (Public Act 93–0617).

State of New Jersey. 2011. "Training." State Ethics Commission. http://www.nj.gov/ethics/training/ (accessed November 11, 2011).

Steinhauer, J. 2010. "Senate, for Just the 8th Time, Votes to Oust a Federal Judge." *New York Times,* December 9, A25.

Stillman, R.J. 1999. *Preface to Public Administration: A Search for Themes and Direction.* 2d ed. Burke, VA: Chatelaine Press.

St. Petersburg Times. 2005a. "Editorial: Ethical Questions." March 20. http://www.sptimes.com/2005/03/20/Opinion/Ethical_questions.shtml.

———. 2005b. "Editorial: Ignorant or Unethical?" March 21.

Stolberg, S.G. 2006. "Fight Looms on Lawmakers' Use of Corporate Jets." *New York Times,* March 8.

Stone, R. 2010. "A Wallet-Sized Code of Ethics." *Governing,* May 5. http://www.governing.com/columns/mgmt-insights/A-Wallet-Sized-Code-of.html (accessed June 28, 2011).

Straus, J.R. 2008. *Honest Leadership and Open Government Act of 2007: The Role of the Clerk of the House and Secretary of the Senate.* CRS Report for Congress, Order Code RL34377, July 22. www.fas.org/sgp/crs/secrecy/RL34377.pdf (accessed March 30, 2011).

The Supreme Court of Florida. 2006. Inquiry Concerning a Judge, No. 02–466, RE: Judge John Renke III. No. SC03–1846, May 25. www.floridasupremecourt.org/decisions/2006/sc03-1846.pdf (accessed April 21, 2011).

The Supreme Court of Ohio. 1997. Code of Judicial Conduct. May 1. www.supremecourt.ohio.gov/LegalResources/Rules/conduct/judcond.pdf.

Tapper, Jake. 2009. "President Obama Sets Rules on Ethics and Transparency." ABC News, January 21. http://blogs.abcnews.com/politicalpunch/2009/01/president-oba-3.html (accessed March 28, 2011).

Taylor, F.W. 1911. *Principles of Scientific Management.* New York: Harper & Brothers.

Tenebaum, J. 2002. "Lobbying Disclosure Act of 1995: A Summary and Overview for Associations." June. www.asaecenter.org/Resources/whitepaperdetail.
cfm?ItemNumber=12224 (accessed January 2, 2006).

Terry, L. 1993. "Why We Should Abandon the Misconceived Quest to Reconcile
Public Entrepreneurship with Democracy." *Public Administration Review* 53
(July/August): 393–395.

———. 1995. *Leadership of Public Bureaucracies.* Thousand Oaks, CA: Sage.

———. 1998. "Administrative Leadership, Neo-Managerialism, and the Public Management Movement." *Public Administration Review* 58 (May/June): 194–200.

Testerman, J. 2005. "LaBrakes Get More Than 8 Years." *St. Petersburg Times,* February 26.

Thompson, D.F. 1985. "The Possibility of Administrative Ethics." *Public Administration Review* 45: 555–561.

———. 1992. "Paradoxes of Government Ethics." *Public Administration Review* 52
(May/June): 254–259.

Thornton, K. 2006. "Vagueness of Statute on Corruption Stirs Dispute." *San Diego
Union-Tribune,* January 12. www.signonsandiego.com/uniontrib/20060112/
news_1n12compare.html (accessed April 17, 2011).

Time. 1971. "Illinois: Paul Powell's Nest Egg." January 18. www.time.com/time/
magazine/article/0,9171,942440–1,00.html (accessed April 15, 2011).

Tocqueville, Alexis de. 1840/2000. *Democracy in America.* Trans. and ed. H. Mansfield
and D. Winthrop. Chicago, IL: University of Chicago Press.

Town of Highland, Indiana. 2005. "Ethics Code of Values." November 21. http://high-
landindiana.org/maindocuments/EthicsCode.pdf (accessed August 26, 2011).

Transparency International. 2005. http://www.transparency.org/regional_pages/
asia_pacific/newsroom/news_archive2/india_corruption_study_2005 (accessed
November 16, 2011).

Treaster, J.B., and J. Desantis. 2005. "Storm and Crisis: The Police." *New York Times,*
September 6.

Troxler, C. 2005. "In Politics, What's Unethical Today Is Legal Tomorrow." *St.
Petersburg Times,* October 20.

Truelson, J.A. 1991. "New Strategies for Institutional Controls." In *Ethical Fron-
tiers in Public Management,* ed. J.S. Bowman. San Francisco, CA: Jossey-Bass,
225–242.

Truman, H.S. 1982. Cited in L. Mosley. *Marshall: Hero for Our Times.* New York:
Hearst Books.

Twain, M. 1897. Pudd'nhead Wilson's New Calendar.

U4 Anti-Corruption Resource Centre. 2006. "Anti-Corruption Tool Kits." Updated
September. www.u4.no/document/toolkits.cfm (accessed January 3, 2006).

UK Committee on Standards in Public Life. 2001. *The First Seven Reports: A Review of Progress.* September. www.public-standards.gov.uk/Library/OurWork/
First7Reports_ProgressReview.pdf.

United Nations. 1999. *Public Service in Transition: Enhancing Its Role, Professionalism and Ethical Values and Standards.* New York: Department of Economic and
Social Affairs, Division for Public Economics and Public Administration.

———. 2001. *Public Service Ethics in Africa,* Vol. 1. ST/ESA/PAD/SER.E/23.
New York: Department of Economic and Social Affairs, Division for Public
Economics and Public Administration. upan1.un.org/intradoc/groups/public/
documents/un/upan000160.pdf (accessed November 16, 2011).

————. 2004. *The United Nations Organizational Integrity Survey 2004: Final Report.* Report prepared by Deloitte Consulting LLP. www.un.org/News/ossg/sg/integritysurvey.pdf (accessed December 29, 2005).

————. 2005. Sixtieth Session: Agenda Items 46 and 120. General Assembly, A/60/568, November 28.

————. 2006. "Starting Operations, New UN Ethics Office Fields Staff Requests for Advice." UN News Centre, January 17. www.un.org/apps/news/story.asp?NewsID=17185&Cr=UN&Cr1=staff (accessed June 26, 2006).

United Nations Economic and Social Council. 1996. Resolution 1996/8. Action Against Corruption (Annex—International Code of Conduct for Public Officials). July 23. www.un.org/documents/ecosoc/res/1996/eres1996–8.htm (accessed February 14, 2011).

United Nations Public Administration Network. n.d. http://www.unpan.org (accessed November 18, 2011).

U.S. Census Bureau. 2009. "Local Governments and Public School Systems by Type and State: 2007." November 2. www.census.gov/govs/cog/GovOrgTab03ss.html (accessed May 30, 2011).

U.S. Courts. 2011. "Code of Conduct for United States Judges." June 2. www.uscourts.gov/rulesandpolicies/codesofconduct/codeconductunitedstatesjudges.aspx.

U.S. Department of Justice (U.S. DOJ). 2005. "Religious Objections to the Postal Service Oath of Office." February 2. http://www.justice.gov/olc/2005/religious-objections.pdf (accessed June 10, 2011).

U.S. House of Representatives. 2008. "Chapter 1. General Ethical Standards." In *House Ethics Manual, 2008 Edition.* Committee on Standards of Official Conduct, 110th Congress, 2d Session. Washington, DC: U.S. Government Printing Office. ethics.house.gov/Media/PDF/2008_House_Ethics_Manual.pdf.

U.S. Office of Government Ethics (U.S. OGE). 1992. Standards of Ethical Conduct for Employees of the Executive Branch. 5 CFR Part 2635 RIN 3209-AA04.

————. 2000. *Executive Branch Employee Ethics Survey 2000: Final Report.* Prepared by Arthur Andersen for the U.S. Office of Government Ethics.

————. 2005. "Employee Training Video." Memorandum, DT-05–003, February 23.

————. 2010. *Performance and Accountability Report FY2010.* November 12. www.usoge.gov/management/admin_mgmt_rpts/par_10.pdf (accessed June 3, 2011).

————. n.d.a. "Agency Program Services." http://www.usoge.gov/about/agency_program_services.aspx.

————. n.d.b. "Frequently Asked Questions." www.usoge.gov/about/frequently_asked_questions.aspx.

————. n.d.c. "OGE Administrative and Management Reports." www.usoge.gov/management/admin_manage_reports.aspx.

U.S. Office of Personnel Management (U.S. OPM). n.d. "Theodore Roosevelt." www.opm.gov/about_opm/tr/ (accessed February 28, 2006).

U.S. Office of Special Counsel. 2010. "Introduction to OSC: Our Mission." January 21. www.osc.gov/Intro.htm.

U.S. Senate. 1884. "Oath of Office." http://www.senate.gov/artandhistory/history/common/briefing/Oath_Office.htm (accessed June 11, 2011).

————. 1987. Joint Hearings Before the Senate Select Committee on Secret Military Assistance to Iran and the Nicaraguan Opposition and the House Select Committee to Investigate Covert Arms Transactions with Iran. 100th Cong., 1st Sess., 100–7 Part I, July 7, 8, 9, and 10.

U.S. Senate Select Committee on Ethics. 2002. "Letter of Admonition to Senator Robert G. Torricelli." July 30. http://ethics.senate.gov/downloads/pdffiles/torricelli.pdf.

———. 2003. *Senate Ethics Manual.* http://ethics.senate.gov/downloads/pdffiles/manual.pdf.

University of Wisconsin–Madison. 1992. "Statement of Professional Responsibility." Policies of the Wisconsin Certified Public Manager Program, October 27, p. 3. www.dcs.wisc.edu/pda/cpm/resources/CPMPolicies.pdf.

Valentine, S., and G. Fleischman. 2004. "Ethics Training and Businesspersons' Perceptions of Organizational Ethics." *Journal of Business Ethics* 52: 381–390.

Valmores, D.J. 2005. "Presentation on Fighting and Preventing Corruption." ASEAN+3 Senior Officials Consultative Meeting on Creative Management for Government, September 30–October 1, Bangkok, Thailand.

Van Blijswijk, J.A.M., R.C.J. van Breukelen, A.L Franklin, J.C.N. Raadschelders, and P. Slump. 2004. "Beyond Ethical Codes: The Management of Integrity in the Netherlands Tax and Customs Administration." *Public Administration Review* 64 (November/December): 718–727.

Van Wart, M. 2005. *Dynamics of Leadership in Public Service: Theory and Practice.* Armonk, NY: M.E. Sharpe.

———. 2008. *Leadership in Public Organizations.* Armonk, NY: M.E. Sharpe.

———. 2011. "Changing Dynamics of Administrative Leadership." In *The State of Public Administration: Issues, Challenges, and Opportunities,* ed. D. Menzel and H. White. Armonk, NY: M.E. Sharpe.

Varian, B. 2005. "E-Mails Get Tampa Workers in Trouble." *St. Petersburg Times,* April 19.

Victor, B., and J.B. Cullen. 1988. "The Organizational Bases of Ethical Work Climates." *Administrative Science Quarterly* 33: 101–125.

Walker, D.M. 2005. "Ethics and Integrity in Government: Putting the Needs of Our Nation First." *Public Integrity* 7 (Fall): 345–352.

Wang, D. 2004. "Striving for Excellence in Civil Service Training." In *Windows on China,* ed. M.T. Gordon et al. Amsterdam: IOS Press, 29–36.

Waring, C.G. 2004. "Measuring Ethical Climate Risk." *Internal Auditor* 61 (December): 71–75.

Washburn, R.H.A. 2011. Personal e-mail communication, August 10.

Wayne, L. 2005. "Boeing Chief Is Ousted After Admitting Affair." *New York Times.* March 8.

Weir, F. 2009. "Russia Corruption Costs $318 Billion—One-Third of GDP." *Christian Science Monitor,* Global News Blog, November 23. www.csmonitor.com/World/Global-News/2009/1123/russia-corruption-costs-318-billion-one-third-of-gdp (accessed 14 February 2011).

West, J. 2005. Personal e-mail communication, August 23.

West, J.P., and E.M. Berman. 2004. "Ethics Training in U.S. Cities: Content, Pedagogy, and Impact." *Public Integrity* 6 (Summer): 189–206.

Wex Articles. n.d. "Judicial Ethics." Cornell University Law School, Legal Information Institute. http://topics.law.cornell.edu/wex/judicial_ethics (accessed July 1, 2011).

White, L.D. 1926. *Introduction to the Study of Public Administration.* New York: Macmillan.

Wikipedia. 2010. "San Diego Pension Scandal." December 25. http://en.wikipedia.
org/wiki/San_Diego_pension_scandal (accessed August 8, 2011).
———. 2011a. "Honest Services Fraud." June 16. http://en.wikipedia.org/wiki/
Honest_services_fraud.
———. 2011b. "Ray Blanton." May 4. http://en.wikipedia.org/wiki/Ray_Blanton.
(accessed November 18, 2011).
———. 2011c. "Thomas Porteous." June 5. http://en.wikipedia.org/wiki/Thomas_
Porteous. (accessed November 18, 2011).
Wiley, C. 1995. "The ABC's of Business Ethics: Definitions, Philosophies, and
Implementation." *Industrial Management* 37 (1): 22–27.
Wilgoren, J. 2005. "Chicago Mayor Questioned in Federal Corruption Inquiry." *New
York Times,* August 27.
Williams, R.L. 1996. "Controlling Ethical Practices Through Laws and Rules: Evaluat-
ing the Florida Commission on Ethics." *Public Integrity Annual,* 65–72.
Wilson, J.Q. 1993. *The Moral Sense.* New York: Free Press.
Wilson, W. 1887/1941. "The Study of Administration." *Political Science Quarterly*
56 (December), 481–506.
Witt, E. 1992. "Is Government Full of Crooks or Are We Just Better at Finding Them?"
In *Essentials of Government Ethics,* ed. P. Madsen and J.M. Shafritz. New York:
Meridian/Penguin.
Wojciechowski, Charlie. 2010. "Four Suburban Officials Busted in Corruption Probe."
NBC Chicago, May 4. www.nbcchicago.com/news/local/Operation-Cookie-
Jar-92797014.html (accessed 25 May 2011).
Wye, C. 1994. "A Framework for Enlarging the Reform Agenda." *Public Manager*
23: 43–46.
Xue, L., and Z. Peng. 2004. "China's Public Administration Education." In *Windows
on China,* ed. M.T. Gordon et al. Amsterdam: IOS Press, 11–28.
Yardley, W., and S. Stowe. 2005. "A Contrite Rowland Gets a Year for Accepting
$107,000 in Gifts" *New York Times,* March 19.
Zajac, G., and L.K. Comfort. 1997. "The Spirit of Watchfulness: Public Ethics as
Organizational Learning." *Journal of Public Administration Research and Theory*
7 (October): 541–569.
Zauderer, D.G. 1994. "Winning with Integrity." *Public Manager* 23: 43–46.
Zhu, Q. 2000. "The Process of Professionalization and the Rebuilding of Administra-
tive Ethics in Post-Mao China." *International Journal of Public Administration*
23 (11): 1943–1965.

Index

Italic page references indicate boxed text and charts.

Pardons, 194, *194*
Paterson, David A., 167
Patronage politics, 33, 47, 140
Peachtree City (Georgia), 58–59
PEERA, 177–179
Pelosi, Nancy, 198–199
Pendleton Act (1883), 34, 47
Peng, Zongchao, 225
Pennsylvania, 170
Pentagon Papers, 190, 192
People, ethical, 23
Perception and ethics, 24
Perelli, Carina, 108
Performance and Accountability Report FY2010 (OGE), 87
Performance and ethics, 11–12
Performance evaluations, 13, 110–111
Perks, Senate, 200, *200*
Personal integrity, 55
Peters, Thomas J., 22
Pevkur, Aive, 218
Peyton, John, 112, 158
Philadelphia (Pennsylvania), 170
Philippines, 213, 215
Pierce, Samuel, 39
Pinellas County (Florida), 94, *95*
Platt, Louis E., 94
Plausible deniability, 40, *40*
Plume, Valerie, 193–194
Plunkitt ethics, 34, 39
Plunkitt, George Washington, 34, *34*, 119
Poindexter, John M., 40, *40*
Policy, ethics, 24
Pope, Jeremy, 217
Porteous, G. Thomas, Jr., 202
Powell, Adam Clayton, Jr., 196
Powell, Colin L., 69
Powell, Paul T., *175*
Pragmatic utilitarianism, *8*
President's Commission on Federal Ethics Law Reform (1989 report), 190
Presidents, U.S., 190, *191–192*, 192–195, *195*
Principles of ethical behavior, *56*
"Principles of Ethical Conduct in Government Officers and Employers," 50
Principles of Scientific Management, The (Taylor), *35*
Prison management privatization, 238

Private censure, 89, 92
Private Provider Law, 239
Privatization, 5–6, 234–239, *235*
Proactive ethical risk taking, 14–15
Professional associations, 87–89, *88, 90–92*, 251–252. *See also specific name*
Professional integrity, 55–56
Progressive Era, 140
Prohibition against reinstatement, 92
Public Administration Review (periodical), 40
Public censure, 92
Public Employee Ethics Reform Act (PEERA), 177–179
Public Ethics Commission (Brazil), 213
Public Law 103-424, 186
Public management, evolution of, 45–46
Public Sector Employment and Management Act (1993; Australia), 212
Public Service and Democracy (Gawthrop), 32, 44
Public Service in Transition (1999 report), 252
Public service oaths, 100, *101*, 102–103, *103*
Public service values, *249*

Quality circles, *42*
Quinn, Pat, 176

Rachman-Moore, D., 114
Radisson hotel chain, 236
Ragghianti, Marie, 71, *71*
Random Audit Program, 180
Rangel, Charles, *198*, 199–200
Rationalization, 62
Reagan administration, 49
Reagan, Ronald, 39–40, *40*, 42, 193
Reflections of a Radical Moderate (Richardson), 69
Reform, ethics, 26, *129*, 196–199
Regulatory-based strategies, 16
Reinventing Government (Osborne and Gaebler), 42, 65, 235
Reinvention movement, 42–44, 65–66, 235
Renke, John III, 169–170
Reprimands, 89, 92, *198*

About the Author

Donald C. Menzel is president of Ethics Management International and emeritus professor of Public Administration, Northern Illinois University. He served as the 2005–2006 president of the American Society for Public Administration. He holds a PhD from Pennsylvania State University (1973), a master's degree (1968) from Miami University (Ohio), and a bachelor's degree in mathematics (1961) from Southern Illinois University. He served in the U.S. Air Force from 1962 to 1967.

Dr. Menzel has published widely in the field of public administration, with particular interest in local government management and ethics. In addition, he has lectured on these subjects in Australia, China, Thailand, France, Germany, The Netherlands, Portugal, and Italy, as well as at many professional conferences in the United States and abroad.

His most recent books are *The State of Public Administration: Issues, Challenges, and Opportunities,* coedited with Harvey White (M.E. Sharpe, 2011) and *Ethics Moments in Government: Cases and Controversies* (CRC Press, 2010). Dr. Menzel also is completing a volume called *Achieving Ethical Competency for Public Service Leadership,* coedited with Terry Cooper (M.E. Sharpe, forthcoming).